The Politics
of Human Nature

The Politics
of Human Nature

Thomas Fleming

Transaction Books
New Brunswick (U.S.A.) and Oxford (U.K.)

Copyright © 1988 by Transaction, Inc.
New Brunswick, New Jersey 08903

All rights reserved under International and Pan-American Copyright Conventions. No part of this book may be reproduced or transmitted in any form or by any means, electronic or mechanical, including photocopy, recording, or any information storage and retrieval system, without prior permission in writing from the publisher. All inquiries should be addressed to Transaction Books, Rutgers – The State University, New Brunswick, New Jersey 08903.

Library of Congress Catalog Number: 87-19149

ISBN: 0-88738-189-8

Printed in the United States of America

Library of Congress Cataloging in Publication Data

Fleming, Thomas, 1945–
  The politics of human nature.

  Bibliography: p.
  Includes index.
  1. Political psychology. I. Title.
JA74.5.F55   1987   320′.01′9   87-19149
ISBN 0-88738-189-8

Contents

Contents

Preface

I began thinking about the roots of political behavior in the late 1970s, under the influence of Maine's *Ancient Law*, Aristotle's *Politics*, and Filmer's *Patriarcha*, all of whom approached political theory in a manner strikingly different from the main stream of Locke, Rousseau, and Bentham. Classical political theory since the time of Hobbes, I thought, took far too much for granted, and those easy assumptions about natural equality and human rights had led to a dead end in theory and to disastrous consequences in practice. What was wanted was a less a priori approach that began with man as he is rather than with the impossibly simple creature of Utopian fantasies.

I began working in earnest, about 1980, on the problem of equality but made little progress until I took the suggestion of two former colleagues and started reading Edward O. Wilson's *Sociobiology* and Evans-Pritchard's studies of the Nuer, a people of the Sudan who came to seem more familiar than my neighbors. It was at that point I realized with some horror that no book, such as I had in mind, could be completed without a thorough investigation of what the social sciences and evolutionary biology had to say on the subject of human nature. Rejecting the larger claims of evolutionary theory and skeptical of the utility of much sociology and psychology, I began to recognize that several generations of patient, sometimes brilliant researchers had succeeded in amassing a wealth of evidence to document Aristotle's definition of man as "the political animal." If I have not always succeeded in integrating the finding of multifarious disciplines into a coherent whole, it may be that success lies beyond the reach of a classicist and literary essayist.

The work was begun in a small village of South Carolina, and it was not until 1984 that a summer teaching position at the University of Colorado gave me the use of a research library. Since then much of the necessary reading was carried out at the University of Wisconsin at Madison, whose superb library is among the glories of the Middle West. During the entire period I neither applied for nor received any fellowship, grant, or stipend to support research or composition. No graduate assistant helped in the preparation of notes or even in the xeroxing of articles. What mistakes there are are due entirely to my own carelessness and ineptitude.

If no direct financial aid was given, my position at The Rockford Institute did afford me sufficient free time to work on the project. Special thanks are due to Anita Fedora for her tireless labor in preparing the manuscript and to Michael Warder for his effort to make sure that it saw the light of day. A number of people have read various parts of the work and made invaluable suggestions: Edward O. Wilson, Robert Nisbet, Stephen R.L. Clark, Thomas Molnar, Grace Goodell, Allan Carlson, Bryce Christensen, and Charles F. Thompson. To all of them I owe a debt of gratitude. Finally, it is to my wife and children, who endured these years of unremunerative labor and an unremitting disruption of family life, that this book is affectionately dedicated.

1

The Part and the Whole

The collapse of Roman authority in the West created a crisis from which political thinking has never quite recovered. The eternal city, settled by the descendants of Trojan Aeneas (Venus' son), the center of empire, was the one permanent fact in a stable world. The world had been at peace, united in a single language (Latin) that conveyed an entire civilization that was both Latin and Greek. A man could travel from Hadrian's Wall in Britain all the way to Egypt and still be bound by the same Roman law.

In the fifth century, most of the European part of the empire fell apart. After the sack of Rome in 410, a bewildered Augustine attempted to shift the blame from the impious Christians to the pagan Romans, but that meant, in effect, denying the divinity of Roman civilization. Augustine's *Civitas Dei* was only the first effort to create a substitute for imperial Rome. After the Western Empire crumbled into the fragments that were reassembled into the nations of Europe, one after another, the great powers attempted to restore the imperial unity. Charlemagne made himself emperor in 800, inaugurating the fantasy of the Holy Roman Empire. The Bourbons in France, the Romanovs in Russia, and the Hapsburgs in Austria made claim to the ancient glory of one kingdom, one leader, and their pretensions were revived by Napoleon, Lenin, and Hitler.[1] But unity remained a dream or, more recently, turned into a nightmare. The casualties of universalist aspirations have been staggering, but after two world wars, the rise of socialism (and national socialism), and forty years of sparring between two churches militant — democracy and Marxism — the world is no more one than it was in 1914. Separatist and nationalist movements disturb the peace of Britain, France, and Spain, while both the United States and the Soviet Union have a hard time holding together their races, nationalities, ethnic groups, religions, and classes into two gigantic bundles.

The creation of unity is not simply a matter of geopolitical tinkerings or thinly disguised imperialism. By nature, human beings are fond of seeking simple

1

answers to complex questions. There is no point in complaining about "reductionism" or oversimplification. We are what we are. "All men by nature are eager to know," as Aristotle began his *Metaphysics*, and since all knowledge requires selection, discrimination, and simplification, we are eternally condemned to imposing our partial and imperfect solutions on the entire universe of problems.

Not all simplifications are harmful. Without arithmetic, geometry, and logic we could not progress very far in analytical thought, and without political abstractions like sovereignty or liberty, legal systems would not get much beyond the notion of custom. The danger lies not so much in simplistic analysis itself but in the application of political abstractions into real situations. Terms like democracy and equality turn into slogans, and slogans become rallying cries in a crusade against complexity.

Modern political thought abounds in such slogans. Most of them revolve around the twin poles of the individual and the state. The individual is said to be possessed of something called "rights," while the state is characterized by the equally abstract "sovereignty." Whole libraries of volumes have been written in an attempt to integrate these two notions. At the center of most modern (that is, liberal) political theory is the idea of obligation—what obedience the citizens owe the state and under what circumstances.

While the contributors to this extended political conversation were often brilliant, their books have an air of unreality. This passage from Locke's *Second Treatise of Civil Government* (V111.95) is only the most familiar example:

> *Men being, as has been said, by nature all free, equal, and independent,* no one can be put out of this estate and subjected to the political power of another without his own consent, which is done by agreeing with other men, to join and unite into a community for their secure enjoyment of their properties, and a greater security against any that are not of it. This any number of men may do, because it injures not the freedom of the rest; they are left, as they were, in the liberty of the state of Nature. When any number of men have so consented to make one community or government, they are thereby presently incorporated, and make one body politic wherein the majority have a right to act and conclude the rest.

Locke, in a series of works, had attempted a bold synthesis of psychology, metaphysics, and political theory that still commands respectful attention. And yet, a newcomer to political philosophy would be baffled by much of his discussion: the state of nature? rights? consent? body politic? What are these things that one so blithely takes for granted? However divorced from everyday living, Locke's myth of nature and rights had an enormous vogue. Its popularity was due, at least in part, to the simplicity and universality of an explanation that could be applied to any situation.

Of course, the problem of discovering unity in diversity is older than Locke, older even than Plato. The Romans, (who are, after all, partly responsible for the one world myth) expressed their proverbial wisdom in a little story about the body and the members. As the story went, the members of the body, grown tired of feeding the lazy and greedy belly, went on strike. The feet would not walk in search of food, the hands refused to carry, the mouth to chew. The inevitable starvation that resulted restored a sense of reality to the revolting members, which quickly resumed their customary and necessary functions. This little tale, according to Livy, was told by a Roman statesman to the common people, when they had withdrawn from the city in protest over the aristocracy's privileges. What it tells us of the Roman habit of mind is more interesting than the historical episode, for it reveals their ecological vision of society as an organic system in which changes cannot be made on one part without affecting the whole. It is quite the reverse of Locke's simplistic myth or our own dreams of imposed or negotiated unification.

Not everyone would agree that a comprehensive and organic vision is needed. Politics, they claim, is like riding a bicycle: If you think too much about it, you may be in danger of losing control. Besides, the organic metaphor of society is declared to be a fallacy that leads to glib generalizations and strained analogies with "health" and "decadence."[2] The alternative would seem to be the machine metaphors, which encourage an approach to social problems that French anthropologists describe as "bricolage" — the primitive art of cobbling together fragments of myth and bits of superstition into what can pass, in a pinch, for a world view.

One common element in much modern thought is the concept of the individual. Almost every writer on social ethics since the seventeenth century takes the individual for granted as the most basic element of society. For Thomas Hobbes, the anarchic passions of human beings made government a natural necessity; for Jeremy Bentham and the Mills, the state's only legitimate raison d'etre was to maximize the potential for satisfaction of the greatest number of individuals in the society. The rules change, but the players remain constant: individual citizens and the state.

The emphasis on individuality is not entirely a bad thing. An important aspect of Protestant culture (not necessarily theology) is the insistence that each mature person be responsible for himself. This is quite the reverse of traditional societies, which rely heavily on status in assessing worth and guilt. The accidental killing of a great man can bring a greater punishment than the murder of a peasant. On the other hand, a nobleman may have to pay a more serious penalty for a crime on the grounds that he knows the law better and has greater influence. In many premodern societies, a criminal's family could be punished for acts in which they had no complicity.

In a very real sense, the virtues of modern civilization depend on the assumption of individual moral responsibility. But not all the consequences have been positive. Since the nineteenth century, a host of important philosophers and social critics have been complaining of "alienation," social dissolution, and moral chaos. While pointing out the failure of fragmentary philosophies and social systems, they have sought, at the same time, a grand unified theory of human social life. Dissatisfaction with modernity is, in fact, one of the hallmarks of modernism.

Karl Marx and his colleague Friedrich Engels are the names that first come to mind. The *Communist Manifesto*, at the same time as it was issuing a call to arms, also included an explosive critique of the moral contradictions inherent in industrial capitalism. Engels, in particular, was wont to lash out at the deterioration of the family when women and children were driven into the work force. In one sense, Marx and Engels exulted in the tragic circumstances, but they were hardly alone in predicting the end of bourgeois individualism and liberal society.

Thomas Carlyle took a less cheerful view of the future, but the charges of his indictment could have been drawn up by the communists: "To whom . . . is this wealth of England wealth?," he asked in *Past and Present*. Carlyle contrasted the unity and purpose of medieval England with the fragmentation of an industrial England, in which the aristocracy was divorced from its responsibilities.

The list of modern jeremiads is practically endless: Friedrich Nietzsche's joyful prophecy of the chaos and disintegration that would result from the atheism he described as "the death of God"; Oswald Spengler's proclamation of the "decline of the West" that made his name a catchword for prophets of doom; Richard Weaver's prediction of inevitable erosion of every principle of right, up to and eventually including property; T.S. Eliot's vision of a rootless Wasteland; and the grimmest of all, the gentle C.S. Lewis's warning against the modern combination of technology and ideology that could lead ultimately to "the abolition of man."

This is only a brief sample. An extensive list would have to include the Catholic existentialist Gabriel Marcel; the ex-Trotskyist James Burnham, who attributed the suicide of the West to the managerial revolution; critics of capitalist technocracy like Jacques Ellul or the Southern Agrarians (Allen Tate, Donald Davidson, Andrew Lytle); disgruntled European liberals like Jose Ortega y Gasset; absurdist playwrights like Eugène Ionesco, and so on. These men had little in common — atheists and Christians, communists and capitalists — but they were unanimous in proclaiming the end of civilization.

There is another link that binds all these criticisms together: Karl Marx and C.S. Lewis, for all their obvious differences, both believed that modern life failed to satisfy important human needs. In fact, every important political theory is also a theory of human nature. Hobbes and Locke both rested their cases on a set of psychological principles. Similarly, Plato developed his theory of the just society (in *The Republic*) as a metaphor for the just man. The most influential method, however, was Aristotle's attempt to base politics on ethics, which he rooted, in turn, in the notion of happiness.

More recent political theorists also derive their systems from a view of human nature, but they rarely take the trouble to make that view explicit. Usually, it is a vulgar version of cultural relativism combined with some form of hedonist psychology. Human nature can be reduced to a few basic "needs" or wants: Food, sex, companionship, etc., since anything more complicated varies so much from culture to culture. While Marx was lucid and explicit in his rejection of human nature, contemporary writers like John Rawls and Robert Nozick (at first glance, poles apart) seem to take such a negation for granted.

This book has a system of natural politics as its aim: the regrounding of political theory in human nature. Such an approach has not been popular for a good many years. Apart from Aristotle, few political philosophers have attempted to use biological or ethnographic evidence, at least not systematically. The exceptions constitute a series of brilliant eccentrics who failed to change the course of ethical and political theory: Lord Kames, Bishop Butler, Walter Bagehot, and—most recently—Stephen Clark.

That some regrounding of politics in nature is necessary should be obvious from all the failed attempts of intellectual revolutionaries, like Marx, Carlyle, and Nietzsche. All of them complained of the hopeless decadence of bourgeois society, but none has succeeded even in providing a common ground for political discussion. Karl Marx was the most effective at making the leap from speculation to a program for action, but the success of Marxism in action has been less than spectacular.

It is possible, of course, that the critics of modern society are all mistaken. After all, every generation believes it has a "rendezvous with destiny," that it is the best of times or the worst of times or preferably (as Dickens describes the period of the French Revolution) both. This generational egocentrism is in part the product of our own experience and the illusion it gives us of our own immortality. From the severely limited perspective of our threescore and ten, personal experiences seem fraught with special meaning for the history of the world. Thousands of years of history appear to converge on the present. Our point of view resembles the old maps of the universe, with earth at the center and Jerusalem at the center of the earth. A learned man knows his own limitations and has a sense of his own insignificance. In any generation, such people are rare, but older societies depended upon tradition to correct the arrogance of the living. What Chesterton called "the democracy of the dead" serves as an obstacle to the tyranny of reformers. The young will always be full of illusions about changing the world, but in a traditional society their impatience is restrained by the constant admonitions to remember the deeds and customs of the ancestors, what the Romans called the *mos maiorum*.

Modern man does not live in a traditional society. In love with tomorrow, with what we are just about to create, we have little patience with any restraint upon our imagination. We like to think of ourselves as the wisest, most powerful, and most humane people that have ever lived. On the other hand, we also take a melancholy pleasure in seeing ourselves as a doomed race: the oceans are dying, the polar ice caps are melting, environmentally caused cancer threatens us all individually, while the entire human race lives under the nuclear threat of the end of all things.[3] We tell ourselves that the nuclear family has disintegrated, that incest is becoming a way of life for a significant portion of our population. As utopian doomsayers, modern Americans magnify our virtues and our vices, our heroes and our villains: only gods can experience a *Götterdämmerung*. When we study history, we seem (to ourselves) a generation of Gullivers confronting an endlessly regressing series of Lilliputs. This illusion is even more serious for the scholars and intellectuals who have isolated themselves from ordinary society.

Even so, it is hard to escape the feeling that things are somehow different now. After conceding the effects of a warped perspective, we have still not addressed the questions raised by social critics. It is possible that our absurd egocentrism is a symptom of a disease, that an infatuation with progress is partly responsible for conditions that no civilized men — perhaps no society of any kind — have ever had to face before. The "problems" described by the modern prophets are more than the usual symptoms of decay: urban crime, political immorality, environmental pollution, free verse, and abstract art. These annoyances are the inevitable accompaniments of a civilization at a certain stage in its development. Like smoke and noise, they are the price we pay for progress and power. But there are more serious, more fundamental problems faced by our civilization: high rates of family dissolution, a breakdown and general confusion in ethical standards, the development of a sensationalistic and homogenized mass culture, and perhaps worst of all an apparent inability to agree on social priorities. The United States today is not so much one nation or even two, the rich and the poor. It is a Balkanized assortment of interest groups based on race, sex, religion, class, and region. Even at this comparatively trivial level, the problem is acute.

One common explanation for this social confusion is the rate of change, especially in America. Never before, it is often said, has a nation risen so rapidly from obscurity to world power. Rapid social changes are unsettling, but that cannot be the whole story. Ancient Athens went through a far more rapid social and political evolution and landed with its feet on the ground, admittedly as a second-class power.

At the beginning of the fifth century, B.C., Athens was a comparatively minor Greek state. She was nowhere near so powerful as Sparta, nor so rich as Corinth. Intellectually, Athens was a backwater compared with the Greek cities on and off the coast of Asia minor. In less than fifty years, however, Athens was the center of a naval and commercial empire that dominated the eastern Mediterranean and was well on her way to becoming the intellectual and artistic center, not just of the Greek world, but of our own civilization, which depends so heavily for its inspiration on the great names of Athenian literature and philosophy. She was, as her leading statesman Pericles is supposed to have expressed it, the "education of Greece."

By the end of the century, the great days of her political empire were over. Within the 100 years of her rise and fall, Athens had experienced the usual crises: discord between rich and poor, between landed aristocracy and commercial interests, a retreat from civic responsibility, a rising skepticism about religion and morality, and yet Athenian — and Greek — culture survived and to some extent flourished, albeit in an altered form. Athens failed as a power but to some extent succeeded as a culture and as a people.

The Athenians possessed many obvious and important advantages that make for social stability. Even at the height of their power, the Athenians were predominantly agricultural and lived in settled communities of kinfolk and family friends. While a small but wealthy part of the population was receptive to the new moral relativism and atheism preached by the "sophists," most Athenians had no time for philosophizing. Their farms depended too much on the weather to reject the great god of sunlight, rain, and wind, Zeus. Five centuries later, when St. Paul made his famous visit, he noted the Athenian addiction to religion: "Ye men of Athens, I perceive that in all things ye are too superstitious."

In their political life, the Athenians made the first great attempt at civilized democracy. Political participation was restricted to adult, freeborn, male citizens; nonetheless, the Athenian democracy was open to the poorer classes. Athens' enemies portrayed her people as bustling, innovative, and dangerous. The Athenian historian Thucydides put this speech in the mouth of a Corinthian:

> They are innovators and sharp to conceive and swift to accomplish whatever they decide . . . they are daring beyond their means and take risks beyond all expectation . . . If they fail to obtain something on which their hearts are set, they consider it just as if they were being deprived of their own property . . .

In their acquisitiveness and love of innovation, the Athenians seem thoroughly modern. On the other hand, they took pride in their national identity, claiming to be "autochthonous," i.e., the original settlers of their territory. Despite their class divisions, they had a sense of unity and of family continuity unknown to any modern society. For them, the state was not an alien power structure that imposed its laws, but an expression of the community will. They were above all profoundly conservative and clung, as well as they could, to the customs of their ancestors and to the continuity of the family. Some of the most interesting and revealing aspects of Athenian law have to do with ensuring the continuity of a household upon the failure of a male heir.[4]

What is most different about the Athenians is what they took for granted: the differences between men and women, the integrity of and the centrality of the family, and the importance of religion. No politician or social reformer could make headway against entrenched attitudes, not just in Athens and Sparta but throughout the Roman Empire that succeeded to their power and lasted in the East until the fall of Constantinople to the Turks in 1453. If this meant the ancients were slow to seize opportunities and resistant to progress, it also meant they were in large measure shielded from the dangers of irresponsible innovation.

The United States is neither so aggressive nor so energetic as Athens in the days of her empire. On the other hand, it does not possess many of the conservative advantages enjoyed by most premodern societies. So far from being a unified, organic whole, the United States is made up of dozens of peoples and cultures. Some of them are compatible with the culture of the original, predominantly British settlers; others are not. We have long since lost our reverence for tradition. If the United States has a national tradition, it is the habit of change and the worship of the dynamo. Our most poignant folkhero is John Henry, the defeated enemy of progress. The ordinary restraints imposed by community and religion survive most powerfully in the distorted forms of intolerance and superstition — much like the bizzare remnants of ancient paganism that endured for several centuries beyond the official Christianization of the Roman Empire. All that seems to bind us together as a nation is a vague ideology of liberty, equality, and progress. Apart from a certain very natural inertia, there are few restraints on social innovation. Far from being unique, the United States has been, much like Athens, the education of the modern world.

Herein lies the special quality and crisis of our civilization. Our original and creative minds seethe with new ideas. A few of them are productive, but in the nature of things, most of them are not. (What fraction of evolutionary mutations are good, either for individuals or for species?) There is nothing wrong with originality, but what is missing from the modern scene are all the powerful restraints, the governors that control the speed of social change, the filters of experience and tradition that sort out the practical from the merely clever. What we lack are the divine oracles that thunder against any trespass upon ancient rights and any invasion of the nature of things. We have our prophets, it is true, but most of them insist on being creative men of original genius. Few of them are as humble as the Marxist songwriter who wanted to be known "as the man who told you what you already knew."

It is possible to overstate the case. Many men and women lead, to all appearances, successful lives and manage to rear children who combine a strong moral sense with civic responsibility.[5] The family or the church have not disappeared.

Far from it.[6] But they survive in isolated and individualized forms, which cannot impose much restraint upon the community or the state. Until recently the family was a force to be reckoned with, so long as it possessed guarantees of its autonomy and integrity, so long as nuclear families were not isolated into intimate fragments but were integrated into wide and powerful networks of extended kin. As recently as the days of the Hatfields and McCoys, the government of West Virginia proved incapable of controlling a clan war. In the 1980s, however, American families cannot even be sure of their right to rear their children without government interference. There is a profamily movement, it is true, but such a movement was never before necessary, and its existence now is strong evidence for the decline of family authority.

The family has not itself actually declined; in fact, it may have changed a great deal less than is commonly supposed. The virtues of modern society are owed in no small measure to the nuclear family,[7] and it may indeed, be pointless to pine for the good old days of multi-generational families or even for the more recent time when the nuclear family was the center of all social life. It is, on the other hand, important to recognize the essential and irreplaceable part played by the family as the one constant and integrative force in every society.

The churches have seen their actual powers reduced even more than the family. The late medieval popes were strong enough to humiliate the kings of Europe. Today, however, the tax-exempt status of churches is regarded as a privilege granted by an indulgent government. Church schools are regularly taken to court in efforts to make them conform to the model of public education. Worst of all, the widening gap between the laity and the official church hierarchies and the declining membership of mainline denominations reduces the possibility of effective church action. Almost everywhere, the church-inspired blue laws and censorship regulations are crumbling before the onslaught of First Amendment crusades. It is not that it is necessarily a good idea to have preachers involved in politics, but what the church used to represent was the higher will of the community. It is more convenient to be able to shop on Sunday. What is unsettling is the idea that community bodies – like local churches – have no part to play in exercising social control, that power is exclusively a function of the government and, perhaps, the mass media.

This hypothesis, that modernism has led to the decay of community institutions and the collapse of moral norms, cannot be tested and proved in the same way that an hypothesis in physics or chemistry can be falsified or verified. It is practically impossible to set up the necessary experiments. There are, however, communities that have been subject to something rather like an experimental process: primitive and premodern societies compelled to undergo rapid modernization.

A great deal has been written about the collision of primitive and modern cultures: some of the most dismal examples come from North American Indians on reservations. The pattern of drunkenness, violence, and family instability is all too familiar. Many Indian communities had the time and the opportunity to adjust slowly. Others, like the Grassy Narrows Ojibwa of Northwestern Ontario, were dragged almost overnight into midtwentieth century life. In *A Poison Stranger Than Love*, Anastasia M. Shkilnyk describes the horror that followed the communities forced to relocate between 1955 and 1963: before the move, 91 percent of the deaths in the community were the result of natural causes; but:

> By the mid-1970s, only 23 percent of all deaths could be traced to old age, illness, or accident. During 1974–78, 75 percent of all deaths were due to alchohol or drug-induced violence directed against others or against the self.

In only one year, one-fifth of the adolescent population (11–19) attempted suicide. Many of the cases involved girls who had been raped by close relatives during the drinking sprees that punctuate existence at Grassy Narrows. The high rates of assault, rape, and incest are partly related both to alchoholism and to sniffing gasoline. But alcoholism is itself a symptom of the underlying problems of a community that has lost its sense of purpose. Some of the problems are clearly related to mercury poisoning in the water, but the Grassy Narrows Ojibwa exhibit only to a more intense degree the social dissolution experienced in housing projects and reservations all over North America.[8]

They are caught tragically in the space between two cultures: the old, traditional ways of the Ojibwa, which were not being transmitted to the children, and a modern society to which they have not adapted. Eventually, the community will either disappear or its members will adjust to modern life. What they will never recover, however, are all the implicit social controls that gave shape and direction to the lives of the Ojibwa. Their spectacular failure to adapt might be read as the predictable debris of cultural collision. On the other hand, the pattern bears a strong resemblance to the routine problems of modern life: parents who no longer seem to care for their children, sexual licentiousness, incest and child abuse, and the conviction, increasingly common, that one's own existence is without purpose. Is the social disintegration at Grassy Narrows simply the result of cultural contamination, or is it an accelerated and magnified representation of the past 150 years? Shkilnyk seems to believe the latter and describes the high rates of suicide, family dissolution, and child abuse of advanced societies as the results of "the loss of our moorings in faith and tradition; the loss of a sense of connection with the earth; alienation from meaningful work; and separation from a nurturing family and communal setting."

There is no question that mainstream society in Europe and the United States is a great deal healthier than the Grassy Narrows Ojibwa, but we have had a far longer time to adjust to conditions which, after all, we have imposed upon ourselves. Still, the long-term trends of social disintegration may indicate that we are not so much healthy as we are like chronic invalids who have grown used to their disease.

The decay of family, community, and religious authority has meant the removal of all obstacles to innovation. As a result, modern Americans and Europeans look less and less to "the wisdom of the past," that is to the accumulated experience of several thousand years, and more and more to the satisfaction of present needs. Our faith, at least until very recently, has been placed not in some transcendent and unchanging divine will but, to adopt a metaphor from Aristophanes, in the ever-changing clouds of the future: "Zeus does not exist, not since Dinos ("whirl") is King, having driven Zeus away."

This modernity requires that everything, especially works of the mind and of the imagination, be subject to fashion. For one reason or another, there are no more classics, no sets of books and principles that connect us — not just with each other — but with our civilized ancestors. The decay of the classics (English as well as ancient) is not the casual byproduct of historical change. It is the result of deliberate policies: even the College Board, apparently, opted for multiple choice aptitude tests because they liberated the curriculum from the tyranny of the classics.[9] The results of our intellectual fragmentation are far too serious to be summed up by glib superficialities like "two cultures." Whatever the cause, there is, in fact, no central humane culture binding the student of the *Vedas* to the interpreter of Baudelaire.

Georg Simmel described this process of fragmentation as the creation of an objective culture that grows to become independent of its original purpose and relates this development to the division of labor so characteristic of modern civilization.[10] But the trouble does not begin with specialization or even with the failure of our public schools. It is the rejection of tradition and contempt for the past that is at work. What every specialist scholar needs — if he wants to make his work serve anything beyond self-promotion — is an integrated vision. Without some philosophical tradition, some common language of discourse, his work must remain an isolated fragment. This isolation is not limited to academic monographs; it extends to nearly every book on politics, ethics, psychology, and social life published in the last fifty years. Few are likely to be read ten years after their date of publication. Why? The most obvious answer is that, whatever their individual merits, they are fragments: like unrelated bits and pieces of a puzzle which, if it ever is put together, turns out to be a Jackson Pollock painting, without form or purpose.

No individual, given this sort of isolation can work out a coherent view of even a part of life. It takes order, system, or at least a set of common prejudices — in a word, tradition. Without it, his insights go unnoticed or, at best, make him a nine-day wonder on television talk shows. Wisdom, usable wisdom, requires the experience of more than one generation. As it is, one fashion succeeds another, and sects blossom and fade with the regularity of the seasons: existentialists, behaviorists, Freudians, libertarians, etc. Between them are no common principles or accepted methods; they share neither a mutually intelligible vocabulary nor even a commitment to a universally accepted logic. Under such circumstances, it is no wonder that intellectuals have so little influence, even on other intellectuals.

Really useful systems—like those of Plato and Aristotle (or of Darwin and Mendel)—are never finished. Even minor thinkers can make themselves useful by perfecting the system, while the occasional genius, an Aquinas or a Plotinus, can change the course of intellectual history. But for many moderns, all that building, all those living traditions have—outside of science—perished, and philosophy has been smashed into a thousand bright ideas. This intellectual isolation from our ancestors and those who should be our colleagues is related to a psychic fragmentation in which rationality subordinates all other elements, including the virtues. With rationalism has come the belief that we can win an easy triumph over the subrational forces of nature. In other words, we have filled the void left by the past with the idea of progress.

The idea of evolution and advancement is nothing new in Western history. Various schools of ancient philosophy taught that man had progressed from a rude, bestial state up to the refinements of civilization. However, the dominant myth was not progress but regress: man had once been free and easy in the golden age of Cronus or in a state of innocence in Eden. A clear conception of progress depends on the linear sense of time provided by Christianity. While most of the ancients believed in cycles of history that repeat themselves, the Christian message centered around certain fixed events: the creation, the fall, the birth and resurrection of the Christ, and, most significantly, his coming again, which would usher in the end of history itself.[11]

Since the Renaissance, the specifically theological (although not mystical) components have been eliminated from this conception of time, but the supernatural aura remains. Since the eighteenth century, it has been believed not only that "every day, in every way, things are getting better and better," but that they have to get better. In matters of technology and the applied sciences, there is some justification for this conviction. But, as Robert Nisbet points out in his *History of the Idea of Progress*,

> Matters become more complicated . . . when we ask what the overall *effects* are—environmental, social, moral, demographic, spiritual, and so forth—of even the kind of progress we see in medicine.[12]

Nisbet goes on to cite the ethical complications that arise from medical technology. Our ability to prolong life helps to foster the illusion that modern men are stronger than other generations because we have in our hands the potential solutions to all the problems the human flesh is heir to and have routed the four horsemen of the apocalypse. We point confidently to the technological achievements of the past two centuries as a self-evident demonstration of our glory. Even more than technology, we pride ourselves on the social and ethical superiority of modern civilization. The easiest way to locate standard views on such a subject is to turn to a high school history text:

> More than ever before men sympathize with the misfortunes of others and feel that it is a duty to help the poor and relieve suffering . . . Along with the increase in humane feelings, there has been an increase in democratic ideas.[13]

The twentieth century has been the culmination of progress and has witnessed the liberation of humanity from the shackles of the past. But what a curious century to pick as an illustration of human improvement!

Any brief survey of the twentieth century would include two of the most terrible and barbaric wars in human history; millions of Jews, Slavs, Gypsies, and political dissidents who died in Hitler's camps; the still greater numbers of millions who starved and froze to death by the order of Lenin, Stalin, and Brezhnev — to say nothing of the apparent record (to date) held by China under Mao. As for democracy, totalitarian governments now control the destinies of the largest nations on earth, where systematic terror and repression are practiced on an unprecedented scale. Historian John Lukacs is fond of pointing out that National Socialism was not destroyed in World War II; in fact, it is a dominant ideology in the world today. As James Hammond said of slavery, "you change the name, not the thing." In their efforts to combine economic centralization with nationalist fervor, the countries of Africa and Asia struggle with mass starvation and a bitter warfare that combines tribal animosity with the glory of modern technology.

If anyone is tempted to retort that Africa, Asia, and Russia are cases of arrested development, he might turn his attention to the enormous social problems engendered by our advanced civilization in Europe and America: the creation of a permanent underclass of welfare recipients, drug and alcohol abuse, spiralling divorce rates, and a disregard for human life that can be measured by the increase in suicides and by the unwillingness of 1.5 million American mothers — a year — to go to the trouble of carrying their unborn babies to term.

And yet, many moderns continue to put their faith in the future — a condition of perpetual possibility. The future is like a science fiction novel, where the author is free to invent — not just plot and characters — but the whole history of the universe. That is the reason so much science fiction is stupid and unreadable and so quickly dated: one writer, no matter how talented, cannot devise a model world with the same richness and variety offered by real life.

The same staleness, the sense of diminished possibilities afflicts visitors to planned communities and utopian settlements. The past, the past of history, teaches us all to be human (and humble), but in the future we are all gods, creating the universe in the image of our own desires.

Sinclair Lewis caught the tone in George Babbitt's famous speech on the greatness of Zenith City, which touches on many popular themes — size, prosperity, and statistics, always statistics:

> We have a right, indeed we have a duty toward our fair city, to broadcast the facts about our high schools, characterized by their complete plants and the finest school-ventilating systems in the country, bar none . . . we have an unparalleled number of miles of paved streets, bathrooms, vacuum cleaners, and all the other signs of civilization . . . we have one motor car for every five and seven-eighths persons in the city . . .

Belief in progress requires a level of abstraction unknown to premodern peoples. We turn away from the windows of sense and experience and prefer the narrow peepholes afforded by theories and charts. Common sense tells us that for most men, life means muddling through much unhappiness shot through with a few moments of joy; their greatest satisfactions are derived from matters little affected by progress in any form. Ask an ordinary man what has given him the greatest pleasure: he will probably mention such things as intimacy with his wife, watching his children grow up, having a few rounds with "the boys" after work, and the occasional lazy weekend of hunting or fishing. The pleasure does not come from inventions like contraceptives, pop-top cans, or infrared rifle scopes, but from experiences we share with our most ancient ancestors. If we think we are happier than a well-fed primitive, it is partly because we believe we have escaped the limitations of primitive life.

Much of our civilization is in fact a refuge we have constructed from our humanity. Consider only the amount of energy and resources we put into bathrooms whose only true function is to dispose of the waste and dirt of our bodies. Although a hole in the ground over a septic tank might serve as well, we have made the modern bathroom more like a Roman bath than an old-fashioned outhouse. It is a place for us to scrub and pluck and oil, disinfect, deodorize, and medicate all the symptoms of our mortality. If communism is Soviet power plus electricity, progress is democracy plus plumbing.

Despite the older view that democracy was against progress, the two have become linked in the popular imagination. What is usually meant by democratic progress, however, is the extension of equality. Any list of the democratic legislation in the United States would surely include the fifteenth amendment giving citizenship rights to blacks, the eighteenth, which did the same for women, the twenty-sixth, which gave the vote to eighteen-year-olds. Other democratic — and egalitarian — landmarks have been the graduated income tax, Brown v. the

Topeka Board of Education, and — should it ever be passed — the Equal Rights Amendment.

Equality is a fine and noble conception, one that has been widely discussed by political philosophers. In application, however, it does not turn out to be all that simple to sort through the jumble of human needs and experiences and make little piles of merits and reward, to boil down the luxuriant organic growth of human life and distill the essences of social justice.

Such a task is obviously impossible. As a result, we fall back on myth and religion, whose rituals are to be performed and pronouncements obeyed without question or analysis. The myth, in this case, is the state of nature. In the natural Eden of liberal philosophers, men were born free and equal. By a process of social evolution and political repression, they surrendered many of these rights, but it is the purpose of government to reclaim at least some of this lost ground and to enforce the natural equality of human individuals.

On the basis of this myth (and a residual religious commitment to social justice) the modern West (led by Britain, France, and the United States) undertook sweeping social and political reforms, many of which affect the status and integrity of families, communities, and religious bodies. In every case, the real and pressing needs of human beings as they actually live and breathe are subordinated to the numerical abstractions of democracy.

In the case of affirmative action, legislation designed to address "the results of centuries of injustice" has meant, in practice, that more qualified young men who happen to be white are turned down by employers, law schools, and fellowship committees in favor of less-qualified women and blacks.

In one contemporary vision of political morality, affirmative action (even when carried to extremes) is a good thing, because justice requires that we equalize as much as possible the conditions of life experienced by our citizens, regardless of race, sex, or religion. If this means that a few individuals have to suffer, it is a small price to pay for the common good.

A majority of Americans seem to object: justice is for them a question of individuals whose rights take precedence over the rights of groups or the desire for equality. This conflict of moral visions is only a small part of the ethical confusion Alisdair MacIntyre describes at the beginning of *After Virtue*: older moral systems have all decayed, but their fossils and bones are jumbled together to create hybrid monstrosities:

> . . . the language and the appearance of morality persist even though the integral substance of normalcy has to a large degree been fragmented and then in part destroyed.[14]

With so many fragments and fossils of moral systems competing for support, it is not surprising that much of our social legislation has been a sort of piecemeal tinkering, more a matter of the cobbler than the shoemaker. The result is that repairs on one section of the machine may mean damage to another. To choose a more organic metaphor, it is as if a man with a sore throat were to take large doses of antibiotics only to realize that the wonder drugs had destroyed the bacteria responsible for his digestion. The patient might then – to cure his diarrhea – resort to morphine, to which he becomes addicted. Meanwhile, the sore throat turns out to be a viral disease unaffected by antibiotics (or simply the result of making too many speeches). Even when they work, social remedies can be, as Tacitus remarked of the Roman Empire, worse than the disease.

Our obsession with technique is also related to the illusion of control. Nothing is immune, not even the nature of man. Belief in progress implies a faith in mankind's destiny to evolve into something higher, in a movement "towards some 'ultra-human' lying ahead in time," as it was expressed by Teilhard de Chardin. It is nothing new for religious people to possess a vision of the future. The Christian Church – to take a once-familiar example – has a fairly concrete picture of the Last Days and Second Coming. But the Christian apocalypse is not a cheerful prospect, that men will "rise on stepping-stones of their dead selves to higher things." It is rather a confession that man, by his own unaided efforts, cannot escape the consequences of his mortal nature.

The Christian vision of life often strikes moderns as gloomy and depressing, but in its view of human nature, Christianity is not all that different from the doctrines of most higher religions and has a great deal in common with the folk wisdom of Europe and the East. A typical example is the maxims inscribed on the temple of Apollo at Delphi: NOTHING IN EXCESS, MEASURE IS BEST, KNOW THYSELF. All of them recommended restraint to the passionate, unrestrained Greeks. The most powerful of them, KNOW THYSELF, was taken up by Socrates. Far from being an invitation to Oriental introspection or adolescent brooding, the *Gnothi Seauton* warned man to resist the temptation to play God, to acknowledge the limits that have been set on human aspirations.

The Delphic note is struck in all the old definitions of man. It was heard over 4,000 years ago by the Sumerian Gilgamesh, who:

> Peered over the wall, saw the dead bodies floating in the river's waters. . . . man, the tallest, cannot reach to heaven, man, the widest, cannot cover the earth.

Poets never grow tired of writing variations on the theme of human futility. The generations of men are "leaves in the wind" (Homer) and we are, variously, "dust and shadow" (Horace), a "quintessence of dust" and "such stuff as dreams are made on" (Shakespeare) and "a shadow's dream" (Pindar).

For the Greeks, at least, the Delphic wisdom was not a doctrine of futility – rather, it was bound up with the sense of shame or face. Shame can be understood as a safety mechanism for society, since it is the fear of ridicule (shame) that prevents us from indulging our appetites at the expense of the community. In a way, shame is the real foundation of morality. While it is true that shame alone may not deter anyone from practicing a secret vice or commiting a crime that avoids detection; nonetheless, once we have conceived of an omnipotent God, "Who sees through doors and darkness, and our thoughts,"[15] our sense of shame begins to act like a moral sense. Moral human beings are something like the nuns who wear a shift in the bath, because God can still see them after they have shut the door.

But shame is one human quality that has been most battered in modern times. It has been many years since women were praised for modesty or delicacy, and it is a rare minister who does not know enough off-color jokes to keep the locker room entertained. Shame is Delphic: it imposes restraint and forces us to recognize our human weakness. While Pindar counseled the great men of his time with the admonition, "Do not seek to become a God," today it is the earnest wish of many people that we all "become as gods." Which god? Preferably one of the shape-changers, like Proteus, or the werewolves of European legend.

The modern age is ideologically diversified, with as many "jarring sects" as are said to have disturbed the peace of Islam. And yet on this one point, there is a reigning orthodoxy. The human species is liberating itself from the unpleasant facts of life that were once thought to constitute its nature; we are — according to the dominant schools of philosophy — the creature that makes his own history (Marxism), whose existence precedes his essence (existentialism), whose nature is given to him by social relations (social psychology including behaviorism), and whose obligation it is to transcend and transform himself.

This faith in the malleability of human clay is more of a political creed than a scientific theory. Marxist ideologues have used it to justify their abolition of private property in the same way that classical liberals used a mythical "state of nature" in their attack on all status based on family and religion. Social Democrats in Europe and the United States have tried to design a world free of any distinctions of sex, class, religion, or nationality. The only moral imperative that was universally recognized was man's need to advance, to improve, to progress beyond the apparent limitations of his species.

Nature has become, in a way, the enemy. John Dewey, for example, argued that democracy — so far from being natural to men — really meant that "the belief in human culture *should* prevail"[16] (italics his). For Dewey, as for most social planners, education was the key. Alter the child's environment, keep him from the age of five to twenty-one, and he will grow up free from the inhibitions and compulsions that have marred human history.

Once human nature is rejected, it will be replaced by something designed by science. The behaviorist B.F. Skinner makes the connection clear: "Behavior can be changed by changing the conditions of which it is a function." Skinner describes the techniques for altering the human condition as "ethically neutral."[17] How are we to judge between the claims of men of good will, like Dewey, and those who are merely neutral? The obvious problem with redesigning the human species does not lie so much in the how as in the whom. In his remarkably prescient *The Abolition of Man*, C.S. Lewis pointed out that the first generation holding such power would also be the last generation of the human race.

The record of previous "ethically neutral" attempts to change the human condition has not been encouraging. Among these experiments, communism is certainly the most significant. In the beginning, communism and socialism were an essentially sentimental and nostalgic reaction against the social disruptions created by capitalism. Communist visionaries wished to restore mankind to its pristine state, when social injustice did not exist, because neither classes nor nations nor even property existed. The French, whose lucidity makes them prone to revolutionary movements, were of course the leaders. St. Simon, Fourier, and even August Comte indulged in speculations about what the world might be like if men once quit squabbling over territory, property, and women.

Earlier utopian communists, like Plato and Sir Thomas More, were prudent enough not to make a practical trial of their theories. The utopian visionaries of the nineteenth century were not so wise. America became the proving (or rather disproving) ground for a number of religious and secular communist sects: New Harmony, the Shaker communities, and the Oneida Colony were all set up along communal lines. The followers of Fourier attempted to set up communist "phalanxes" in several places. The most famous was the Brook Farm experiment, which included the cream of the New England intelligentsia. The socialist experiments of the philanthropist, Robert Owen, are particularly instructive. Owen, a wealthy British industrialist, set up a series of utopian communities, which all failed. In each case, the community worked only so long as Owen remained on hand, supplying money and — what was far more important — strong leadership. Every time Owen left, the settlers would immediately begin squabbling over their rights. Two centuries earlier, Captain John Smith's description of communism at Jamestown makes the deficiency clear: no one worked so long as the fruits of labor were divided up "according to need," and no one, except under the compulsion of a powerful leader (like Owen or Smith) was willing to lift a finger for the common good.

The followers of Karl Marx did, in fact, learn one of the necessary lessons. Marxist leaders — beginning with Marx himself — quickly moved to establish an absolute power over their political movement. As W.H. Mallock was pointing out before the Russian Revolution, Marx ran the *Internationale* as a complete autocrat. His successors in the Soviet Union stifled all controversy and tried to impose an almost religious discipline upon their followers. To the extent that communist revolutions have been successful, it has been due to the exercise of complete control over the parties and nations they have taken over, and not to any virtues in their social or economic theories.

Even so, despite their strictly political successes, the record of Marxist regimes has not been encouraging: slow industrial growth, food shortages, and a general technological backwardness that leads visitors to regard the Soviet Union as an industrial museum. Already in 1921, only four years after the Russian Revolution, Lenin was forced to adopt a New Economic Policy, which reintroduced a market economy in farming, trade, and small industry. The results were an immediate and impressive acceleration of the growth rate.[18]

Lenin's successes were only temporary, because he and the other Soviet ideologues were determined to do away with all vestiges of capitalism. Since they could not entirely eliminate such ordinary human motives as the desire for power and prestige, the pride in working for one's own, they have set up an elaborate piecework system that predominates in Soviet industry. The system is based on a set of production norms that the workers seem to regard as unfairly high. Workers who do not produce up to the norm are penalized, while those who overproduce are rewarded. Even with 'capitalist' incentives, Soviet industry has a dismal record. In 1984, almost half of the enterprises in Leningrad failed to reach output goals; only 70–75 percent of shoe orders could be fulfilled (and only 20 percent of the demand for copy machines).[19]

Bleaker still is the story of Soviet collective agriculture. The annual crop failure in the Soviet Union has become as predictable as their pronouncements on world peace or nuclear disarmament. Under Stalin, Nikita Khruschev had been a stalwart promoter — and enforcer — of collectivization, but after he came to power, he began to vocalize concerns for agricultural failures. At the Central Committee Meeting in 1958, Khruschev exploded at the Azerbaijan party secretary who complained that the peasants were resisting collectivization and that they needed more time to educate the peasants in "the principles of socialist agriculture."

"And how much time do you need?" was the First Secretary's withering reply. "Haven't forty-one years of Soviet power been enough?"

In fact, as Khruschev confessed, the Soviet Union was not producing much more grain than Russia of 1910–14, despite the increase in population.[20] A survey of travellers returning from the Soviet Union in 1981 indicated that only three out of nineteen food products were regularly available in the cities where they lived — vodka, bread, and sugar.[21] The presence of vodka on the list is ominous, since alcohol-related deaths occur at a frequency of 88 times the rate experienced in the United States — a good index to the hopelessness of Soviet life. After one memorable drinking bout that left his face numb, *New York Times* reporter Hedrick Smith concluded that his companions "and the millions upon millions of Russians who drink that way" had "set out deliberately to destroy me and themselves from the very beginning."[22]

The usual communist excuses — bad weather, sabotage, hooliganism, wartime/postwar economy, etc. — might be accepted if Marxism were not a failure everywhere it has been tried. In fact, as Milovan Djilas (a once passionate Marxist) points out in *The New Class*, communism is simply another form of private ownership under which economic development has come to be guided mainly in the interest of the ruling class. Despite experiments with incentives and the partial introduction of free enterprise into Yugoslavia (and recently, tentatively in Czechoslovakia), "the abolition of all forms of private ownership *except their own* is their unchanging purpose".[23]

It goes without saying that the abolition of property is a futile ambition. There appears to be no known society in which some form of personal possession was not normal. The Marxist mistake is to confuse ownership of land with personal possession. There have been many societies, some of them fairly advanced, where land was held in common by the family or tribe. And yet, this communism bears little resemblance to Marxism. In the first place, the family — rather than the individual — is the real social unit for such peoples. Even the legal identity of the individual is a vague, ill-defined concept in a society where a criminal's family shares the burden of guilt. In the second place, individuals — in every society — do possess articles of value: hunting implements, tools, musical instruments, clothes, etc. Personal wealth exists.

The Soviets' attempt to create a classless society has failed even more miserably. As early as the 1930s, James Burnham was arguing (against Trotsky) that Lenin, no less than Stalin, was guilty of creating a hierarchy with rigid class boundaries. Trotsky, in defense of the Soviet system, was forced to concede that not much more than 10 percent, 11 percent, or 12 percent of the Soviet population was receiving more than half of the national income — a disparity in excess of anything in the United States during that time or any time since.[24] David Shipler found himself depressed by the cynicism of young Russians who assumed that "nothing was done truly on merit." Party membership by itself means little, but party professionals find the doors to pleasant living gradually opened to them and their families.[25]

The communist attack on differences is not restricted to economics and class divisions. It includes the elimination of nation states (the brotherhood of man) as well as the destruction of family and religion. Their efforts to promote international harmony and the abolition of nations have, unfortunately, met with as much success as their attack on private property and personal initiative. The first generation of Soviet leaders appear to have taken their internationalist ideals seriously. However, by the end of the 1930s, Burnham was able to describe their "ever growing nationalism which has come . . . to exceed anything present under the czars themselves."[26] Other communist countries have experienced a similar outbreak of extreme nationalism.

It would be wrong to attribute Soviet nationalism to the Russian character. A sense of place, of local identity is part of human nature:

> In general primitive men divide the world into two tangible parts, the near environment of home, local villages, kin, friends, tame animals, and witches, and the more distant universe of neighboring villages, intertribal allies, enemies, wild animals, and ghosts.[27]

To an individual, a territory can be as small as the home place—even his own room—or as wide as the borders of a nation state. However, it always involves a distinction between us/here and them/there. To the extent that we have a group identity—the Jones family, of St. Stephens, South Carolina, the South, the United States—we have a corresponding sense of territory.

A sense of territory can obviously be enlarged. We grow up with horizons no broader than our own neighborhood, but find ourselves in a war fighting to defend the lives of over 200 million people. Historical circumstances can also broaden our allegiances. The sons and grandsons of Confederate soldiers, who had fought for Virginia and Alabama, enlisted in the Army to defend the United States during the Spanish-American and First World War. The citizens of Rome succeeded in enlarging the *imperium romanum* until it included first Latium, then Italy, and eventually most of the civilized world—at the expense, it must be said, of the territorialities of Sabines, Etruscans, Gauls, and Greeks. All internationalism is at bottom a form of imperialism—the cultural, economic, and political domination that the strong exert over the weak.

There is nothing necessarily wrong with imperialism—so long as it provides security, stability, and prosperity—and so long as we recognize it for what it is. But what has happened to our sense of reality, when we begin talking of a world state, of international tribunals, of putting an end to national boundaries?

The purpose of international cooperation is to ensure peace, but the League of Nations failed to prevent the great powers from taking a second crack at each other in World War II, while the United Nations has had similar failures in keeping the peace in Korea, Vietnam, Africa, and the Middle East. Given the "territorial imperative," we shall never be able to guarantee a peaceful international unity until we face a common, extraterrestrial enemy.

There is, of course, a purpose to internationalism. The Russians have, from time to time, promoted the idea of Pan-Slavism—the union of all Slavic peoples under the benevolent protection of the Great Russians. The United States has also flirted with promises of stability and prosperity to various peoples, to the Mexican province of Yucatan during the Mexican War, to the territories Spain lost in the Spanish-American War, and to remnants of the Japanese Empire after World War II. In fairness to the United States, it must be said that Americans lack the force of character necessary to form and maintain an empire.

A real internationalist movement always turns out to be nationalism. What is the U.S.S.R. but a union of republics? Ask an Estonian or a Lithuanian or an Armenian how much he appreciates Russian internationalism. As Zbigniew Brzezinski puts it, "The Soviet Union is the political expression of Russian nationalism," in which "135 million Great Russians control a political empire that includes almost 400 million people."[28] In that case, movements that espouse peaceful international cooperation only accelerate the process of imperialism by discouraging Western resistance and enheartening Russian expansionism. Nothing has changed since the time of the Romans, who did succeed in creating their own one-world state. Tacitus must have expressed the feelings of many internationalized peoples in the accusations he puts into the mouth of an independent Scot: *solitudinem faciunt, pacem appellant* — they make a desert and call it peace.

The great paradox of human nature is that by trying to transcend its limitations, we most often sink beneath it and become the victims of a terrible revenge. By seeking to become international, we only lose our nationhood. By giving up private property, we become slaves, not only to a greedier set of masters, but also to our basest material desires. By promoting universal human rights, we lose the hard-won legal and civil rights of our national traditions. By seeking freedom from nature and death through a misapplication of genetic engineering, we shall fall prey to the tyranny of technocrats. The ancient wisdom said: do not seek to become a god. The new wisdom informs us that godhead is only a generation away. Sherlock Holmes knew better. The wise logician once warned his friend Dr. Watson on the perils of immortality:

> When one tries to rise above nature, one is liable to fall below it. The highest type of man may revert to the animal if he leaves the straight road of destiny. . . . Consider, Watson, that the material, the sensual, the worldly would all prolong their worthless lives. The spiritual would not avoid the call to something higher. It would be the survival of the least fit. What sort of cesspool may not our poor world become.

Nearly every attempt to transcend the human is aimed at the individual — at liberating his potential, of increasing his fitness, of adding to his intelligence. The result is always the same — an increase in the power of the rulers over their subjects. It now seems that by escaping from the restraints of the family, the village, and the church, we inevitably put our lives in the hands of tyranny.

The nineteenth century was much taken with the ideas of democracy and capitalism. By changing the form of government and subjecting everything to the laws of the marketplace, the peoples of Europe and America were supposed to enjoy peace and prosperity. Above all, the democratic process would minimize the power of government over its citizens. And yet, the democratic ideas of Locke, Rousseau, and Bentham seemed to lead inexorably to the creation of powerful nation states in which individuals are increasingly dependent upon the government for the necessities of life. This is dramatically clear in the case of revolutionary movements. As Sorel observed in his *Reflections on Violence*, "All of the revolutionary disturbances of the last century ended up reinforcing state power."

As an ideology capitalism, almost as much as communism, wages war upon natural institutions. Under the conditions of what Marxists call "late capitalism," we have reached the stage at which household functions are increasingly absorbed by the state, which succeeds in "transforming duties performed by women in the household into capitalistically organized services, or . . . replacing them with capitalistically produced commodities."[29] This is not to say that a free-market economic system is inconsistent with human sociability and competitiveness — on the contrary. But a society that recognizes none but economic goods will end up poisoning its own wells: deracinated hedonists do not make good workers or good citizens.

The fault of much social legislation lies not in the details, but in the absence of an organic vision of society. We possess a naive faith in partial solutions to particular problems. It is part of our self-conception as moderns that we are men of action who get things done. Our slogan is "It doesn't matter so much what you do, so long as you do something." If there is a problem, we must fix it, usually by "catching the shortest way" — as Macbeth expressed it — quickly, directly, and efficiently. Confronted with something we don't quite understand, our first temptation is to eliminate it. This temptation arises from our habit of treating society as a machine. In the introduction to his *Leviathan*, Hobbes described the state as a metaphorical man, but men themselves were *automata* — "engines that move themselves by springs and wheels as doth a watch." By a similar art is the state created, "an artificial man." Paradoxically, it is our very ability to fix things that is at the root of our malaise. As Walker Percy observes, our belief that, whatever is wrong, "they can fix it," is not unreasonable in technical matters. "But what happens when one feels in the deepest sense possible that something has gone wrong with one's very self?"[30]

Whether ideas "have consequences," as Richard Weaver insisted, or are the by-product of historical circumstances is the chicken-and-egg dilemma of epistemology. Which came first, the ideas of individual and state or the social and political pressures that demanded articulation? If ideas, indeed all conscious experience, are mere epiphenomena in a mechanical world, then any political theory makes little difference. If, however, ideas are as much a part of the universe as photons and chlorophyl, then the reduction of all political elements to state and individual can properly be held responsible for whatever good and whatever ill it may have engendered.

What we do not need in modern times are more easy solutions. It is an age when everyone has the answer: Marxists, behaviorists, Freudians, radical feminists, racialists, all claim to have the key that will unlock the secret treasure chest. It is more likely to be a collective Pandora's box. No, something more modest is needed; not a new ideology, or even a philosophy, but a broadly ecological approach that looks at society not as a machine, a few simple mechanisms easy to repair, but as a natural system: organic, complex, and interdependent. What follows is no more than a rough sketch. It is a very fallible attempt to discover the parameters of human social and political life. The information came from a variety of disciplines: history, anthropology, psychology, sociology, biology, and philosophy. It is a difficult task. To do it well would be almost impossible without assigning chapters to a committee — which would mean an end to the hope for an integrated vision.

Fortunately, there is an important precedent for this attempt: the *Nicomachean Ethics* and the *Politics* of Aristotle. By training, Aristotle seems to have been more of a biologist than anything else. He devoted much of his best efforts to observing and classifying natural phenomena. In fact, Aristotle's political thought cannot be properly understood outside the context of his biology. His most famous statement on politics, the definition of man as *zoon politikon* — a political lifeform — makes the connection explicit. If Aristotle were alive today and teaching at Harvard, he would be more likely to be found in the Museum of Comparative Zoology than in the philosophy department.

Aristotle brought the natural history approach to bear on human questions and nearly always began his investigation of a problem by trying to find out the common opinions and practices of the world he knew. His ethical writings take happiness as their point of departure because most people agree that happiness is the most important object of living. When he came to write on politics, he sent his students all over the Mediterranean world to collect information on the constitutions.

It will be clear that Aristotle has served as a model for more than methodology. His comments on social evolution provide a skeleton for the central argument of this book. Above all, the inspiration for discussing the politics of human nature derives from Aristotle's insistence on relating phenomena like poetry and politics to the demonstrable needs of human nature. A unified theory of politics is possible, but only when it is grounded in the reality of human life. Only such a theory would fully deserve the name "natural politics."

Notes

1. See Friedrich Heer, *The Holy Roman Empire*, trans. by Janet Sondheimer (New York: Praeger, 1967).
2. For the metaphor, see Brigitte and Peter L. Berger, *The War Over the Family: Capturing the Middle Ground* (Garden City, NY: Anchor/Doubleday, 1983), 1–8.
3. Marshall Berman, *All That is Solid Melts into Air: The Experience of Modernity* (New York: Simon and Schuster, 1982), views this cultural self-criticism as an essential aspect of modern thought.
4. On the ancient Greek family in general, see W.K. Lacey, *The Family in Classical Greece* (Ithaca, NY: Cornell University Press, 1968); for bourgeois domesticity, see Sally Humphreys, *The Family, Women, and Death: Comparative Studies* (London: Routledge & Kegan Paul, 1983).
5. See Stephen R.L. Clark, "Morals, Moore, and MacIntyre", *Inquiry* 26 (1984) 425–45.
6. For the enduring influence of religion in the U.S., see A. James Reichley, *Religion in American Public Life* (Washington, DC: The Brookings Institution, 1985).
7. The virtues of the bourgeois family are the constant theme of welfare state critics, most of whom are unfamiliar with the wide variety of successful family patterns.
8. Anastasia M. Shkilnyk, *A Poison Stronger than Love: The Destruction of an Ojibwa Community* (New Haven, CT: Yale University Press, 1985), 12–13.
9. David Owen, *None of the Above: Behind the Myth of Scholastic Aptitude* (Boston: Houghton-Mifflin, 1985), 18ff.
10. Georg Simmel, *The Philosophy of Money*, trans. by Tom Bottomore and David Frisby (London: Routledge & Kegan Paul, 1978).
11. For the classic statement on the idea of progress, See J.B. Bury, *The Idea of Progress: An Inquiry into Its Origin and Growth* (London: Macmillan, 1920).
12. Robert Nisbet, *History of the Idea of Progress* (New York: Basic Books, 1980), 6.
13. Carl L. Becker and Kenneth Cooper, *Modern History* (Morristown, NJ: Silver Burdett, 1977), 4–5.
14. Alisdair MacIntyre, *After Virtue*, 2d ed. (Notre Dame, IN: University of Notre Dame Press, 1984), 2.
15. George Chapman's *Bussy D'Ambois* Act II, scene 2.
16. John Dewey, *Freedom and Culture* (New York: G.P. Putnam's Sons, 1939), 124.
17. B.F. Skinner, *Beyond Freedom and Dignity* (New York: Alfred Knopff, 1972), 150.
18. For Soviet economic performance, see G. Warren Nutter, "The Soviet Economy: Retrospect and Prospect" in M.M. Drachkovitch, ed., *Fifty Years of Communism* (University Park, PA: Pennsylvania State University Press, 1986), and most recently Mikhail Heller and Aleksandr Nekrich, *Utopia in Power: The History of the Soviet Union from 1917 to the Present*, translated from the Russian by Phyllis B. Carlos (New York: Summit Books, 1986).
19. John L. Scherer, USSR: *Facts and Figures Annual* (Gulf Breeze, FL: Academic International Press, 1985), 135 ff; cf. Alex Inkeles and Raymond A. Bauer, *The Soviet Citizen: Daily Life in a Totalitarian Society* (New York: Atheneum, 1968), 109–10.
20. Adam B. Ulam, *The New Face of Soviet Totalitarianism* (New York: Praeger, 1965), 93 ff.
21. Seweryn Bialer, *The Soviet Paradox: External Expansion, Internal Decline* (New York: Alfred Knopff, 1986), 58–59.
22. Hedrick Smith, *The Russians* (London: Sphere Books, 1976), 158.

23. Milovan Djilas, *The New Class: An Analysis of the Communist System* (New York: Praeger, 1957), 106.
24. James Burnham, *The Managerial Revolution*, repr. from 1st ed. (Bloomington: Indiana University Press, 1960), 46.
25. David K. Shipler, *Russia: Broken Idols, Solemn Dreams* (New York: New York Times Books, 1983), 163 ff.
26. James Burnham, op. cit., 47.
27. Edward O. Wilson, *On Human Nature* (Cambridge, MA: Harvard University Press, 1978), 111.
28. Zbigniew Brzezinski, "The Soviet Union: World Power of a New Type," in Erik P. Hoffmann, *The Soviet Union in the 1980s* (New York: The Academy of Political Science, 1984), 148.
29. Ernst Mandel, *Late Capitalism*, trans. by Joris de Bres (Thetford, Norfolk: Lowe Brydone Printers, Ltd., 1975), 391.
30. Walker Percy, "The Diagnostic Novel: On the Use of Modern Fiction," *Harpers*, June 1986, 39–45.

2

Against the Grain

Human nature is an idea that dies hard. Its persistence can be measured by the proverbs and platitudes that reflect our belief in an unvarying, universal human type. English is full of them: a fool and his money are soon parted; you can't teach an old dog new tricks; it's only human nature (or you can't change human nature). Our view of life is neatly packaged into categories of age and sex — impetuous youth and cautious old age, the bravery of men and the tenderness of women . . . all in the apparent belief that these qualities do not, on the whole, change from age to age or suffer by translation into other languages.

The persistence of such opinions is remarkable. The modern age has little use for received wisdom of any sort, especially the stereotypes and generalizations that seem to give a color to sexism, agism, and racism. The modern wisdom — the opposite in every respect of the old, proverbial wisdom — is dead set against all the categories by which individuals may be "put in their place." Such categories tend to promote discrimination and snobbery, while at the same time interfering with our appreciation of every man as a unique individual. If Shakespeare were composing *As You Like It* for a modern audience, he could scarcely have included Jacques' speech on the seven ages of man, since it is offensive alike to the very young — "the infant mewling and puking," "the whining schoolboy" — and to the very old — "second childishness and mere oblivion, sans teeth, sans eyes, sans taste, sans everything." An author writing such stuff today would face the combined fury of the Gray Panthers, the advocates of children's rights, and — inevitably — the feminists (Why the seven ages of *man*?).

The argument over man's nature enters into every arena of public debate. Scientists who speak of innate characteristics or of intelligence as genetically transmitted are reviled as agents of neofascism and racism. Economists and politicians who base their assumptions on the universal human desires for wealth and power are attacked as low-minded agents of the New Right. A similar fate

27

awaits religious leaders who continue to speak of original sin, the old Adam, and the "desperately wicked" heart of man.

In the face of all our education and indoctrination, most of us continue to believe nonetheless in a constant human nature. This tendency, which is itself a kind of universal, constitutes a powerful testimony to the existence of an innate, specifically human set of predispositions that direct the individual behavior and social life of human beings. No matter how hard we try to avoid it, we cannot escape thinking of ourselves as only human. It is a little like a children's game described by Tolstoy: try not to think of a white bear. Try as they might, Tolstoy and his playmates would come upon the bear in the most obscure nooks and crannies of their minds. So, in all our struggles to evade the Old Adam of human nature, the little beast is forever slipping out of the trees and making gestures we regard as obscene.

This belief in human nature is an old story, as old as there are written records. The oldest literary documents — Sumerian, Egyptian, Indian, and Greek — are filled with generalizations about human life. Many Sumerian proverbs could be written on a men's room wall: "For his pleasure — marriage, upon reflection — divorce;" "The Poor have no power"; "Who has not supported a wife or child has not borne a leash"; "Friendship lasts a day, kinship endures forever." Such proverbs, which can be paralleled in most cultures, imply the obvious conviction that human beings are pretty much the same in essential matters. In fact, their comprehensibility to a modern European or American five thousand years later is itself a sign of universal social traits.

David Hume took this ability to understand other periods of history as the strongest kind of evidence for the constancy of human nature:

> It is universally acknowledged that there is a great uniformity among the actions of men, in all nations and ages, and that human nature remains still the same, in its principles and operations. The same motives always produce the same actions: the same events follow the same causes. Ambition, avarice, self-love, vanity, friendship, generosity, public spirit: these passions, mixed in various degrees, and distributed throughout society, have been, from the beginning of the world, and still are, the source of all the actions and enterprises, which have ever been observed among mankind. Would you know the sentiments, inclinations and course of life of the Greeks and Romans? Study well the temper and actions of the French and English: you cannot be much mistaken in transferring to the former *most* of the observations which you have made with regard to the latter. Mankind are so much the same, in all times and places, that history informs us of nothing new or strange in this particular. Its chief use is only to discover the constant and universal principles of human nature, by showing men in all varieties of circumstances and situations, and furnishing us with materials from which we may form our observations and become acquainted with the regular springs of human action and behaviour.[1]

Obviously, manners and customs change, and in Hume's day it was common to speak of the "national" character of the English, the French, and the Germans. But when modern historians reject Hume's argument, they put themselves in a difficult position. It becomes almost impossible to speak of "the lessons"— or even the usefulness of history, if men of other times are fundamentally different from ourselves.

In R. G. Collingwood's philosophy of history, human nature is impervious to empirical disciplines like psychology. While criticizing the older philosophers who tried to create a science of human nature, he still maintained that the work of such a science was possible, but it "is actively done, and can only be done, by history."

For Collingwood, the prime task of the historian was to think himself into the mind of other ages. Whatever the whole duty of the historian might be, it ought to enable us to understand the minds of other generations. What good would it do to do current events, or calculate the impact of geographical and economic forces, if we failed to appreciate the motives and aspirations of the agents of historical change? But, how is it possible to understand "the thought in the mind of the person by whose agency the event came about," if there is no substratum of humanity that connects our generation with those of the past?[2]

If Cromwell's roundheads or Julius Caesar's legionaries are utterly alien to us, history would have to become a natural science — an ethological discipline that assumed no more about the human mind than about the mind of rats. H. G. Gadamer makes something of the same point. Seeing the contradictions in Collingwood's thought, he draws the only reasonable conclusion: no historian can escape his age. By interpreting the past, we are really only talking about ourselves.[3]

A great deal of historical writing is, in fact, about the present. The more philosophical the historian is, the more he is writing about his own concerns. But why restrict this alienation and isolation to our place in time? From Gadamer's perspective, there is no evidence of our ability to understand each other in our own age. Of course, it might be possible to examine the data provided by psychology and neurophysiology, but most radical historians — particularly Gadamer — reject the evidence of the natural sciences. Their only alternative, it would seem, is to take refuge in mysticism. In the tradition of the German idealists, they might speak of "the spirit of the age" or perhaps even "the national will."

The one fact we do have to go on is the near universality of human nature as an idea. The concept of human nature may be as old as man himself. After all, the ability to conceptualize and make what is now called "value judgments" — to put things in their place — is one of the powers that distinguish us from the beasts we resemble the most. Homo sapiens is the intelligent human primarily because he is the rational animal. The modern view, that environment is predominantly responsible for molding individuals, is far more recent. While there were, even in ancient times, writers who emphasized the variability of cultures and the openness of man's nature to environmental influences, (Herodotus, Plato and Epicurus, for example) John Locke is among the first philosophers to articulate the robust environmental position, that men are made and molded by their experiences.

Locke wrote a great deal about nature and set great store by the rights enjoyed by men "in a state of nature": life, liberty, and property (by which he meant everything you can call your own, including life and liberty). At the same time, Locke did his best to undermine belief in a specifically human nature. In *An Essay Concerning Human Understanding,* Locke argued that man is not born with an already formed intellect — one that is prewired (to use a modern metaphor) to interpret experience in certain ways. Rather, the human mind is a tabula rasa, or blank slate, upon which experience is free to write any sort of message it likes. In that same essay, Locke suggested that our concept or definition of man "is nothing else but of an animal of such a certain form," irrespective of any other so-called human characteristics like rationality.

Locke was himself a social and political reformer, and his blank slate gave a great deal of encouragement to the political theorists of the Enlightenment. Reformers became convinced that it was possible to alter and improve the nature of man by providing the right social atmosphere. In France, the idea of social progress became gospel for many of the lawyers and journalists who brought down the monarchy and began dating the history of the world from the French Revolution. The English took their time in making up their minds, but already in the 1790s, William Godwin (who later married Mary Woolstonecraft, the first feminist, and fathered Mary Shelley) was outlining the basic dogma of the age to come: the inevitability of progress and the perfectibility of human nature. In his highly successful *Political Justice,* Godwin went so far as to endorse Ben Franklin's speculation that the human mind might triumph over death.

This notion of human perfectibility helps to explain the obsession that modern man has had with education. Such diverse political thinkers as Rousseau, Jefferson, and Wordsworth firmly believed that in education lay the salvation of the world. Locke took up the idea of educational reform in a modest way, but his disciples, Helvetius in the eighteenth century and John Dewey in the twentieth, drew the comforting conclusion that mankind is capable of infinite progress, so long as he is subjected to sufficient doses of positive education. As Helvetius put it in *De l'homme,* "Education is capable of changing everything."[4]

The opposition to human nature is not a conspiracy of one or two crank philosophers and a handful of devoted followers. The mainstream of modern thought flows inexorably against any notion of humanness, whether it takes the form of Platonic ideas, Kantian categories, original sin, or genetic constraints. With the very partial exceptions of Freudian psychoanalysis and structuralism, all the modern -isms and -ologies are based on the belittlement or repudiation of human nature. Each school of thought has its own set of arguments. However, most of them are variations or restatements of one of the following types.

Psychological Arguments

Man may or may not possess innate predispositions (like the sucking reflex or sexual desires). However, all such instincts are subordinate to the pressures of environment. "Babies, whatever their potential may be, have few inborn abilities. They can grasp . . . but probably have to learn to utilize the capacity. They have to be taught to suck . . ."[5] This argument, as old as Locke's "blank slate" and associated in this century with John Dewey, is really the heart of the matter. It is not necessary to deny the existence of all "instincts" (as Helvetius did), but Dewey regarded them as the "raw materials" for which "custom furnishes the machinery and designs." Customs, habits, and traditions can be modified in such a way as to transform the operations of our primitive nature into something quite different. In the decade before World War II, Dewey actually proclaimed that mankind was on the threshold of learning to do without war, inequalities of wealth, and even private property.[6]

The weakness of Dewey's approach is clear: the strength and quality of "instincts" is exactly what he needed to determine. Not only did Dewey overlook that problem, he was capable of appealing to human nature when it suited his purpose. Egalitarian democracy is inevitable, he argued, because children are "born with a natural desire to give out, to do, to serve."[7] However, openness had to be a primary human characteristic, because it fostered the belief in democratic progress. This paradox in blank slate theories is met head-on by the behaviorists whose learning theories were once enormously influential. All animal behavior is merely a question of physiosociological stimulus and response patterns of the sort Pavlov demonstrated in dogs and Skinner in pigeons and rats. The central doctrine of behaviorism was formulated by John B. Watson. Watson reduced unconditional response, that is human nature, to three primitive emotions: fear, love, and rage. Everything else was determined by environmental stimuli.

Watson's disciple, B.F. Skinner, was more successful than his master in establishing a school of thought. All that human nature comes down to, according to Skinner, is "what a person . . . would have been like if we had seen him before his behavior was subjected to the action of an environment."[8] Skinner (like Locke, whom he so much resembles) eventually adopted what we shall call the Nominalist position — that the human species is itself only an abstraction. Like Dewey, Skinner was convinced that apparently fundamental aspects of our social life could be changed or eliminated simply by redesigning the environment. His utopian novel, *Walden II*, was designed to illustrate such a possibly optimum environment. The novel was a modest success, but in the great flowering of utopian communes during the 1960s, no one seemed eager to create the sterile conditions of *Walden II*. The communards were mostly interested in rejecting the state and the rationalized conditions of life in a country redesigned by progressives. Perhaps man's "animal" nature had greater strength and appeal than Skinner supposed.

In fact, the behaviorists devised a great many experiments to show the impact of environmental forces on human behavior. They do not seem to have lavished much attention on the (null) hypothesis of human nature.

One of the weaknesses in their approach is its universality. Behaviorist theory assumes that individuals (whether rats, pigeons, or humans) learn their behavior in the same way. While there may be certain common patterns, it would be a strange world if chickens and chimpanzees followed the same path in social development, even allowing for the great difference in intelligence. In fact, much learning is species-specific: animals can only be trained to perform tasks consistent with the needs of their ordinary existence in the wild. E. O. Wilson makes this point against Skinner: "The full range of learning potential of each species appears to be separately programmed."[9]

Behaviorism depends both on the universality of "operant conditioning" and on the absence of powerful, specifically human predispositions. More than one school of psychological thought — Aristotle and Kant, for example — take the opposite view that human understanding is possible if and only if men are born with certain innate categories of time, space, and relation. Others have looked for norms in the universal principles of human language. This train of thought, found in Descartes and Thomas Reid, was revived by the linguist, Noam Chomsky.

Chomsky, who turned out to be Skinner's most trenchant critic, argues that by studying what he calls the deep structures of language, we are in fact learning about the basic processes of the human mind. Chomsky's argument against behaviorism has been made several times, with variations. The essential point is "creativity": young children (five or six years old) constantly come up with new sentences and are able to understand the sentences of other people in ways that cannot be predicted on the simplistic model of stimulus/response patterns. Children are able to use language creatively and with infinite variety, because there are "formal universals" that determine the basic forms and rules of grammar in real or "natural" languages. In recent years, Chomsky has devoted his efforts to outlining the principles of a universal grammar. While much of his work is debated — even by his former students — he has succeeded in pushing linguistics in a new direction.[10]

An entire new discipline, cognitive psychology, has grown up partly in response to Chomsky's central principles and partly under the stimulus of computers. Most cognitive psychologists emphasize the innateness of mental structures. Jerry Fodor probably represents the extreme "nativist" position. Fodor argues that the everyday language we speak — "natural languages" — cannot be the language of thought, because in that case we could not have had access to the thought processes we need to acquire a natural language. Put simply, learning English would be impossible if our minds did not somehow have a universal language built into them. Experiments conducted by cognitive psychologists, while they are not conclusive, do show that the mind tends to learn in some ways and not in others.[11]

Consider a characteristic (albeit inconclusive) series of experiments conducted by Saul Sternberg. Sternberg wanted to find out how recent memories are retrieved. He had his subjects memorize various lists of numbers, which they were allowed to see for just over a second. After a brief pause, they were shown a number and asked to decide if it was on the list. What Sternberg measured was the time it took to answer. He found that reaction time was related to the number's position on the list. The farther down the list, the longer it took subjects to retrieve it. Sternberg concluded, perhaps prematurely, that in retrieving short-term memories our minds work by scanning the whole list, starting at the beginning. On a broader level, what this and similar experiments tend to show is that the mind works according to certain preordained patterns and is not simply "open to experience."[12] There are difficulties with this sort of experiment: not only are they hard to replicate, but counterexperiments have been devised to show that under some circumstances, at least, information is processed differently.

The most serious criticism of cognitive psychology does not come from behaviorists or other advocates of the blank slate, but from philosophers and natural scientists who are impatient with any talk of mind, as opposed to brain. Philosopher John Searle, probably the most prominent critic of cognitive science, concedes that there are features common to all languages but argues that there is a simpler explanation than universal grammar: "That the physiological structure of the brain contains possible grammars without the intervention of an intermediate level of rules or theories."[13]

Some of the strongest arguments against the blank state come from an unexpected quarter: color perception. Color terms do, in fact, vary from language to language. They used to be particularly troublesome to students of the classics. Consider the word *Xanthos*, generally translated as yellow or tawny. It is often applied to the Homeric heroes, but what do we make of Aeschylus' "yellow olive"? A more familiar puzzle is the Homeric expression, wine-dark (actually, wine-appearing) sea. The general assumption has been that the Greeks — and, indeed, most other cultures — perceived color differently.

Recent studies, however, seem to show that color vocabularies and color perception are biased toward discriminating the four basic colors: blue, green, yellow, and red. What is more, even people without any color words are able to learn a 'natural' vocabulary twice as quickly as an unnatural. The naturalness of the basic colors is physiological, since the retina is designed to be roughly sensitive to the wave lengths that correspond to blue, green, yellow-green.[14]

What is more, the evolution of color terms in a language appears to proceed along certain naturally determined lines. In the Mexican language Tarahumara, blue-green may be undergoing a process that will end in discrimination between blue and green.[15] Finally, we seem to make new distinctions along these evolutionary lines. James Boster asked a group of American subjects to subdivide colors over and over. They actually recapitulated "the evolution of color lexicons." Boster concluded that his research "supports the position that the source of cross-cultural universals can often be found in the cognition of individuals."[16]

Emotions are, perhaps, even more obviously universal. Cross-cultural studies indicate a degree of agreement on interpreting facial expressions: happiness, anger, fear, surprise, and disgust can be correctly guessed from pictures of facial expressions, and even children born deaf and blind exhibit a standard repertory of expression. Even many chimpanzee facial expressions can be correctly interpreted by students — although the "smile" is usually misinterpreted as a sign of pleasure rather than as a fear reaction.

It also appears that such essential features of perception as constancy of shape and size and object permanence are present in newborn children, and cannot, therefore, be acquired by experience. Newborns also seem programmed to respond to the human face and voice (especially female), and children — when they are first beginning to talk — display a knowledge of grammar (with their very first words) never attained by chimpanzees that have been trained to communicate.[17] Freedman sums up the results of these researches in a striking sentence: "Learning proceeds easiest in directions determined by phylogenetic evolution, i.e., evolution has dug the major channels through which the river of experience runs."[18] The blank slate turns out to be more like a commonplace book, with pages numbered and ruled and with all headings printed in bold face.

Nominalist Arguments

Research on perception and cognition tends to show man as a creature whose identity is partially determined by his central nervous system, whose characteristics are universal (but to some extent unique) in the human species. However, some philosophers have suggested that there is no such thing as Man: only individual men exist, and the species is nothing more than an abstraction.

This approach might be termed individualist, since it is based on treating all men as unique, undefinable individuals. Since Rousseau, individualist arguments have tended to be highly romantic and rhetorical, of the sort "I am not like anyone I have ever met. . . ." The more general term nominalism refers to those medieval philosophers who insisted on the primacy of individual things, as opposed to the class, genus, or universal, and reduced all universals like whiteness or humanness to the status of mere names (*nomina*). Applied to man, such a doctrine constitutes a denial of general human nature and even of the human species. There is no species, only generalizations made about individuals. This was the view of Marx and Engels in *The German Ideology* and remains the standard Marxist position: "The human essence is no abstraction inherent in each separate individual. . . . It is the ensemble of the social relations." When we speak of general human traits, we really only mean "like us."[19] Marxists concede that men possess certain traits that distinguish them from other animals, but these are differences of degree, not of kind. The chief difference lies in the fact that man, unlike subhuman animals, "makes his own history." This Marxist commonplace means that human beings are to a great extent free from the biological constraints that govern the behavior of other animals.

Marx's nominalism is less well-advertised than that of his political disciple, Jean-Paul Sartre. The cardinal point in Sartre's philosophy of existentialism is that for man "existence precedes essence," that is, there is no general, universal human type to which individuals tend to conform. A similar position is taken by Ernst Cassirer: "We cannot define man by an inherent principle." For Sartre, man is free to define his own "essence," because God does not exist. There is, therefore, no mind in which the idea of man can be located, unlike manufactured objects whose essence, i.e., conception, exists in the mind of the designer. On the contrary, man is free and alone.[20]

Existentialists typically resist any idea of innateness, not merely the theistic arguments used to support such ideas. Sartre speaks disdainfully of people who remark "It's only human nature," when they are faced with some unpleasant piece of misbehavior. For Sartre, as for Marx, the point is freedom and revolution. Man must be by his very nature free to throw off the shackles of history and create a new society. Neither Sartre nor Marx made any attempt to prove their assumption. Sartre's proof — denial of God's existence — is not a philosophical argument; it is only a premise, a fashionable prejudice, which even Sartre grew uncomfortable with in his last days. It will scarcely do for a first principle. In addition, existentialism does not follow from the assumption of atheism. No one would describe most evolutionary biologists as defenders of the faith, and yet some of them are devoting their careers to proving that social behavior is partly determined by genetic factors. It will take more that a denial of God to prove that man is exempt from the same kind of rules that dictate the social behavior of other species. In fact, the strongest traditional argument made for human freedom is that we have a special relationship with a Creator, or at least a source of values lying outside nature.

The most radical form of the nominalist argument, which was used by Marx and goes back as far as Leibniz, is that the concept of a species is itself only a rough generalization, a sort of statistical average that has no real influence on the behavior of individuals. Of course, it is difficult to make precise distinctions between species and subspecies. The old rule, that breeding takes place within the species, is subject to all sorts of caveats and exceptions. But the fact that it is hard to define the species is no argument against the inheritance of social behavior. The subspecies of a widely distributed species like the herring gull may vary widely in color and even in certain behavioral patterns (especially at the geographical extremes), so much so that serious disagreement may arise about their status, i.e., whether species or subspecies. Yet no one would argue that the social behavior of such a species is any the less genetically transmitted.

The most intriguing nominalist arguments have been made recently by Michael Ghiselin and David L. Hull in a number of articles in which they redefine the species in terms of evolutionary theory. Is the species a class (like planet) in particular, the sort of class that functions in scientific laws, or simply a lineage, i.e., a sequence "of entities that usually produce one another"? The distinction is crucial, if we accept the common view that scientific laws apply only to classes unrestricted in space and time. Hull insists that species are, in fact, only "lineages" and count, therefore, as individuals. As "historical entities," in an evolutionary process, they cannot be the subject of laws.[21]

Hull spells out the implications for human nature in no uncertain terms:

> If species are interpreted as historical entities, then particular organisms belong in a particular species because they are part of that genealogical nexus, not because they possess any essential traits. No species has an essence in this sense. Hence there is no such thing as human nature. There may be characteristics which all and only extant human beings possess, but this state of affairs is contingent, depending on the current evolutionary state of *Homo sapiens*. Just as not all crows are black (even potentially), it may well be the case that not all people are rational (even potentially). On the historical entity interpretation, retarded people are just as much instances of *Homo sapiens* as are their brighter congeners. The same can be said for women, blacks, homosexuals and human fetuses. Some people may be incapable of speaking or understanding a genuine language; perhaps bees can. It makes no difference. Bees and people remain biologically distinct species. On other, non-biological interpretations of the human species, problems arise (and have arisen) with all of the groups mentioned. Possibly women and blacks are human beings but do not "participate fully" in human nature. Homosexuals, retardates, and fetuses are somehow less than human. And if bees use language, then it seems we run the danger of considering them human. The biological interpretation has much to say in its favor, even from the humanistic point of view.[22]

Hull is quite correct in his insistence on the historical quality of species, but his conclusions are too sweeping. There is, after all, a very strong counter-argument: life itself evolved on earth under specific circumstances of space and time. This would seem to exclude all life on earth from the province of scientific laws. Hull's escape from this dilemma is reminiscent of a Carl Sagan: "Things which biologists would recognize as organisms could develop (and probably have developed) elsewhere in the universe." If we are going to engage in science fiction, there is no reason to suppose Homo sapiens is restricted to terra. Hull would respond, quite properly, that identical intelligent bipeds from another star system would not be human, because they do not share our evolutionary history. But the same restrictions can be applied to terms like "life" or "organisms."

In an absolute sense, there are no laws of nature that concern organic life, much less the human species. There are, however, law-like regularities. It would be more useful to imagine a descending scale of scientific law from mathematics through physics and chemistry to evolutionary principles and, finally, to the species themselves. In any event, it really does not make a great deal of difference whether there is an essential human nature, so long as we are subject to behavioral "laws" that derive from the evolutionary history of the species.

Contrary to Hull's assertion of humanism, the real effect of any form of nominalism would be to accentuate the differences between the subspecies of man, i.e., the races, and to revive the old racist theories that blacks and whites were the products of separate evolutionary developments. To counter such racist presumptions, Skinner once tried to argue that if thirty Hottentot babies were exchanged with thirty European aristocratic infants, the children would grow up as members of their new adopted culture. To a very great extent, that may be true but irrelevant to his conclusion that there is no real "man qua man" whose freedom and dignity are imperiled by totalitarian social planners.

Cultural Arguments

Skinner is far from unique in using cultural diversity to justify a wholesale reconstruction of the human race. In general, cultural arguments portray man as a species defined by reason, by symbolic communication, and above all by culture through which he transcends the limitations of his genetic heritage. Cultural arguments, employed by many anthropologists, social psychologists, and sociologists, are the most widespread and the most convincing. At bottom, they are simply the psychological argument restated in relation to culture. This way of thinking goes back, in the United States, to the pioneers in social psychology, Ellsworth Faris, Charles H. Cooley, and John Dewey. According to Faris, our "nature" (such as it is) is not given at birth but is developed in an individual as "others are emotional towards him." Cultural arguments are not, however, simply psychological. The emphasis is always on culture or society. As Charles H. Cooley expressed it, individuals do not make society: "Society makes persons."[23]

There is more than a little truth in Cooley's once-famous declaration. It is the essential insight of the French school of sociology. It is to the credit of Auguste Comte (and, to some extent, the utopian socialists who preceded him) that society began to be recognized as more than a collection of competing individuals. The dominant trend in ethics since the time of Hobbes had been converging on individualism. Locke's view of society as based on consent, Adam Smith's economic and moral theories, the utilitarian philosophies of Jeremy Bentham and the Mills — all had this in common: their unit of analysis was the individual. Comte was hardly immune from these influences, and yet his primary concern — the creation of a "science" of society as an instrument of international harmony — led him to rediscover the social nature of men and to repudiate any social analysis that began with the individual:

> La décomposition de l'humanité en individus proprement dits ne constitue qu'une analyse anarchique, autant irrationelle qu'immorale, et qui tend à dissoudre l'existence sociale au lieu d'expliquer. . . . Elle est aussi vicieuse en sociologie que le serait en biologie, la décomposition chimique de l'indivu lui-même en molecules irreductibles, dont la séparation n'a jamais lieu pendant la vie.[24]

Emile Durkheim appropriated this organic conception of society while repudiating Comte's psychology and his view of history. Durkheim established sociology as an independent discipline by asserting the independence of social facts. If society somehow transcends the individuals who compose it, it is because society makes us into what we are — just as a child is molded by education. Over and over, Durkheim rang the changes on this basic theme: "Social phenomena are extensive to individuals," "Social facts are in a sense independent of individuals and exterior to individual minds." For this to be radically true, the mind itself has to be independent of the brain (as Durkheim realized). Otherwise, we should in principle be able to derive social laws ultimately from the nature of the brain, a position that most sociologists and anthropologists strenuously reject.[25]

A less extreme sociological view can coexist with a belief in human nature, especially if man is — in Aristotle's famous phrase — a *zoon politikon*, a social animal. However, the most influential tradition of American anthropology has sought to minimize both universal patterns of behavior and innateness. Franz Boas and his students insisted on the point, and Boas devoted his career to dissociating anthropology from biology. His motives, while admirable, were not strictly scientific, since Boas' main objective was to counter the racial theories that predominated in early twentieth century thought, and with the bathwater of racism went the baby of human nature.[26] The greatest success of Boas' school was probably Margaret Mead, whose work is constantly cited as proof that sexual roles and practices vary so enormously from culture to culture that generalizations are useless or at best trivial. Mead went to Samoa in the 1920s, and in *Coming of Age in Samoa* she reported that there was no adolescent sexual crisis among these simple Polynesians who accepted their sexuality as simply and naturally as they accepted the weather. Mead was to follow up the implications in later works, like *Sex and Temperament in Three Primitive Societies*, in which she tried to demonstrate an extreme cultural variability in the roles assigned to males and females.

Recently, Mead's methods have come under serious attack, especially for her fundamental Samoan research. In 1983, Derek Freeman created a virtual scandal by suggesting that Mead had never learned the language, spent much of her time in the very unSamoan home of a Mr. and Mrs. Holt, and allowed herself to be taken in by the off-color jokes typical of nearly every society but the genteel Philadelphia in which she grew up. Like many earnest young researchers, Mead went to Samoa to collect evidence that would corroborate her mentor's theories.[27]

In a very real sense, she found what she set out to find. It would be interesting to discover how much the progress of anthropology owes to an anti-Western impetus. Primitive cultures have been exploited repeatedly (since Montaigne's essay on the cannibals) for evidence of golden age simplicity in contrast with our own overcivilized degeneracy. The contrast, the shock of seeing how alien another culture is, tends to unsettle the conviction that the human personality is fixed and permanent. Boas himself conceded the existence of "general human characteristics," some of which were derived from our animal nature, but his hostility to racial theories made him anxious to restrict the list to basic needs: sex, food, and protection against the weather.

The most impressive Boasian, A.L. Kroeber, vacillated on the question. He originally took the position that culture was "superorganic," that is, transcends genetic limitations. The "notorious . . . variability of human cultures" he took as a proof of our "exemption from heredity."[28] (Kroeber's best work, it goes without saying, does not depend on the shallow philosophizing he picked up from Boas). For obvious reasons, most social scientists resent any attempt to explain away their subject on a lower, more basic level. They rely, at least implicitly, on Durkheim's distinction between the psychobiological self (endowed by nature) and the sociocultural self (determined by membership in society). As social scientists they are predisposed to emphasize what can be discovered through the methods of their disciplines — the sociocultural self.

Clifford Geertz, the most philosophical of contemporary American anthropologists, observes that "Men unmodified by the customs of particular places do not in fact exist." This is a valuable point, which needs to be stressed, since man as we know him does not exist outside history. Unfortunately, from this solid ground Geertz leaps to the unjustified conclusion that any apparently universal human trait has a different content in different societies (a central doctrine with Boas.) As a result, "there is no such thing as a human nature independent of culture."[29] Some, although by no means all, advocates of culture over nature draw social and political conclusions that are remarkably similar to Dewey, Sartre, Skinner, and Marx. Margaret Mead's early advocacy of progressive causes is too well known to dwell upon, but others are equally candid. The once-prominent Ralph Linton, who dedicated *The Study of Man* "to the next generation," believed the human species was characterized by "extreme teachability." Innate tendencies, to the extent that they exist, "can be inhibited or modified in such a way that the tendency will find indirect, socially acceptable expression."[30] This means the range of human behavior is practically unlimited. Linton could even imagine a future society that will have transcended the admittedly universal pattern of male dominance. In the same vein, Geertz describes men as "unfinished animals who . . . finish ourselves through culture." Who or what is to determine the finished product is usually omitted.

There is something reactionary even about Geertz, a subtle and original anthropological theorist. It is not so much that the culturalist positions are unjustifiable, but it is the consistency of their bias that is peculiar. Man is, after all, a living organism. There are branches of science devoted to the study of life. In them, the dominant "paradigm" for research is the neo-Darwinist synthesis. Put crudely, zoologists generally assume that species are adapted to live and reproduce in their natural environments; their behavior patterns, which are to some extent transmitted genetically, have evolved (just like their anatomies) to maximize reproductive success. It is strange that most social scientists do not avail themselves of methods that have proved to be productive in studying every other species.

The older, competing hypothesis — inaccurately called Lamarckism — appears to be more congenial: the belief that a creature's life experiences would affect its descendants. In the example always used in high school biology classes, it does not matter how many generations of rats have their tails cut off, their offspring will still be born with tails. If the Lamarckians were right, the tails should get progressively shorter. It was August Wiesmann, in the 1880s, who first solved the problem by positing the separation of "germ plasm" from the rest of the body. (It is now known that the DNA of the cell nucleus is completely separate from the cytoplasm.)

Despite all the empirical evidence, neo-Darwinism proved offensive to Marxists. The Soviet Union was, after all, attempting to create a new world within one generation. Soviet authorities assumed that Russian children, if they were given the proper environment and a correct education, could transcend the ordinary human frailties of greed, snobbery, and the lust for power. In this atmosphere, it was easy for T. D. Lysenko to convince Stalin that it was possible to "harden" strains of wheat against frost by exposing seeds to low temperatures. Scientists who disagreed found themselves hardening their own bodies against the Siberian cold, serving life sentences in labor camps where the life expectancy was less than a year. (In all fairness, it should be noted that, before Lysenko, Soviet geneticists were in the main stream and the younger biologists in the Soviet Union are even becoming sympathetic to sociobiology.)

There are, of course, evolutionary anthropologists like Leslie White, Morton Fried, Elman Service, and Marshall Sahlins, but most of them shy away from an explicitly Darwinist approach. Sahlins, one of the most interesting anthropologists of any period, devoted a very superficial book to attacking sociobiology. If Sahlins, a very bright and flexible-minded social evolutionist, responds so vehemently, it is not hard to imagine the reaction of the less gifted.

When sociologists and anthropologists set their minds against human nature, they are really rebelling against Darwin. They become guilty not only of wishful thinking but of fostering a cultural Lysenkoism that sees limitless possibilities in the human species to change the conditions — and nature — of its existence. Since even politically biased social scientists can produce important work, it becomes important to separate cultural arguments from the political ideologies that often contaminate them. Many social scientists have, in fact, searched for universals of social behavior. The search for universals is in the nature of science and of man. Emile Durkheim (like his predecessor, Comte) believed in universal patterns of cultural evolution, and he used the cultural argument as a weapon against the nominalist/psychological approach: Individuals are not responsible for social institutions like marriage. The explanation of social life must be found in "the nature of society itself."

Certain British anthropologists, Malinowski and his disciples, looked for universal social functions, cultural processes that are dictated, to some extent, by biological needs. George Homans, the American sociologist, even went so far as to speak of "elementary forms of social behavior," at which level "there is neither Jew nor Gentile, Greek nor barbarian but only man." While Homans was originally thinking primarily of things like eating and copulation, seen from the behaviorist perspective of Watson and Skinner, his attempts to formulate the rules of social structure had to depend on some sort of universal human tendencies. Increasingly, Homans has tended to see these rules as biological in origin, but most social scientists shrink from such conclusions.[31]

The reasons for this reluctance (apart from ideological rigidity) are not hard to discover. Anthropologists spend much of their time in direct observation of exotic people. They study isolated cultured fragments containing only hundreds (sometimes only dozens) of men and women who may have developed strange, not to say pathological, habits: cannibalism, incest, and chronic child neglect. Even well-established and stable cultures seem remarkably alien. Robert Redfield has written perceptively on the impact of such experiences:

> At first the people . . . seem very alien. . . . Later, the strange customs fall into the background, and one sees the same kinds of people one has known at home. . . . Still later, the ways in which these people *are* different from one's own people emerge . . . but now more subtly, as if demanding that they be truly reported against the background of the common human.[32]

The common human. Redfield, in fact, comes closer than most anthropologists to a clear idea of what might constitute humanity. This common human he finds not in instincts but as those characteristics that are "inevitably developed or acquired," a solution that puts aside the whole nature/nurture debate.

It would be a serious mistake to cast anthropology in the role of an "enemy." Some anthropologists are open to the idea of human universals and even innateness; most, perhaps, go about their useful work without troubling themselves overmuch with theoretical speculation. The most extreme expressions of the cultural argument were made most frequently in the early part of this century, but pioneers like Boas blazed certain trails that it is hard to avoid taking, even when the destination is some place he would never have approved of. There is a bias, a certain contour to the social sciences, which can influence our thought in the direction of cultural relativism. And, while glib and superficial generalities about human nature are hardly typical of contemporary anthropologists, such arguments are part of the arsenal used by social engineers in defending their projects.

There is no denying it. Man is different from other animals, and some of the differences can be explained by his possession of culture. That cultural evolution replaces biological evolution is an important point, especially if culture can be seen as continuing the tendencies that appear so prominently in the evolution of the primates. The fact of culture, far from constituting a refutation of human nature, may provide confirming evidence. Human social forms are varied, but not infinitely so. Marriage and the family come close to being as universal as anything in the human make-up. Of the infinity of theoretically possible forms of family life, a very few predominate. The striking fact is that, despite the plethora of logical conceivable arrangements, "the essentials show little, if any, variation."

Anthropologists do sometimes concede the existence of basic aptitudes, emotions, and even social forms. Even in his most radical phase, Kroeber conceived of human nature as a "theoretically separable and essentially constant component." Like most social scientists, Kroeber treated these universals as trivial in comparison with the pressure exerted by cultural institutions — what Durkheim called "social facts." But this is the point at issue: the existence and persistence of a substratum of natural aptitudes and dispositions and the degree to which they influence or even determine our social behavior. The dividing line between culture and human nature cannot be simply assumed or drawn at will. It is in the most vital sense the *quod est demonstrandum* of the social sciences.

Notes

1. Hume, *Enquiry Concerning Human Understanding*, L.A. Selby-Bigge, ed., 3d ed. (Oxford: Oxford University Press, 1975), 83.
2. R.G. Collingwood, *The Idea of History* (Oxford: Oxford University Press, 1946), especially 224 ff., cf. *Human Nature and Human History* (Brooklyn: Haskell House, 1976).
3. Hans Georg Gadamer, *Truth and Method*, trans. from *Wahrheit und Methode*, Tubingen, 1960 (New York: Seabury Press, 1976).
4. Claude A. Helvétius, *De l'homme, de ses Facultés Intellectuells et de son Éducation* (London: La Société Typographique, 1774), Vol. II, 402.
5. Paul Bohannon, *Social Anthropology* (New York: Holt, Rinehart and Winston, 1963), 17.
6. John Dewey, *Human Nature and Conduct: An Introduction to Social Psychology*, repr. of 1922 ed. (New York: Random House/Modern Library, 1957), 107–8.
7. John Dewey, *Freedom and Culture* (New York: G.P. Putnam's Sons, 1939), 124.
8. B.F. Skinner, *About Behaviorism* (New York: Alfred Knopf, 1974), 150.
9. Edward O. Wilson, "Biology and the Social Sciences," *Daedalus* 106 (1977), 125.
10. See especially *Language and Mind* (New York: Harcourt Brace, 1968); cf. John Lyons' remarkably lucid discussion in *Noam Chomsky* (New York: The Viking Press, 1970).
11. Jerry A. Fodor, *The Language of Thought* (Cambridge, MA: Harvard University Press, 1975), 82ff.; cf. Owen J. Flanagan, Jr., *The Science of the Mind* (Cambridge, MA: MIT Press, 1984).
12. Saul Sternberg, "High Speed Scanning in Human Memory," *Science* 153 (1966), 652–54. There are difficulties with such experiments: not only are they hard to replicate, but counter-experiments seem to indicate that under some circumstances, at least, information is processed differently; cf. Howard Gardner, *The Mind's New Science: A History of the Cognitive Revolution* (New York: Basic Books, 1985), 121–23.
13. John Searle, *Minds, Brains, and Science* (London: The BBC, 1984).
14. Brent Berlin and Paul Kay, *Basic Color Terms: Their Universality and Evolution* (Berkeley: University of California Press, 1969).
15. Don Burgess, Kempton Willett, and Robert E. MacLaury, "Tarahumara Color Modifiers: Individual Variation and Evolutionary Change," *American Ethnologist* 10 (1983), 133–49.
16. James Boster, "Can Individuals Recapitulate the Evolutionary Development of Color Lexicons?," *Ethnology* 25 (1986), 61–74.
17. Peter C. Reynolds, *On the Evolution of Human Behavior: The Argument from Animals to Man* (Berkeley, CA: University of California Press, 1981), 89ff.; cf. Irenäus Eibl-Eibesfeldt, "The Expressive Behavior of the Deaf-and-Blind Born" in M. Van Cranach and I. Vine, eds., *Social Communication and Movement* (New York: Academic Press, 1973), 163–94.

18. Daniel G. Freedman, *Human Infancy: An Evolutionary Perspective* (Hillsdale, NJ: Lawrence Erlbaum, 1974).
19. See, in general, Vernon Venable: *Human Nature: The Marxian View* (New York: Alfred Knopf, 1945); F. Tönnies, *Karl Marx: Leben und Lehre* (Berlin: Verlag Karl Curtius, n.d.); cf. Karl Marx "Zur Juden Frage" in *Werke* (Berlin: Dietz Verlag, 1976), I, 366 ff.
20. See especially *L'Existentialisme est un humanisme* (Paris: Nagel, 1968), and Ernst Cassirer, *An Essay on Man* (New Haven: Yale University Press, 1944).
21. Michael Ghiselin, "Categories, Life, and Thinking," *Behaviorial and Brain Sciences* 4 (1981), 269–83; and D.L. Hull, "The Ontological Status of Species as Evolutionary Units" in R.E. Botts and J. Hintikka, eds., *Foundational Problems in the Special Sciences* (Dordrecht-Holland: D. Reidel, 1977), 91–102.
22. D.L. Hull, "A Matter of Individuality," *Philosophy of Science* 45 (1978), 358.
23. Ellsworth Faris, *The Nature of Human Nature*, repr. (Chicago: University of Chicago Press, 1976), 17 ff; Charles H. Cooley, *Human Nature and the Social Order* (New York: Scribners, 1922), cf. the illuminating discussion in David Bidney, *Theoretical Anthropology* (New York: Columbia University Press, 1953), 125 ff.
24. Auguste Comte, *Système de Politique Positive*, II, 3. (Paris: Librairie Scientifique - Industrielle de L. Mathias, 1851–54.
25. Emile Durkheim, *The Rules of Sociological Method*, translated by Sarah A. Solovay and John H. Mueller (New York: The Free Press, 1938), 90 ff, cf. *Sociology and Philosophy*, translated by D.F. Pocock, (New York: Free Press, 1974), 24.
26. See especially the 1930 essay "Some Problems of Methodology in the Social Sciences," repr. in Franz Boas, *Race, Language, and Culture* (New York: Macmillan, 1948), 260 ff.
27. Derek Freeman, *Margaret Mead and Samoa: The Making and Unmaking of an Anthropological Myth* (Cambridge, MA: Harvard University Press, 1983). Roy A. Rappaport seems to defend Mead on the curious grounds that she was really engaged in creating a myth to counter patriarchal sexual mores, "Desecrating the Holy Woman: Derek Freeman's Attack on Margaret Mead," *American Scholar* (Summer 1986), 313–47.
28. See Julian H. Steward, ed. *Alfred Kroeber* (New York: Columbia University Press, 1973), 119 ff. (repr. from Southwestern *Journal of Anthropology* II), 195–204).
29. Clifford Geertz, *The Interpretation of Cultures: Selected Essays* (New York: Basic Books, 1973), 35 ff.
30. Ralph Linton, *The Study of Man: An Introduction*, repr. of 1936 ed. (New York: Appleton-Century-Crofts, 1964), 137 ff.
31. George C. Homans, *Social Behavior: Its Elementary Forms* (New York: Harcourt Brace, 1961), 6; *Coming to My Senses: The Autobiography of a Sociologist* (New Brunswick, NJ: Transaction Books, 1984), 346 ff.
32. Robert Redfield, "The Universally Human and the Culturally Variable," in *The Papers of Robert Redfield: Human Nature and the Study of Society* (Chicago: University of Chicago Press, 1962), Vol. I, 440 ff.

3

Natural Law and Laws of Nature

None of the modern schools of thought has succeeded in breaking down the common conviction that there is a nature proper to human beings. Their arguments serve a useful purpose by preventing us from falling back on nativist cliches or the excesses of vulgarized social Darwinism, but skepticism loses all utility when it is made into a religion. Was it ever really conceivable that man was somehow not a natural being? If we say man has no nature, we should have to mean he is outside nature. Man may, of course, be viewed as a compound of natural and supernatural elements, and endowed with mind as something distinct from the brain. But philosophers who take this position are either religious (like St. Thomas) or committed (like Cicero) to the idea of a definite human nature.

Perhaps we are cheating, or at least punning, by playing off two senses of nature: nature can mean "life, the universe, and everything," especially in the sense that phenomena behave in a lawful manner, but when we speak of human nature we usually are talking about the essence or special property of mankind. In this sense, human beings would have a nature in the same way that ethyl alcohol has a nature: a liquid, volatile at certain temperatures, narcotic in moderate quantities, and poisonous at higher levels. Human beings might not have the second kind of nature, while still remaining a part of the first.

But are the two uses of nature really so distinct? When ordinary people speak of nature's laws, they generally have universal properties in mind. D.M. Armstrong recently refers to "the utterly natural idea that the laws of nature link properties with properties," and defines the laws of nature as "relations between universals."[1] The laws of gravity or thermodynamics could easily be restated in terms of the nature of bodies, because both senses of nature imply that something natural or with a nature is part of the universe and subject to its laws. If we discovered a chemical element on Pluto, one that did not have natural properties — if, for example, it "defied" all the ordinary laws governing natural substances — we should be tempted to call it an unnatural element, especially if its "irregularities" were neither predictable nor explicable. If human beings really had no nature, that is, no set of roughly universal properties, it should be impossible to understand the behavior of others. Other cultures, in particular, would remain a closed book.

Imagine what the world would be like if human beings actually did come into life completely open to experience; if societies really were free to go off on any tangent that struck their collective fancies. In the hundreds of known societies, one might predict that roughly half would have ended up under the political control of females or would have developed means of sharing power between the sexes. A nonsexist Rome might have emerged, with two consuls — one male, one female. Some of them would have solved the problems of aggression and violence — or, rather, they would have avoided them altogether. Others might have learned to do without private property, marriage, and religion. Without letting our imaginations run too wild, we can conceive of turning political control over to the innocent — preadolescent children, or a community in which men freely copulate with mothers, daughters, and sisters: "Imagine everybody living life in peace. . . ."

It all sounds something like a popular tune lyric or a script for a science fiction film, but there is no apparent reason why a human society could not ignore distinctions like left/right, right/wrong, and me/thee. In *Promethean Fire*, Lumsden and Wilson make a similar thought experiment and outline an imaginary race of blank-slate beings, the Xenidrins, whose "genes direct the construction of their body and brain but not their behavior." Their minds are the product of "the accidents of history."[2] (Even on the improbable assumption that such a species could come into existence, they point out, competition soon would operate on the population to bias their behavioral patterns in certain directions, but not in others.) We could devise an infinite number of social arrangements and intellectual systems, each more bizarre than the last. Unfortunately, they would be like the tribes of dog-headed men and upside-down men described in early travellers' tales: sheer fantasy. On the face of it, man has to possess a distinct nature, but what is more, no species could be as malleable as the humanity described by social scientists.

Man is obviously a part of nature — to say otherwise is to speak to no purpose. Whether all of what we are is natural is another matter, but for a natural politics it will be enough if we can locate man's place in nature. In such an enterprise, mathematical or logical precision is out of the question. As Aristotle and, more recently, John Searle have observed, no social science can be exact, because part of its content is what goes on in the minds of other people. We are more in the position of the early African explorers: without maps or reliable information, they set out to discover the source of the Nile — not that they knew where they were going. On the contrary, all they knew was that rivers have sources and since the source existed, it had to be somewhere. In the same way, if mankind has a place in nature, as it must, then there is also a human "somewhere" in the scheme of things.

Popular histories of science project the impression that before Darwin men had thought of themselves as creatures separate from nature rather than as members of the animal kingdom. This is simply not the case. Man has always known that he is an animal. Many older philosophers made the explicit point that man was the animal at the apex of the *scala naturae* (nature's ladder) and only distinguished from the rest of the animal kingdom by the endowment of reason. Even in the Middle Ages, when philosophy and theology were sometimes indistinguishable, scholastics followed Aristotle's lead in considering man as an animal. The habit was ingrained. John of Salisbury, a moderate nominalist, argues that, since man is "a certain kind of animal," it is necessary "to understand what an animal is to understand man."[3] When the very Christian Linnaeus drew up his *systema naturae* in the eighteenth century, he displayed few qualms about fitting in man at the top, right above the apes — in other words, where Aristotle had placed him.[4] The archaeological record suggests that even early man was "aware of his affinity with other animals."[5]

The "Darwinism" of primitive man is tragically illustrated by the case of Yali, a religious leader in New Guinea. Yali was a prophet in one of New Guinea's cargo cults, whose believers expect the gods or the ancestors to return — like Santa Claus — bearing all the wealth and goods of European society. Summoned to Port Moresby, Yali was told that Europeans didn't believe in Cargo. Yali, a former sergeant-major in World War II, was impressed, but what he wanted to know was, what did Europeans believe? Bitter experience had taught him that it wasn't Christianity, since even the missions managed to reconcile indentured labor with the Gospel. At last, he was shown a book on evolution. Yali was deeply shaken. Descent from animals? That was what his people had always believed. He returned to his village with a violent hatred for the lying missionaries.[6]

Men like Yali have always known they were part of the animal kingdom: it takes philosophy to teach them otherwise. It was Descartes, with his dualism of body and soul, who first "discovered" that animals were mere animated machines, a position that never succeeded in winning universal acceptance.[7] Despite Descartes' enormous influence, his view of the beasts was rejected almost immediately by the atomist Gassendi in the seventeenth century, and in the eighteenth, Scottish philosophers like Kames and Monboddo were deriving human qualities from other animals. Loren Eiseley to the contrary,[8] 1859 (when Darwin published *The Origin of Species*) was not the year "in which scientists discovered that man was an animal." It was hardly a fact that could be kept hidden. Most of the old definitions of men included him in the genus *animal* or *zoon*. Cicero[9] refers to "animal hoc providem, sagax, multiplex, acutum, plenum rationis et consilii, vocamus hominem" (this animal, foreseeing, clever, various, sharp-witted, full of reason, and deliberation we call man). The most famous definitions came from Aristotle: the rational animal, the *zoon politikon* — "social/political animal" or, what brings out the flavor better, "born for citizenship."

The first term, animal, seems obvious enough. It is the second term of *Zoon Politikon* that requires elaboration. In what sense is man a social or political animal? Aristotle may have been thinking of social insects like the bees, (although he says man is more social), but it would be unwise to push the analogy. Most of the first book of the *Politics* can be read as an extended commentary upon his definition. What he clearly meant was that nature compelled men to live in families (for the bearing and rearing of children) and families to form villages, and villages to join together into cities for us to fulfill our nature. As a species, we are naturally sociable. Lord Kames was not unique in observing, "That there is in man an appetite for society, never was called in question."[10]

Beyond the urge to procreate and enjoy the companionship of his fellows, what is the social component of our nature? Most of the older discussions were centered on the idea of the natural law. Any doctrine with over 2300 years of history behind it is bound to have undergone transformation, but most natural law advocates would argue along these lines: While laws and customs vary from place to place and from period to period, there are certain universal prohibitions against incest, murder, and theft; these "shalt nots" are instances of a natural law that is : 1) universally observed, 2) innate in mankind, whose provisions 3) can be grasped by any rational person, and whose 4) source is supernatural or transcendent. One or another variety of natural law doctrine helped to form the ethical consensus of two millennia, especially through the vehicles of Roman law and scholastic philosophy.

During the seventeenth century, however, natural law theory gradually degenerated into a theory of rights: Human behavior, on this view, may or may not be guided by social instincts, but — and this is the crux — human reason is able to discern the existence of certain rights (like life and liberty), which would have been enjoyed in the state of nature. Many political philosophers felt free to ignore natural rights by 1800, and after Hegel's attack in the early nineteenth century, natural law gradually withered away into an object of study for predominantly Catholic scholars. The reason for its decay, I would suggest, lies in an excessive reliance on only one of the four elements — rationality. Natural law, once it is reduced to a set of simple abstract principles like "to each his own," opens itself to the criticism of legal positivists, like Hans Kelsen, who pointed out that such "empty formulas" "have the effect of justifying any positive legal order," because they presuppose some pat answer.[11] What is, after all, the "own" to which each man is entitled? Socialists and capitalists will answer differently, but each is free to use the formula to bolster his own system. A rationalized natural law is one that has given up all of its distinctive advantage.

Rationality, which lies at the center of most modern ethical systems, is now the primary characteristic of most natural law theories. As Michael Novak writes of the Catholic theologian Bernard Lonergan's theory of moral insight, "the ground of ethical inquiry is not descriptive but prescriptive." In applying this principle to natural law, Novak concludes:

> Natural law then, is not a set of general descriptive regularities like the law of gravity, nor a set of necessary logical relationships like the law of inverse squares.[12]

This raises one of the most perplexing things about natural law: the words themselves. Turn them around a bit and you end up with law of nature (lex naturae). Is there any relationship between the two? The usual answer is a resounding NO. Passerin d'Entrèves warns against confusing the two:

> The notion of natural law . . . is a notion which refers to human behavior, not to physical phenomena. Our concern is with ethics and politics, not with the natural sciences.[13]

This criticism is representative, and it reflects the modern philosophical consensus that there is a split between the realm of fact and the realm of value. On the one side is the realm of nature, facts, and observable scientific laws, while on the other stand rational human beings, making judgments of value and erecting systems of morality and law. Between the two there is as great a gulf as is fixed between heaven and hell. Bentham and Mill were among the first to apply such a distinction to natural law. While the laws of nature are perceptible regularities that are open to a process of rational investigation, human laws—including the misnamed natural laws—are simply commands. Because of an unbridgeable chasm between the realms of fact and value, there can be no natural basis for morality. In this connection, several sentences of David Hume are often quoted:

> In every system of morality . . . I have always remarked that the author proceeds for some time in the ordinary way of reasoning, and establishes the being of a God, or makes observations concerning human affairs; when of a sudden I am surprised to find, that instead of the usual copulations of propositions, *is*, and is not, I meet with no proposition that is not connected with an *ought*, or an *ought not*.

Quoted out of context, Hume seems to be arguing that ethical judgments cannot be deduced from the nature of things, when in fact, his main object was to discredit rational judgment as a basis for morality. In Hume's defense, Alisdair MacIntyre argued that the philosopher has been badly misinterpreted in the twentieth century. In fact, Hume consistently violated the principle that "no set of nonmoral premises can entail a moral conclusion." MacIntyre concluded that Hume, by deriving morality from the human desire for happiness, was the last Aristotelian.[14]

It does not matter a great deal who is to blame — Hume, Bentham, or G.E. Moore — for the fact/value split. Once any ethical or legal system is cut off from the natural soil of human nature, it is bound to wither either into pseudomathematical formulas or the naked imperatives of raw power. While academic philosophers have been debating the nature of legitimacy and the meaning of meaning, ambitious politicians employ the language of political morality as a cloak for their own schemes. There is hardly a major tyrant (like Stalin) or a petty dictator (like Peron) who has not felt himself free to redefine law and morality. In retrospect, an internationally recognized system of natural law begins to look, at least in principle, like a good idea.

A number of efforts have been made to reconstitute natural law. The legal philosopher, H.L.A. Hart proposes to salvage a simplified version, which would rest on the recognition that men have certain needs that must be met if they are to survive. Although Hart repudiates the metaphysical status of natural law, his approach has the merit of being grounded in observation. That human social behavior is rooted in certain universal needs is hardly a new idea. In Britain, it dominated the social anthropology of Malinowski and his disciples. Malinowski rejected universalist theories like Freud's Oedipus complex and preferred to see only natural necessities as the basis for social life: food, procreation, shelter, and so on. This argument goes back to Epicurus, the fountainhead of so much materialist thought, through David Hume to Karl Marx. For Epicurus, natural law (or justice) was only a *façon de parler*. Since all justice is based on agreements, only human beings are capable of any kind of law, including natural law. All that is actually universal are our natural and necessary desires, which may lead us into conflict and competition with others. Laws are, therefore, based on need and expediency.

From the Epicurean perspective, "value" only comes into existence with human reason. There can be no moral values in nature itself. Value would then have to enter the world through supernatural means as the transcendent, like rays of sunlight, slips through the cracks and illumines the moral world. For human beings, this realm is accessible through right reason. But few philosophers would accept such a supernaturalist account, which is also, for that matter, at odds with the Christian doctrine of the logos, which makes the second person of the trinity not only a participant in the Creation but also — even before assuming flesh — accessible to all humanity. The easiest way out of this fact/value dilemma is to assume a connection between ethical judgments and the real world.

"Human moral reason is trustworthy because it is in touch with reality."[15] But is moral reason completely an affair of spirit? If the brain is involved or makes a contribution, then at least some bits of natural matter have a connection with morality. Apart from the crudest superstitions, it is hard to imagine a universe with morality in it, unless moral judgments are grounded in nature. The alternative would seem to be a gnostic or Manichean rejection of all matter, as somehow evil. The exercise of reason or spiritual discipline then becomes an avenue of escape from an inherently wicked universe. When nature and reason are seen as antagonists (as they are, for example, by Freud and Marx), then "naturalism," in Michael Polanyi's words, "is thus transformed from a moral command into a doctrine of moral skepticism," because nature has been stripped of any moral implications. Good and evil are replaced by health and sickness or by the conflict of class interests.[16]

The assumed tear in nature's fabric virtually compels us to grasp one side or the other: the diminishing spiritual fragment or the more palpable universe of things. It is all very well for Epicurus and Hart to speak of natural needs — such needs manifestly are an aspect of human nature, but how we get from another man's needs to how I should behave toward him is a process beyond many ordinary people. It does no good to drag in Kant's categorial imperative — a formal restatement of the Golden Rule, which says our ethical judgments must apply to everyone. An immoralist or a legal positivist will have a quick and effective answer to that one, especially if he is armed. It is more reasonable to assume with J.L. Mackie that "there are no objective values. First, because human values vary so much from culture to culture and second, because we have no way of knowing how these moral qualities could affect the natural world. It is because reason fails us that we cannot accept a merely rationalistic account of ethics."[17]

To consider the needs of others and frame a system of ethics and law to match them is an essentially rational procedure, but this requires that a person be in touch with nature. So much seems certain. How exactly do we imagine the contact taking place? Most people these days believe the brain plays a part — many would say the only part — in the exercise of reason, and the brain, it is assumed, is a natural organ, the product of natural selection. Now, since the brain evolved along with the rest of our natural world, it is "reasonable" that its reasoning processes should be accommodated to "reality," but does that say anything more than a statement like, "the calculator is programmed to perform division"? Unless we assume there is a master-electrician, designing plugs, sockets, and programs, and rationality, there is no obvious reason for us to subordinate the inclinations of our glands to the inclinations of our brain. Of course, it might be in our best interest, but that is another matter.

The problem comes with the assumption that nature itself is not normative. As the rational animal, man becomes either an alien in the universe, a mutant that can never be at home, or else the victim of a delusion, because we — no more than a bath sponge (alive or dead) — are nothing more than puppets whose strings are jerked by necessities and forces we can never escape or even understand.

The fate of natural law theory is linked, inextricably, with the rest of legal theory. Law has become, in general, a matter of rational decision-making aimed at upholding social interest and/or abstract principles of equity. This attitude toward the law either rules out natural law or reduces it to a set of universal principles of "right" or "fairness."

Other views of law, however, are less abstract. Like many premodern peoples, the Greeks regarded law more as an outgrowth of custom than as a set of rigid principles. Most words translated as "law" and "justice"—like *themis, dike,* or *nomos,* which Pindar declared to be the king of all—meant originally something like "the way things are." When King Agamemnon returns the captive girl Briseis to her rightful master, he swears (*Iliad* IX 133 ff) he never entered her bed or joined with her, "which is the custom (*themis*) of humans—of men and women."

It is a natural step from custom as "the way things are" to what E.R. Service calls "sanctioned customs." When the swine-herd Eumaeus reassures the disguised Odysseus (*Odyssey* XIV 55 ff) that he will be treated hospitably, he explains:

> It is not my *themis*—not even if someone lower than you comes—to dishonor a stranger. For all strangers and beggars belong to Zeus. What I can give you is little—but you are welcome to it. For that is the *dike* (natural habit) of slaves.

It is hard for most of us to distinguish between old habits and the divine will, although the Greeks did succeed in turning *dike* into a principle of reciprocity and *nomos* into something like "prescriptive right." Still, down to the Classical period, these words did not entirely lose their original flavor. Even *dike* remained a natural principle, more like gravity than our modern sense of justice.

Compared with the better-developed and universalized Roman law, the laws of the Greek states had serious shortcomings; however, there were advantages: Greeks were less susceptible to the common temptation to deify the law. Idolatry invites iconoclasm, as the modern rejection of natural law suggests. For all its inelegance, the Greek approach to law cuts closer to the bone than modern jurisprudence. If laws were only the commands of sovereigns or the decisions of judges, they could not command obedience, much less respect. Legal systems are a living record of civilization, the cumulation, in outline form, of its painfully acquired wisdom. Like the religious rituals they so much resemble, legal forms and pronouncements must be couched in a solemn and archaic language, because they bear the heavy burden of the past. Every people has its own history, and its laws must be viewed not as abstract solutions to even more abstract problems, but as particular, local, and idiosyncratic answers to urgent questions. If laws are a record of a society's history, natural law is the more general record of the human species. If the old natural lawyers were right, it is only at those points where legal customs converge that a universal code is to be found, a code that is both innate within the human species and yet derived from some source beyond our nature. Before settling for a rationalist view of natural law (or rejecting it altogether) we might try to rediscover the older view of law by looking at the other provisions — universality, innateness, and transcendence.

Universality

The most important statements come from Roman law, which recognized — in addition to its own law (*ius civile*) — a law of nations (*ius gentium*), which might have originally meant the law applying to foreigners[18] but generally meant a code of rules universally observed.[19] In Justinian's *Digest*, Gaius equates the *ius gentium* with natural law (*ius naturale*):

> What natural reason has determined among all men, it is guarded and called upon among all peoples, the law of nations, just as that law all nations employ.

But are there actually any universal rules? The incest prohibition is almost universal, although it has been systematically violated in a small number of cultures — notably by the Egyptian Pharaohs and their Greek successors, the Ptolemies. Parents almost always are expected to take care of their children, but among the Ik (an African people described by Colin Turnbull) the constant pressure of starvation has caused parents to become pathologically indifferent to the welfare of their children. In fact, there is no item of natural law that is quite universal.

This situation is hardly surprising. "There is no fine thing/since Adam's fall but needs much laboring" — and Yeats' pronouncement holds as true for law as it does for poetry. There are several responses to this problem. St. Thomas suggests that the first principles of natural law are the same everywhere, but that there are also derived norms, "conclusions of these common principles . . . valid and acknowledged by all men only in the majority of cases." Respect for parents and family are virtually universal norms, but how such respect is shown varies. When sick and elderly Eskimos went out to die on the ice, it was not because they were being brutally expelled from the family; in fact, their self-sacrifice (giving up their share of food to children) is a powerful affirmation of family ties. The human reason can, of course, be distorted by passion, and Thomas instances the Germans, who are reported to have condoned theft.[20]

Since the first principles are based on reason and self-preservation, their content is not much richer than Hart's version of minimal natural law, Malinowski's functionalism, or Epicurus' natural and necessary desires. What do we mean, then, by considering sodomy or paricide as unnatural?

Aristotle gives a careful answer in his discussion of natural justice:

> Of political justice (or right) part is natural, part is conventional; the natural being that which has the same Force everywhere and does not depend upon opinion; . . . Some believe everything is conventional, because that which is unchangeable and has everywhere the same quality is like fire: it burns in Greece here as it does in Persia, but they see that justice is variable. That is not the way it is, but rather like this: Perhaps among the gods at least there is no change, but with us there is something natural — although everything is changeable — but nonetheless there is some aspect of justice that is natural, others not.[21]

Aristotle's difficulties with this notion of a universal justice are shown by his equivocating prose. Ultimately, he hits upon a good analogy: The right hand is stronger by nature, but people can by effort become ambidexterous. He may have had in mind a passage of the *Laws* (vii) in which Plato asserts — against all evidence and experience — that it is only habit that makes us right-handed. With sufficient practice we can all be ambidexterous. Aristotle's cautious answer is a qualified no: There are universal tendencies of *natural justice*, but they can be modified or even overriden by custom. (There is, however, a price. Naturally left-handed individuals compelled to favor their right hands often exhibit learning difficulties that arise from "mixed brain dominance.")

A structuralist anthropologist like Lévi-Strauss must insist that universal laws are very elementary — preferably structural — because of "the observable diversity" anthropologists insist upon.[22] But the cultural relativists present the case as too cut-and-dried. Just as there are social norms within societies, we might expect there to be cross-cultural norms. Crimes of violence violate the norms of American and European civilization, and yet in 1981 there were an estimated 3,461 violent offenses for every 100,000 Americans. While this represents a significant increase even from 1969, it still means that less than 4% of the population deviates from the social norm. If we were to narrow the focus to certain groups in certain neighborhoods, we might discover a subculture or subsociety in which violent crime was not viewed as seriously abnormal. Would this damage the argument that Americans regard murder and rape as immoral? As Lumsden and Wilson suggest, the question is one of statistics:

> . . . cultural diversity can be generated in the presence of even rigid genetic controls. What is determined is not a particular social response but rather the statistical *pattern* of response across many societies.[23]

This statistical approach to human nature was at least partly anticipated by Hume:

> ... there may often arise disputes concerning what is natural or unnatural. .... Frequent and rare depend upon the number of examples we have observed; and as this number may gradually increase or diminish, it will be impossible to fix any exact boundaries betwixt them. We may only affirm on this head, that if ever there was anything, which could be called natural in this sense, the sentiments of morality certainly may. . . . [24]

This idea of social universals — the *ius gentium* — received a new lease on life as ethnographers began to assemble and compare the results of field reports from all over the globe. Most prominent in this movement was George P. Murdoch, whose *Social Structure* remains the most convenient starting place for comparing cultures. While Murdoch was emphatically not an advocate of universal human nature, he did establish an inventory of social behavior found in every culture — everything from age-grading to weather control. They include sports, funeral rites, magic, marriage, property rights, sexual restrictions, and religious rituals. In the almost fifty years since his cross-cultural survey was first established, comparative studies have been done on family organization, sex roles, deference patterns and many other subjects. Reviewing the sometimes bewildering results, Lévi-Strauss puts the matter succinctly:

> As posed by anthropologists today, the problem of culture — hence, the problem of the human condition — is to discover the consistent laws underlying the observable diversity of beliefs and institutions. [25]

Innateness

It is an easy step from the notion of universality to innateness, but since Hume we have been taught to regard the passage from regular coincidence to causation as a perilous transition. Roman lawyers were bolder. According to Ulpian, natural law was what nature taught all animals. It included the union of male and female and the procreation and rearing of children. [26]

The Stoics had taught much the same thing: The variability of laws was no argument against the universality of justice; social relationships, because they were based on the instinct to reproduce, were natural. Chrysippus seems to have argued that justice, law, and right reason existed by nature. These arguments eventually were absorbed into medieval philosophy and underlie the thought of St. Thomas. While Thomas frequently associates natural law with rationality — "the participation of the Eternal law in rational creatures," he was not blind to the more natural view of innateness. Thomas repeatedly draws our attention to the inclination of nature as it exists in infants as well as in the damned. Most significantly, in discussing the "fomes" of sin, he observes that various creatures have different natural inclinations. What is lawful for one is unlawful for another. Ferocity is a law for dogs but not for sheep. Man's specific nature is to act according to reason. But since the fall, we are subject to sensual impulses, which are for other species a law. But as a punishment, our sensuality has the force of law.[27]

Aquinas was wrestling with a very difficult problem and deliberately decided against any view of sin that did not include sexual desires among the natural inclinations. Moreover, he takes the sensible position that natural law can vary in its dictates from species to species. Put another way, Thomas comes close to committing the mistake modern theologians and legal philosophers thunder against — viewing natural law as descriptive as much as prescriptive.

A search for the elements of the natural law should begin, therefore, not with a set of ethical precepts derived from reason or revelation. It must seek to find out the actual behavior and conditions of human life. In such an investigation, ethics and theology would play little if any part. This is not to say the object is not ultimately theological. Those who believe that the universe and man were created for a purpose should be interested in what observation can tell us about that purpose. This approach, which used to be known as natural theology, has fallen into disrepute for over a hundred years on the mistaken impression that the findings of biology were incompatible with theology. Bishop Butler assumed that, although the creation was ultimately beyond our comprehension, it was framed to teach us certain lessons. Butler viewed the universe in terms that can only be described as ecological:

> In this great scheme of the natural world, individuals have various peculiar relations to other individuals of their own species. And whole species are, we find, variously related to other species, upon this earth. . . . As there is not any action, or natural event, which we are acquainted with, so single and unconnected as not to have a respect to some other actions and events, so possibly, each of them, when it has not an immediate, may yet have a remote, natural relation to other actions and events, much beyond the compass of this present world.

In essence, Butler's object was to look at human life as it is lived and — like a critic interpreting a novel — to deduce the rough moral lessons taught by experience.[28]

Most common ethical prescriptions can be restated as general descriptions. Respect for parents: In most human societies, *Pater* (the male family head) is treated with respect, while the mother-child bond is the one social universal that knows no cultural exceptions; Care for children: Parents almost everywhere devote time, energy, and economic resources to child-rearing. The "shalt nots" are a bit more complicated. Men regularly commit theft, adultery, and murder, but with what results? In societies without government or law, the transgressor is routinely punished by the victim, his family and friends, or by the entire village or band. There are, of course, exceptional cases of unpunished villainy, but it is not the norm. In reality, elementary ethical rules can be expressed as statements of cause and effect: Murderers are killed, thieves are deprived of their property, adulterers pay damages. The simplest formula is given by Aeschylus: *drasanta pathein*, the doer suffers (not should suffer, but *does* suffer).

There is a sense in which the "good" must be good for us, that is, must satisfy our natural needs. This naturalism must narrow (if not close) the gap between fact and value:

> To know what we ought to do, what is good for us to do, we must understand our natures as social, rational, and choosing creatures, with distinctive needs for friendship and intellectual stimulus and some conviction of internal harmony.[29]

Natural needs are not the same thing as natural law, but they are a component. Epicurus and his modern descendants manage to combine a belief in material needs with a rejection of human nature, but for Aristotle human sociability was bound up with the inability of individuals to provide for their own wants. To some extent, our needs define our nature.

Needs are, to be sure, a matter of perception rather than reason. We don't convince ourselves, by rational argument, that we want food and drink or companionship. We feel hunger and thirst, "love and desire and hate." Hume was correct, up to a point: our moral sense must be derived from natural passions.

An Aristotelian or observational approach to natural law cannot rest ultimately on cross-cultural comparisons alone. Putting to one side all supernatural questions of mind, reason, and God, we are left with man the animal, the species Homo sapiens. Both the stoics and St. Thomas believed that some tendencies were shared by most common animals, such as the domestic and wild mammals and birds they had observed, while others were restricted to man alone. By the late eighteenth century, it was possible to consider human social behavior in the light of animal parallels. The Scottish jurist, Lord Kames, made a cautious and humble attempt in this direction. He thought it probable "that the social laws by which social animals are governed, might open views into the social nature of man."[30] Kames was unable to satisfy his curiosity on these points. It was not until the triumph of Darwinism that serious attention could be given to the roots of human behavior. Unfortunately, much of the early social Darwinist writings were based on sweeping generalizations nad seemed, at times, composed for the sole purpose of justifying the civilization and economic system of white Europeans. The application of social Darwinist theories in Nazi Germany cast a pall over any application of biology to human social life.

Serious interest in the human implications of evolutionary biology did not revive until the 1960s, with the publication of *On Aggression* by the ethologist Konrad Lorenz, *The Imperial Animal* by the anthropologists Robin Fox and Lionel Tiger, and the popular books of the playwright Robert Ardrey: *African Genesis, The Territorial Imperative,* and *The Social Contract.*

Of these pioneers, Lorenz is by far the most important. Before taking up the human question, he had a distinguished career as a student of animal behavior, for which he received the Nobel Prize. *On Aggression* is a study of aggressive impulses in a number of species. Man, so Lorenz argued, was not by nature a particularly violent creature, especially against members of his own species. The real predatory species like wolves and tigers are born with special mechanisms which limit aggression against members of their own species. Two male wolves in a fight, for example, will struggle only up to a point. When the weaker one surrenders, the victor ceases to attack. Men, unfortunately, are not designed for violent aggression. As a result, we lack the necessary mechanisms to regulate it. However, when men became hunters and warriors, they had to rely on their uncontrolled aggressive impulses. For this reason, according to Lorenz, we need such cultural institutions as clearly defined lines of authority (rank order of hierarchy) and rituals (sometimes religious) to defuse our violent impulses once they have been aroused.

Others of these early writers — Ardrey, Fox and Tiger, and Desmond Morris — compared human behavioral patterns with what is known of other primates, especially the baboons that live in large troops. They painted an unattractive picture of males domineering over females, fighting to establish pecking order, and defining and maintaining territorial boundaries. Man is, to use Desmond Morris's title, "a naked ape" or in Ardrey's phrase, the "killer ape."

Arguments from analogy, however persuasive, can settle nothing. Scienfific explanations as Aristotle noted, involve a middle term — some quality that necessarily links two classes of phenomena. In the model syllogism:

All men are mortal
Socrates is a man
therefore Socrates is mortal.

It is humanity that links Socrates to mortality. In behavioral studies the missing link was not supplied until the early 1970s when a number of researchers were taking a new approach to certain facets of animal behavior. W. D. Hamilton, Robert Trivers, E. O. Wilson, and Richard Dawkins were looking at such phenomena as sex ratios among social insects, for example bees and wasps, and altruism from the perspective of genetics. In principle, they argued, animal behavior should contribute to the reproductive success of the individual. This meant, in effect, that one set of genes was winning out in a competition with other sets. Therefore, the willingness of an animal to risk its life (or even sacrifice it) should be related to the probable amount of genetic material they had in common, that is to their degree of relatedness. Years before, the geneticist J. B. S. Haldane had been asked in a pub if he would lay down his life to save a brother. No, he replied, not for *one*, but he would do it for three brothers or nine cousins. The point of his joke is simply this: I share with a brother — or parent or child — 50% of the same genes and with a cousin 12.5%. By saving three brothers or nine cousins, I shall actually be enhancing the reproductive success of my genes.

The most radical statement of this position was made by Richard Dawkins in *The Selfish Gene* and *The Extended Phenotype*. For Dawkins, everything is in the genes. Organisms are simply vehicles which these replicating bits of DNA have adopted to ensure their survival and propagation. While critics have portrayed Dawkins' most extreme statements as the *reductio ad absurdum* of social Darwinists, he is neither contrite nor defensive. In his view, genetic reductionism, however erroneous, illuminates one aspect of life that is usually ignored.

The publication of Edward O. Wilson's *Sociobiology: The New Synthesis* (1975) gave a name to the new movement and sent a·clear signal that something of a revolution was taking place in the sciences that study man. Wilson defined the new synthesis of genetics, ethology, evolutionary anthropology, and population ecology, as "the systematic study of the biological basis of all social behavior." While Wilson's primary research interests lay with the social insects, he devoted a controversial last chapter (and later a book *On Human Nature*) to Homo sapiens.

Wilson and his colleagues were from the very first subjected to blistering attacks from social scientists who thought their disciplines were imperiled. While some anthropologists (like Napoleon Chagnon), a few sociologists (particularly Pierre Van den Berghe and Joseph Lopreato), and at least two political scientists (Roger Masters and Robert Axelrod) have risen to the challenge, Marxist scholars have uniformly rejected the whole idea — which is strange, given Marx's keen interest in Darwin. In their efforts to discredit sociobiologists, Marxists and other leftists have not hesitated to misrepresent their views or blacken their character. Konrad Lorenz in his youth had written in praise of Nazi eugenics laws — laws, it must be added, which were copied from progressive American legislation. Dawkins has been found guilty of letting his books fall into the hands of the racist National Front in Britain. The most systematic attack is contained in *Not In Our Genes* by Steven Rose, R.C. Lewontin, and Leon Kamin, a book that is, despite the authors' credentials, a work of political ideology rather than scientific criticism.

Christian conservatives, on the other hand, are wary of the possibility of applied sociobiology. Thomas Molnar, a Catholic philosopher, reacted strongly to Lionel Tiger's call for a "veterinarian view of the species" by concluding that sociobiology reduces human conduct to a "mechanical act." As a consequence, "the moral judgment is pulverized and the political community joins the anthill."[31]

The charge of genetic determinism, i.e., of giving genetic explanations for the whole of human life, is only partly accurate. While this may be true of some younger writers, it is certainly not true of E.O. Wilson. In his earlier works, Wilson did appear to view the relationship between genes and culture as a one-way influence, but in two later books, written with Charles J. Lumsden, he worked out a gene-culture theory that provided for a coevolutionary process in which culture is determined by biological traits, which are at the same time constantly being refashioned in response to cultural changes. During the same period, Richard Dawkins was considering the extended effects of genes on environment, and the sociologist Joseph Lopreato was independently developing a theory of culture remarkably similar to Lumsden and Wilson's.

Biocultural methods can be as varied as the disciplines from which sociobiologists are drawn. However, most of the research depends on the notion of inclusive fitness: a successful individual not only will survive, it will have a greater reproductive success than competitors. Many studies focus on the adaptation of populations to a specific environment, while others make extensive use of comparative data, both cross-cultural within the human species and interspecific. Comparisons with other primates have stimulated a great deal of speculation and controversy, and particular attention has been paid to man's closest relations, the great apes, gibbons, orangutans, gorillas, and especially our first cousin, the chimpanzee. Comparison between species is always a risky business, but many of the objections to using animal parallels beg the question by denying the relevance of man's place in nature. Perhaps the real reason for not comparing ourselves with other species is a sense of shame. As Davenant writes of the hunted stag denied shelter by his former friends, "We blush to see our politics in beasts."

Bernard Williams recently summed up the case against natural ethics very succinctly. It is impossible, he argues, to prove that an individual's well-being is related to his moral goodness. Biology can tell us little on the subject because it is concerned with fitness, not well-being, but this objection begs a central question: Is the moral behavior of human beings exclusively a matter of rational decisions made by individuals? That remains to be demonstrated. Two areas of moral behavior that cannot be analyzed in exclusively individualist terms are: a) sex and the family and b) the social order. Both have received a great deal of attention from sociobiologists.

Sex

Darwin viewed sexual selection as a variety of natural selection: males engage in combats for the prize of a mate, while females may choose between males on the basis of attractiveness. At the most elementary level of gametes (reproductive cells), males and females are different. Human females produce a small number of comparatively large eggs (only about 400 in a lifetime are sent into the uterus), while the average male can send out millions of sperm in a single ejaculation. This "basic asymmetry" means females have a greater stake in children. Additionally (or consequently), women spend nine months pregnant before experiencing the rigors of childbirth; they nurse (for several years in many primitive cultures) and are primarily responsible for providing child care.[32]

In most species, the females are predictably coy, the males aggressive. It is possible to imagine a number of "strategies" by which each sex would try to manipulate the other. However, a stable social arrangement obviously depends on some degree of mutual satisfaction. Prolonged courtship, for example, may benefit both partners: the male can ensure that his mate is not pregnant by another male (cuckolds are among the biggest losers in the "survival of the fittest," because they devote their resources to the welfare of another's genes). On the other hand, the female—and, perhaps, her family—has time to study the qualities of the fiance. Among the possible male assets are aggressiveness, fondness of children, and skill as a provider—all of which would help to ensure the survival and success of offspring.[33]

To this extent, there is a genetic basis for sex roles and for marriage; both parents maximize their "fitness" by ensuring the survival and success of more children than competitors can manage. Each of them sacrifices time and energy that could have been devoted to improving and prolonging their own life, but from the perspective of their genes, three children may be worth more than one adult: they represent three times approximately 50 percent of each parent's genotype. There must be a nice adjustment of costs and benefits in which the loss of other options is compensated for by the relative certainty of reproductive success.

Individuals do not always restrict acts of "altruism" to their children. It used to be argued that individuals had to sacrifice their own self-interest in order to benefit the group, but by definition the tendency to make such a sacrifice would be selected against, because the altruist is the loser. The exception comes in the case of kindred. According to W.D. Hamilton's theory of "kin selection," an organism's willingness to give help to another depends on the probable degree of relatedness. Altruistic behavior would be most likely to evolve in a "family-structured population" in which individuals could recognize each other or, at least, be in a position to reciprocate acts of kindness. Mankind has the best opportunity to develop group-related characteristics of more generalized altruism, since human beings have the intelligence and foresight needed to "transcend the limits of family relationships."

How does a genetic theory of altruism explain supererogatory acts of charity — the dying Sir Philip Sydney giving his last drink of water to a soldier? It doesn't, although Robert Trivers has tried to make a case for reciprocal altruism even between individuals of two different species. But when both parties benefit from a transaction, (even if one of the benefits is postponed) altruism seems hardly the *mot juste*. What seems more likely is that man, whose original social organization was a small band of genetically related members, has been translating his elementary social codes into the infinitely richer languages of advanced societies. Some of us learn to identify our neighbors, fellow citizens, and even fellow humans as kin. This cosmopolitan principle was developed even in the ancient world in such proverbial expressions as "to a wise man, the whole world is his city." However, the experience of modern urban civilization does not suggest that universalized benevolence flourishes in a society of mobile and deracinated individualists.

Social Control

The three terms used most often in studies of social behavior in animals are aggression, territory, and dominance. While earlier writers, like Robert Ardrey, gave the impression that animals (including men) were driven by simple and universal instincts to seek power and stake out territory, the response of their critics, like Ashley Montagu, was the flat denial of such "instincts." The complexity of human behavior and the variability of cultures seemed to exclude any explanation based on drives. Besides, the old picture of brutal and ferocious apes was gradually being replaced. By the 1960's chimpanzees and gorillas were typically being described as peace-loving vegetarians. Social anthropologists eagerly pointed to primitive human cultures that seemed to resemble the egalitarian apes — the bushmen and pygmies of Africa, the Eskimos of Alaska. The truth lies in neither extreme — nor between them. What is beginning to emerge is a complex pattern that involves physiological elements (central nervous system and hormones) as well as environmental factors (population density, availability and predictability of resources, etc.) and species parameters.[34]

It is, for example, misleading to speak of aggression as if it were a simple behavior. Even if we exclude predatory aggression, there are at least half a dozen separate types, as displayed, for example, in struggles for dominance within a group, sexual aggression, and fights over territory.[35] The differences depend on more than the social setting; separate brain structures and hormones are often involved.[36]

Many "primitive" emotions, like fear and aggression, are located in the limbic system of the brain, whose primary functions involve the regulation of body temperature, blood pressure, sugar levels, etc., and the emotional reactions required for survival (sexual desire, fighting, and fleeing). In simple fight-or-flee situations, the limbic system causes the adrenal glands to secrete cortisone, which in turn affects the brain. The male sex hormone testosterone also has a complex role in promoting aggression. Winners in athletic contests often have higher levels of testosterone in their blood, but an enduring generalized stress can cause a decrease.[37]

Competition of any kind usually leads to victory for one party, defeat for the other. After a series of such contests, a pattern of dominance begins to emerge. The human race, as we know it historically, shows a marked inclination to develop social hierarchy. Rousseau and Marx (like his socialist predecessors) would have us believe that social distinctions are a historical development rather than a fulfillment of natural inclinations: in the original golden age, men were free and equal, sharing land, wealth, and responsibility. If this were so, Homo sapiens would be an unusual animal. Most social mammals and birds sort themselves out in some kind of "pecking order" — an expression derived from watching chickens in the poultry yard. Many descriptions of dominance hierarchies focus on contests between two individuals in which A dominates over B, but the actual process of formation must involve at least three parties. A defeats B in the presence of C who goes on to defeat B, then challenge A, until a stable pattern emerges.[38] Since dominance is an historical relationship, there can be no single gene or set of genes that determine it. On the other hand, in a social species, some hierarchical order is an almost inevitable product of aggressive competition under certain circumstances; namely, whenever individuals stand to win by gaining and maintaining easier access to valuable resources.

Most of our nearest primate relatives have a social order in which males dominate over females, and males in the prime of life dominate over immature and aging males. Despite earlier claims to the contrary, it is now known that chimpanzees exhibit a "fairly well-defined, social hierarchy amongst the adult males," in which there is, at any time, a clear head or "alpha."[39] Social status is maintained more often by threats than attack.

Among most higher primates, the social situation is not simple. While earlier observers tried to establish a uniform order based on "attention structures," this should mean that individuals of higher rank would be the object of more eye contact and grooming. It was also believed the nonsexual mounting was an expression of dominance. In practice, however, none of this works out so neatly. It turns out that patterns of grooming and nonsexual mounting are not at all consistent. Primates groom and mount each other for a variety of reasons: maternal comfort, appeasement, play, as well as sex and dominance. Patterns of dominance do, however, evolve from play bouts between older juveniles and young adults. Something like inherited status also plays a part, since to some extent a young chimpanzee's rise in the social scale is also affected by his mother's social standing.[40]

A chimpanzee social group is never static. Some males are always on the way up, others are on the way down. The cohesiveness of the group can vary with the season: it increases with the advent of dry weather, when large groups are formed.[41] In fact, cohesiveness is generally more pronounced in larger groups, especially when other groups are nearby. Taking all these elements into consideration, social dominance in chimpanzees can be viewed as "an adaptation to increase the inclusive fitness of individual males and their male community relatives threatened by males of adjacent communities."[42]

The chimpanzee is, of course, man's closest primate relative, and it would be strange if human beings did not display some tendencies toward social hierarchy. There are, in fact, very few human societies that lack leadership and social status. The most frequently cited exceptions include Pygmies, Eskimos, and !Kung Bushmen, all of whom have been marginalized by more successful neighbors. Irenaus Eibl-Eibesfeldt has made a thorough review of the peaceful peoples and discovered that most of them look back to the good old days, when circumstances allowed them to be as violent as other peoples.[43] While the !Kung have been described as "the harmless people" and a "people who devalue aggression,"[44] their level of violence exceeds that of suburban America. In her two years of study, Patricia Draper observed or heard four real fights—this in a population of only 120.[45] Despite their social informality and political anarchy, the small groups of bushmen do display "patterns of leadership," which include deference toward elders or toward heads of large families.[46] Most significantly, certain family heads have particular claims over specific water-holes—the one predictable and essential resource available to the !Kung.

The concept of territoriality is, however, very little developed among the hunting bands of the !Kung or the Hazda of Tanzania,[47] but it does exist. In general, territorial behavior can be described as an aggressive response to valuable resources. Such behavior is almost infinitely flexible, varying from species to species and within species, depending upon the abundance and predictability of resources.[48]

Chimpanzees are decidedly territorial. Adult males keep watch on the boundaries and assault strange intruders,[49] and similar behavior is observed of almost every human society, wherever it is in a situation where the cost/benefit trade-off works to the advantage of territorial defense. Obviously, no one would ordinarily need to stake out a claim on the desert—although an oasis is a different matter. Similarly, a small group of hunters following migratory animals can hardly claim, much less defend, thousands of square miles of hunting range. Does this mean that territoriality is not innate in human beings? In one sense, it cannot be innate, if by innate we mean a simple drive to hold and expand the space on which we live. On the other hand, we do seem to possess a mechanism that almost automatically responds to the most common environmental circumstances in which we find ourselves.

It would be dangerous, however, to conclude that nationalism is an innate territorial response. While it is true that any society that practices agriculture — to say nothing of heavy industry — will inevitably defend its investment of time and energy against competitors, that is not quite what we mean, ordinarily, by nationalism or patriotism.

The words we have used for "country" may reveal something of our attitude: European nations since the Greeks have called their country the fatherland (*Patris, Patria, Vaterland*). In ancient times, it was conventional to speak not of Athens (unless the topography was meant) but of the Athenians; not Rome but the Romans. This was particularly appropriate for the mighty herds of barbarians — Franks, Burgundins, Goths, and Vandals — who took so long to settle down. But at a deeper level, a nation is a family (as expressed in the Latin *gens*, which can refer both to a descent group and a nation). In the most primitive societies, kinship is often of greater significance than territory. This does not mean that every people goes through the transition from kinship to territory that Sir Henry Sumner Maine posited for Indo-European nations, only that it is hard to disentangle the sentiment of kinship from national identity.

There are other elements of human social life that can be subjected to sociobiological analysis, but these suffice to show the possible range of applications. It almost goes without saying that evolutionary biology is only the beginning point. Despite the fears that sociobiology is going to swallow up the social sciences, nothing could be farther from the truth. The emergence of language and culture make the human species in many respects unique. To a large extent, cultural evolution has replaced biological evolution. Nevertheless, it is a safe bet that no serious research in the social sciences can afford to neglect the biological foundations of human nature.

The results of such neglect are particularly obvious in the proliferation of political philosophies that practice a studied contempt for those observable habits of mankind. Plato, in many senses, began the mischief. In the *Republic* and *The Laws* he tried to construct an ideal (and a less than ideal) society based on absolute sexual equality and severe restrictions on the citizens' ability to acquire property, rise in the social scale, and rear their children.

Fortunately for Western civilization, the political ideas of Aristotle and Cicero — a biologist and a practical politician — had a greater impact than those of Plato and Augustine. Still, since the Renaissance, system after theoretical system of political philosophy have been created on the basis of a priori, abstractions about "rights" of the state as well as the individual — and a state of nature. The Marxist-Leninist attempt to eliminate property, sexual distinctions, social classes, and nationality has produced a stratified imperialist bureaucracy that rivals Byzantium in complexity and Attilla in ferocity. Natural law, like all laws of nature, cannot be violated any more than jumping off a cliff proves that man can defy the laws of gravity. Any attempt to defy the laws demonstrates their validity.

Transcendence

Once we have granted the universality and innateness of human social behavior, the natural law is still not binding. A prudent man, knowing what is at stake, would not wish to construct a society in open defiance of the most basic facts of human nature; nonetheless, the natural law cannot be regarded as a set of commandments so long as it is entirely natural. In ordinary speech, we sometimes speak as if statements — promises, for example — had a binding force, but these depend on prior moral assumptions, e.g. the belief that it is right to keep promises. A.J. Ayer, who uses this example, insists, "in cases where purely factual premises appear to yield a definite normative conclusion . . . a normative premise has been tacitly assumed."[50] The other side of the coin is equally interesting: Is it ever possible for human beings to make a statement of fact — "You're wearing that red dress, my dear" — that does not imply a judgment? Outside of thought experiments, mathematical statements are rarely value free. Most are on the order of, "Your account is out of balance," or else, "Figures don't lie."

On this problem, evolutionary biology sheds only a feeble light. *Ex definitione* a transcendent basis for the good is not a subject of any natural science. The religious impulse is apparently as universal as sex roles and private property. At the very least, it can be argued that the idea of God has "survival value," as Richard Dawkins has suggested. E.O. Wilson takes the argument a step further by pointing out a general human incapacity for life without religion. In the twentieth century, which has made every effort to fulfill Nietzsche's terrifying prophecies about a world in which "God is dead," nonbelievers have turned to every imaginable surrogate:

> The self-fulfilling cults of the present day, including Esalen, est, arica, and scientology, are the vulgar replacements of the traditional forms. Their leaders receive a degree of obedience from otherwise intelligent Americans that would wring smiles of admiration from the most fanatical sufi *shaykh*.[51]

Wilson and most other sociobiologists would like to explain away the religious impulse as an evolutionary relic. But in the case of our other desires — for food, sex, companionship — there is a basis in real needs: nutrition, procreation, and cooperation. It is not unreasonable to speculate that the desire for God has a genuine object. If religiosity confers fitness on individuals possessing that inclination, then it might be possible to restate Anselm's ontological proof for the existence of God in Darwinist terms. God might be said to exist not only because we can conceive of him also but because our ability to do so increases our chances of survival and reproduction.

Some physicists like to speak of an anthropic principle in the universe, by which they mean that the slightest difference in "the beginning" fraction of millisecond would have meant no solar system, no earth, no life, and no mind capable of understanding the universe. In this sense, they argue, man was fore-ordained. As a corollary to this argument, we might add that man is the only organic creature capable of knowing and worshipping a creator.

None of these speculations, it goes without saying, proves anything. They are introduced to illustrate a simple point: The unbelief of sociobiologists does not constitute a sufficient reason for religious believers to reject their views out of hand. Christians, who worship the son of God who called himself "the way, the truth, and the life," can have nothing to fear from a dispassionate investigation into the mystery of creation. At least one important religious philosopher has tried to incorporate an ethological perspective. In *The Nature of the Beast*, Stephen Clark tries to derive a basis for social ethics from the observed habits of other animals. "By seeing what constrains and motivates our kindred," he suggests, "we may, perhaps discover what the morals and manners of the human beasts might be." While sharply criticizing sociobiology as dangerous reductionism, Clark still concludes:

> Affection towards clan-mates, love of children, deference to authority, disinclination to kill those who have reminded us of common humanity, even some respect for property: these features of human life do not, it seems, stem from our intellectual gifts. We share them with our cousins.[52]

In practical terms, there are many problems in applying natural law to the everyday circumstances of personal life and public policy. The relationship between nature and an assumed super-nature is only one obstacle. Even if one can make the leap from is to ought, would this justify an imposition of natural law principles by way of legislation? In fact, most serious crimes — murder, theft, assault, rape, arson, kidnapping, and treason — are violations of natural law. The question only becomes problematic in those areas in which there is a current political debate, especially in the matter of sex roles and the family. Does a natural theory of politics dictate, for example, the subjugation of women or a rule of *Patria Potestas*, by which a father might legitimately put his children to death?

In an obvious sense, the answer is no. Positive law is rooted in natural law, but it is also a response to the infinite variation of local customs and circumstances. A man cannot legislate for all mankind without making himself as foolish as the *philosophes* and "citizens of the world" who adorned the eighteenth century. In patterns of sex roles and family life there is a great diversity; however, most of the variants are within a rather narrow range. Societies and nations are free to develop along lines that take them well beyond the norms. In doing so, however, they ought to be aware of potential consequences. Legislation against private property will not render men less acquisitive, and no affirmative action legislation can annihilate the special bond between mothers and children. Epigenetic rules cannot proscribe or prescribe legislation, but even in the near future sociobiology may have important legal ramifications. One legal scholar has already suggested it should be used as a tool in rewriting inheritance laws.

A theory of natural politics is not a blueprint for legislation. It is more like a set of specifications that determines the ratio of height to circumference in a column. Gravity imposes limits on the size of land animals and the tallness of trees. New building materials and construction techniques enable human beings to stretch beyond the limits without actually defying the law of gravity. However, the construction of a Sears Tower or an Empire State Building requires the active participation and coordinated efforts of thousands of workers beyond the reach of simpler societies. Similarly, the Western variants of social organization rely heavily on individual autonomy, nuclear households, and citizen participation. In so complex a society, the burden of history becomes almost overwhelming, and we begin to long for simpler times. Utopian communes, stressing sexual and social equality, are an understandable reaction to urban complexity, but it is important to bear in mind that the choice may well be either/or: either a highly articulated complexity of well-developed sexual and social roles or the egalitarian simplicity of the pygmies. Primitives do not build 100-story buildings, compose symphonies, or structure their lives much beyond tomorrow or next week. When it rains, they shiver. When the game leaves, they follow or they go hungry. When they face enemies, they either abandon whatever small advantages they possess in their homeland or else they fight. If they lose, they may all be either dead or enslaved, and if they win they will have taken the first faltering step toward a higher level of social organization. Exiled from the Eden of simplicity, they will rise to fight or flee, again and again, until they are either civilized or extinct. Only in art can they allow themselves the luxury of looking back.

For the purpose of understanding natural politics, it may not matter much how we derived our human nature — from Adam and Eve in the Garden or from Australopithecus in the savannahs of Southern Africa. But to insist on this point of "the common human" is not the same thing as denying the great diversity and variety of human cultures. The role of cultural and material forces in shaping social behavior is too obvious to ignore. Even so, the claims made by some anthropologists are too extravagant to accept outside of science fiction. Even in the wildest accounts of the most alien societies, a reader can see his own lineaments reflected — or distorted as in a funhouse mirror.

The great difficulty lies in deciding just what constitutes the natural element in social and political organization. Short of supernatural revelation, nothing human can ever be absolute. The border between nature and culture is as hard to fix as the border between two states divided by a river. Rivers change their course, and the vicissitudes of arms and diplomacy will cause one side to possess sometimes one or both, sometimes neither, bank. There are, however, a few guidelines — surveyor's tools — which might be useful in a rough way. Three considerations might lead us to consider some item of social life as natural: primate (and mammalian) parallels, universality (or even prevalence) in human societies, and the tendency for cultural evolution to accentuate and develop (rather than diminish) a trait.

The primary data of natural law consist of the customs and institutions that seem universal in human societies. It is, admittedly, hard to make a generalization to which there are no exceptions. Male dominance is universal, but there are societies in which women are permitted a high degree of autonomy within the family and some, like certain Indian tribes, which allowed women to vote in tribal assemblies or, as in Europe, to inherit royal power. The incest taboo was violated by Egyptian kings and even aristocrats, while certain African peoples encourage fathers to have intercourse with a daughter before setting out on a raid. Such exceptions do not necessarily invalidate the idea of natural law or natural politics.

Similar exceptions might, after all, be applied to individual cases. Any number of acts are almost universally regarded as not-normal, that is, not to be practiced or even thought of, except under extreme or very special conditions. Such violations of the moral code as murder (killing without legal or social justification), incest, sexual relations with children and animals lie under the general condemnation of the human race. To be sure, individuals do commit murder; sons do — on the rarest of occasions — sleep with their mothers; and some men and women seem to prefer the company of sheep. Such acts are possible in nature and actually occur, but no one would describe such behavior as natural or deny that it violated natural law. Aristotle made a useful distinction in literature between the real or actual (including the bizarre events that make the careers of tabloid journalists) and the probable. Literature, he claimed, was concerned only with the probable, that is, with what is consistent with nature. Likewise, natural politics does not concern itself with the exceptional, but with the normal and the probable. There is nothing to prevent a society, like an individual, from falling into "bad habits": cannibalism, incest, regular infanticide, and so on, but social scientists would do well to follow the example of Gilbert's little Oliver:

> The simple truth is my detective
> with me sensation can't abide.
> The likely beats the mere effective
> And Nature is my only guide.

Anthropologists are fond of pointing out that in man, cultural evolution replaces biological evolution. This should not mean that culture reverses or even replaces nature. Traits that have remained constant throughout primate evolution will not be overturned by social whim. For example, the essential facts of maternity — birth, lactation, and the need for prolonged care — cannot be overridden by custom or legislation. If cultural evolution really does replace natural selection, then it ought to continue or fulfill some of the tendencies already present in the evolution of primates. In the same way, cultural evolution might "choose to emphasize," in Ruth Benedict's phrase, primate traits that are biologically well developed in man. Wilson describes this general phenomenon as hypertrophy. Ordinarily, hypertrophy refers to the exaggerated development of a simple organ or structure — the elephant's trunk or the caribou's antlers. In the case of maternity, there is a pronounced tendency in primate evolution to extend all phases of development — pregnancy, nursing, and dependence of children upon mother. Even the least developed human societies represent a great advance over chimpanzees; however, the requirements for prolonged child care continue to increase as societies become more developed and more complex. The lavish attention bestowed on children in such "high cultures" as traditional China and modern Europe suggest that cultural evolution has carried out the tendencies of biological evolution.

Sexual dimorphism is more complicated. It has been argued, on the basis of size, that gorillas and chimpanzees display greater differences between the sexes than are exhibited by men and women. While men are 20–30 percent bigger than women — and considerably more muscular — gorilla males are proportionally much larger than females. In other features, however, men and women in the natural state do seem — to a casual human observer — more different. At all events, this dimorphism is not repressed by culture; on the contrary, it is generally enhanced — by customs of hair style, clothing, jewelry, and cosmetics. Once again, the "high cultures" of the Orient and the West agree in emphasizing the physical, emotional, and social differences between the sexes. This agreement might be regarded as convergence, an additional argument in favor of the naturalness of sexual distinctions. In this sense, elaborate codes of chivalry could be seen as entirely natural development, whereas radical feminism, which seeks to reduce these differences to a minimum, is at best a false and unnatural atavism, and at its worst, an assault upon the foundations of all human social life.

Notes

1. D.M. Armstrong, *What Is a Law of Nature?* (Cambridge, MA: Cambridge University Press, 1983), 85.
2. Charles J. Lumsden and Edward O. Wilson, *Promethean Fire: Reflections on the Origin of Minds* (Cambridge, MA: Harvard University Press, 1983), 56–57.
3. *Metalogicon* II, 20.

4. See Heinz Happ, "Die Scala Naturae und die Schichtung des Seelischen bei Aristoteles" in Ruth Stiehl and H.E. Stiehl, eds., *Beiträge zur Alten Geschichte und denen Nachleben: Festschrift Für F. Altheim* (Berlin: de Gruyter 1969–70), 220–44.

5. William S. Laughlin, "Acquisition of Anatomical Knowledge by Ancient Man" in Sherwood Washburn, *Social Life of Early Man* (New York: Wenner-Gren Foundation, 1961), 150–75.

6. Peter Worsley, *The Trumpet Shall Sound: A Study of Cargo Cults in Melanesia* (London: MacGibbon & Kee, 1957), 216–17.

7. In a letter to the Marquess of Newcastle (23 November 1646) Descartes admitted that animals could be trained to mimic human feelings or behavior, but only as machines.

8. Loren Eiseley, *Darwin's Century: Evolution and the Men Who Discovered It* (Garden City, NY: Doubleday, 1958), 225.

9. *De Legibus* I.7.22.

10. Henry Home, Lord Kames, *Sketches of the History of Man* (Edinburgh and London: Creech, Strahan, and Cadell, 1778), Book II (Vol. II), 153 ff.

11. Hans Kelsen, *General Theory of Law and State* (New York: Russell and Russell, 1961), 8ff.

12. Michael Novak, "A New Approach to Natural Law," *Proceedings, American Catholic Philosophical Association* 41 (1967), 246–49.

13. A. Passerin d'Entreves, *Natural Law: An Historical Survey*, repr. of 1951 ed. (New York: Harper & Row, 1965).

14. A.C. MacIntyre, "Hume on 'is' and 'ought,'" *The Philosophical Review* 68 (1959).

15. Anthony Battaglia, *Toward a Reformulation of Natural Law* (New York: Seabury Press, 1981), 15ff.

16. Michael Polanyi, *Knowing and Being: Essays by Michael Polanyi,* Marjorie Grene, ed. (Chicago: University of Chicago Press, 1969), 42–43.

17. J.L. Mackie, *Ethics: Inventing Right and Wrong* (New York: Penguin, 1977), 18ff.

18. Cf. Cicero, *De Officiis* III. 17.69.

19. *Digest*, I.1.1.

20. See his discussion in *Summa Theologiae* I-II. 94.

21. *Eth. Nich.* V. 7, 1134b.

22. Claude Lévi-Strauss, *The View from Afar*, trans. by Joachim Neugroschel and Phoebe Hoss (New York: Basic Books, 1985), 28 ff.

23. Lumsden and Wilson, *op. cit.*, 137.

24. David Hume, *A Treatise of Human Nature* III.1.2. (p. 474).

25. Claude Lévi-Strauss, *op. cit.*, 137.

26. Digest 1.1.3.

27. See especially *Summa Theologiae* I-II, 93.

28. Joseph Butler, *The Analogy of Religion, Natural and Revealed, to the Constitution and The Course of Nature*, repr. with Introduction (New York: F. Ungar, 1961), I.VII.

29. Stephen R.L. Clark, "The Absence of a Gap Between Facts and Values," *Proceedings of the Aristotelian Society*, Suppl. Vol. 54 (1980), 207ff.

30. Kames, *op. cit.*, 154.

31. Thomas Molnar, "Ethology and Environmentalism: Man as Animal and Mechanism," *Intercollegiate Review* (Fall 1977), 25–43.

32. For sexual selection and sexual strategies, see W.D. Hamilton, "The Genetic Evolution of Social Behavior," *The Journal of Theoretical Biology*, 7: 1–25 repr. in James H. Hunt, *Selected Readings in Sociobiology* (New York: McGraw-Hill, 1980), 7–30;

and in the same volume Robert L. Trivers, "The Evolution of Reciprocal Altruism," 38–68 as well as standard works by Richard Dawkins and E.O. Wilson.

33. Cf. Robin Fox's list in Bernard G. Campbell, *Sexual Selection and the Descent of Man 1871–1971* (Chicago: Aldine, 1974).

34. J.H. Crook, J.E. Ellis and J.D. Goss Custard, "Mammalian Social Systems: Structure and Function" in James H. Hunt, *op. cit.*, 307.

35. For the varieties of aggressive behavior see, for example, Junichiro Itani, "Intraspecific Killing Among Non-Human Primates," *Journal of Social and Biological Structures* 5 (1982), 361–68; and E.O. Wilson, *On Human Nature* (Cambridge, MA; Harvard University Press, 1978), 101.

36. K.E. Moyer, "Kinds of Aggression and Their Physiological Basis," *Communications in Behavioral Biology* 2 (1968), 65–87.

37. For a general discussion, see Melvin Konner, *The Tangled Wing: Biological Constraints on the Human Spirit* (New York: Holt, Rinehart, and Winston, 1982), 192–99.

38. Ivan D. Chase, "Social Process and Hierarchy Formation in Small Groups: A Comparative Perspective," *American Sociological Review* 45 (1980), 905–24.

39. Jane Van Lawick-Goodall, "The Chimp" in Vanne Goodall, ed., *The Quest for Man* (New York: Praeger, 1975), 134.

40. See especially Paul E. Simonds, "The Bonnet Macaque in South India" in L.A. Rosenblum, *Primate Behavior: Developments in Field and Laboratory Research* (New York: Academic Press, 1970), 183; and in the same volume, Irwin S. Bernstein's "Primate Status Hierarchies," cf. his "Dominance: The Baby and the Bathwater," *Behavioral and Brain Sciences* 4 (1981), 419–29. Bernstein sometimes appears to confuse the question of complexity with the more basic question of causation.

41. Yukimaru Sugiyama, "Social Characteristics and Socialization of Wild Chimpanzees" in Frank E. Poirier, *Primate Socialization* (New York: Random House, 1972), 151.

42. Harold R. Bauer, "Chimpanzee Society and Social Dominance in Evolutionary Perspective" in Donald R. Omark, F.F. Strayer, and Daniel G. Freedman, eds. *Dominance Relations: An Ethological View of Human Conflict and Social Interaction* (New York: Garland STPM Press, 1980), 118.

43. *The Biology of Peace and War: Man, Animals, and Aggression* (New York: Viking, 1979).

44. Patricia Draper, "The Learning Environment for Aggression and Anti-Social Behavior Among the !Kung" in Ashley Montagu, ed., *Learning Non-Aggression* (New York: Oxford University Press, 1978), 32–33.

45. Draper, loc. cit.

46. Richard B. Lee, *The !Kung San: Men, Women, and Work in a Foraging Society* (Cambridge: Cambridge University Press, 1979), 343 ff.

47. James Woodburn, "Stability and Flexibility in Hazda Residential Groupings," in Richard B. Lee and Irven DeVore, eds. *Man the Hunter* (Chicago: Aldine, 1968).

48. Rada Dyson-Hudson and Eric Alden-Smith, "Human Territoriality: An Ecological Reassessment," *American Anthropologist* 80 (1978), 21–41; and Elizabeth Cashden, "Territoriality Among Human Foragers: Ecological Models and an Application to Four Bushmen Groups," *Current Anthropology* 24 (1983), 47–66.

49. Jane van Lawick-Goodall, "Order Without Law," *Journal of Social and Biological Structures* 5 (1982), 353–60.

50. A.J. Ayer, *Freedom and Morality and Other Essays* (Oxford: Oxford at the Clarendon Press, 1984), 23.

51. E.O. Wilson, *op. cit.*, 185.

52. Stephen R.L. Clark, *The Nature of the Beast: Are Animals Moral?*, repr. in paper (Oxford: Oxford University Press, 1984), 109.

4

"Male and Female Created He Them"

Men and women are different. Until recently, this difference was one of those things the proverbial "any schoolboy" could be expected to know. Males and females, so it was thought, differed in size, shape, temperament, and intellectual abilities. These differences were related to the distinct functions that nature (and the Creator of nature) had assigned to the sexes. Aristotle, for example, describes the male sex as more savage, courageous, and masterful; the female as softer, more modest yet more impulsive, sooner tamed and more devoted to the nurture of children. These qualities, in his view, fitted men and women for their different responsibilities: men ruled, women nurtured.

This division of labor had the sanction of religion. Man was created master of everything on earth, while woman was his assistant, an "help meet for him." Myths and folktales abound in which the Fall of man is attributed to an Eve or Pandora, whose beauty was the vehicle by which evil came into the world. As one proper Victorian (W.S. Gilbert) put it,

> In all the woes that curse our race
> There is a lady in the case.

The greatest mistake a man might make would be to give way to the weaker sex. Political power was, in the course of nature, a perquisite of the male gender. The right to vote, to hold office, and to attend most schools of higher learning — all were exclusively male prerogatives.

There were tales of other times and places, in which women ruled or shared power. The Athenians celebrated mythical victories over the man-hating Amazons and entertained themselves with stories of a prehistoric Athens where women voted — before being put in their place by a coalition of men and gods. But the myths were just that. What is more, they were part of the "propaganda" used to support a society run by men. As one feminist scholar recently expressed it, these Athenian tales "functioned as a tool for thinking, explaining, and validating patriarchal customs, institutions, and values by postulating the absurdities and horrors of its opposite."[1] The fact is that women have never held political power over men by virtue of their sex, not even in the modern United States.

Any talk of male dominance or sexual differences is sure to bring down a hail of curses from those who have made a profitable business out of women's studies and female liberation. In response to the myths of Hesiod and Genesis, they have constructed countermyths of female equality and even superiority. The more moderate version of the myth is often advanced by older feminists and respectable women scientists and scholars: Men and women are different in some important respects; women are adapted to the bearing and rearing of children, and men are born to develop a stronger musculature; these differences, accentuated by the economic pressures on preindustrial societies, made the subordination of women an inevitable fact of history, until recently. Simone de Beauvoir wrote movingly of the female sex in the grip of natural forces: "From birth the species has taken possession of her" and at puberty it "reaffirms its rights."[2] However, the argument now runs, the continuation of sexual discrimination in modern industrial societies is "increasingly maladaptive."[3] Social and technological progress now make it possible for men and women to redivide the pie — political power and domestic responsibility — in a manner more consistent with modern ideas of freedom and equality. This moderate feminist version of reality is part of the more general myth of ameliorative progress.

Increasingly, many feminists have come to reject moderation. Resurrecting the long-dead theories of Bachofen and Engels, they dream of lost civilizations in which "women had played a dominant role." They discover that it was woman "who had first tamed and then re-educated man."[4]

It is not just harmless cranks and feminist ideologues who embrace such views. Book after book is issued by women professing to be classical scholars, historians, and anthropologists, all of them dedicated to proving either the existence of Amazons, mother-right, and matriarchal societies, or the sinister machinations of the male sex. Honest and open discussion is out of the question. As psychologist Joseph Adelson describes the situation in the social sciences, "A certain frivolousness in dealing even with simple facts is now so commonplace as to be nearly normative,"[5] and of feminist history, Sir Geoffrey Elton has written, "The combination of passionate assault and conscience-stricken response produced, predictably, a state of affairs in which women's history has received little serious criticism."[6]

The more sober feminists are wise enough to avoid prehistory and prefer to make up their own quasi-Marxist versions of human history. Women, as Betty Friedan writes, are "an oppressed people" who have been "forced to be mothers — and only mothers — against their will."[7] Men may have bigger muscles, but, claims Kate Millet in *Sexual Politics*, such an advantage is "hardly an adequate category on which to base political relations *within civilization*."[8] The threat of rape and violent assault is the only cement that holds men and women together in society, so much so that Susan Brownmiller seems afraid to enter an elevator. Black feminist Shirley Chisolm has a tragic vision of women programmed for subordination from the moment of birth, when a girl-child is wrapped in a pink blanket.[9] It is the task of modern women to confront their oppressors and wrest power from the imperial male.

It is not necessary to rehearse the absurd fantasies of feminist organizations with names like ALLECTO and WITCH or to repeat their demands for revenge upon all the hapless men who have strayed into the second half of the twentieth century. It is to be hoped that at least some of them will have the luck of Turandot, the Chinese fairy-tale princess Puccini put in his last opera. For the sake of a remote ancestress' sufferings, the princess defied "l'aspro dominio," the harsh dominion of the male sex, until she succumbed to love — and reality.

A prime example of feminist scholarship is Gerda Lerner's *The Creation of Patriarchy*.[10] Lerner's thesis is simple: While women were central to the creation of society, they have been "kept from knowing their history," a phenomenon she calls "the dialectic of women's history." Without training in the languages or methods of Assyriology, she explains the rise of patriarchy in the ancient Near East. Undaunted by ignorance, Lerner rejected the professional suggestions of sympathetic colleagues in constructing her myth and took pains to base her arguments on generally frivolous feminist historians and literary critics.[11] Of the wealth of cross-cultural studies tending to indicate the universality of sex roles, there is hardly a word. Despite the book's obvious silliness, praise came pouring in from all sides. Typical is Germaine Brée's defiant, "The scholarship is impeccable." What Brée, a critic of French literature, may be supposed to know about cuneiform texts, it is hard to imagine, but the publisher (Oxford) thought enough of her opinion to include it on the dust jacket.

More serious feminist writers do glance from time to time at some of the research into sex differences, but they usually succeed in finding only what they are looking for. Kate Millet concluded that "experimentation regarding the connection between hormones and animal behavior . . . yields highly ambiguous results."[12] Many take refuge in an obscurantism unbecoming to scholars and scientists. One feminist anthropologist insists that there might have been matriarchies, since "no one can ever penetrate into the facts about [sic] 99 per cent of human life on earth."[13] This is not the only example of a feminist scholar for whom facts are not things in themselves but are "about things." One apparently competent neurophysiologist has devoted an entire book to casting ideological doubt on dispassionate research into sex differences. For her, Amazons do not exist, but something called "heterosexism" does, and it is responsible for preventing millions of women from fulfilling themselves — as lesbians.[14] Germaine Greer has read just enough of the evidence to confirm her belief that culture is the main culprit. Her chapter on "baby" is devoted to showing how the socialization process turns sex-neutral babies into men and women — with almost no mention of the most important fact: maternity.[15]

No serious person has ever argued that all sex differences are attributable to biological destiny. Even some of the most apparent physical differences are subject to cultural influence. The longer hair and fairer complexions of women owe much to fashion. The softer and less muscular bodies of Western women are partly the result of cultural traditions that have specified football for boys and dolls for girls. On Bali, where neither sex performs hard labor, they differ little in muscle development. But once a Balinese man begins to perform Coolie labor, he begins to assume the universal male physical type. There have been efforts to explain absolute differences in size as products of cultural adaptation; however, height difference between men and women seems to be universal.[16]

On the other hand, there is an irreducible core of anatomical differences that are resistant, if not impervious, to cultural processes.[17] Cross-cultural studies confirm the common impression that men are, on the average, taller, heavier, and more muscled. Reported variations in height turn out to be more a function of sampling inaccuracy than a result of cultural influences. Even at birth, boy babies are longer and heavier, and their muscle-to-fat ratio is higher than that of girls — a gap that widens as they grow older. While only 15 per cent of a young adult male's body weight is in adipose tissue, it is 27 per cent in a young adult female. On the other hand, 52 per cent of a man's body is muscle — as opposed to only 40 per cent of a woman's. A crude idea of the order of difference can be derived from realizing that, in total body volume, sexual dimorphism is the order of 20 percent.[18] Since male lungs and hearts are proportionally larger and their blood is able to carry more oxygen, men are able to sustain greater exertions. Their heavier skeletons and specially designed hip-sockets fit them for the hard labor that is the lot of men who were told almost from the beginning: "In the sweat of thy face shalt thou eat bread." The physical advantages of the male sex have obviously played a part in determining the allocation of social roles to men and women.

It is interesting to compare the development of sexual dimorphism among apes and hominids. Among the higher apes, dimorphism of canine tooth size is a function of increasing social organization, but among hominids, canine teeth functions are taken over by tools. This tool use in turn leads to development of need for heavier male bodies — clearly a case of gene/culture interaction.[19] Ever since Darwin, it has been argued that sexual selection is the main cause of dimorphism: the sex that invests less in its offspring will end up competing for mates and developing certain secondary characteristics. The theory has been able to validate some of its predictions. For example, in species where males invest more in parenting than females, courtship patterns should be reversed: Females will vie with each other for male favors. This is precisely what happens in the case of Mormon crickets: The male provides a large spermatophore that is an essential nutrient for a reproducing female. Predictably, females compete for access to males, and the chosen females appear to be more fecund than the rejects.[20] In the case of certain baboons that live in multi-male troops, females compete for mates — especially dominant males — and emphasize their availability by means of bright-colored hair on the rump. Similarly, human cultures develop bizarre forms of cosmetics, dress, and even body shape in response to competition for mates. Most such ornamentation can be shown to be an advertisement of fitness. Shoulder pads are a sign of masculine strength, while most female padding attempts to persuade us that a woman will make a good mother.[21]

Human males invest less in their offspring than females. The disparity is very basic: While females produce few but large eggs, males provide millions of small sperm; while women carry the fetus for nine months, nurse and take care of the baby for years, a man's natural responsibility is confined to being a provider. To some extent, therefore, the special development of male characteristics is a result of the competition for women.

Even more striking are the different paths of development taken by male and female reproductive systems. The basic process by which we become male and female is now fairly well understood. Conception determines the chromosomal sex. In normal humans, it is either XX (female) or XY (male). In about the sixth week after conception, the fetal child begins to develop sexual glands (gonads): ovaries in females, testes in males. If the testes develop normally, their secretions induce the formation of male sexual characteristics, the marks of the male "phenotype." If, however, ovaries develop — or no gonads at all — then the phenotype is female. Female hormones secreted by the ovaries continue the process of differentiation.[22]

From the perspective of embryology, the basic theme is female, upon which the male is a variation. After birth, the process of differentiation remains very slow until the onset of puberty, which takes place at about the age of eleven in girls, twelve in boys. At this time, the familiar metamorphosis of children into men and women is triggered by sexually appropriate gonadal hormones.

This normal process of development affects more than the reproductive organs. Evidence is mounting that a parallel process of sexual differentiation takes place in the brain and nerves that make up the central nervous system of higher vertebrates like man. Once again, "the intrinsic pattern is female," as the specifically male characteristics take shape under the influence of androgens, although the differences seem to be of a lower order of magnitude.[23] There is some evidence to indicate that female hormones may also play a role in the development of the specifically female mammalian brain. For obvious reasons, most of the research has been done on laboratory animals, especially rats, and the results can only be provisionally applied to humans. However, the same caveats apply to a good deal of research on human behavior. It now appears that the brains of female rats are structurally different from the males'. If a male rat is castrated just after birth, it will display typically female brain patterns. On the other hand, injection of testosterone (a male testicular hormone) into newborn females can induce a male brain pattern.[24]

It takes very little reflection to realize that in some respects men and women must behave differently if they are going to survive. The sexually dimorphic human anatomy means that our mating behavior, at least, must be dimorphic enough to permit conception to take place. Since the circuitry for our behavioral mechanisms lies in the central nervous system, it too must be sufficiently different in men and women to allow them to reproduce.

When we come to the influence of sex hormones on behavior, we are on firmer ground. These hormones, which circulate in the blood, appear to have a direct effect on the brain and concentrate in the highest levels in those regions of the brain that are most important in mating, mothering, and aggression (i.e. in the limbic system).[25] The male hormone testosterone, in addition to promoting muscle growth, plays some role in exciting aggressive and violent behavior. While there is no direct correlation between levels of testosterone and levels of violence, it turns out that prisoners with "long and vivid histories" of violence do have higher-than-normal levels of testosterone circulating in their bloodstream.[26] If these levels are reduced, aggressiveness — along with the sexual appetite — is lowered. Men are, in general, more violent and more aggressive than women. In most societies, boys are more prone to engage in mock fighting and more ready to meet an attack with a counterattack.

The impact of hormones on behavior is clearest in the case of abnormal development. Men suffering from Kleinfelter's syndrome possess an extra X chromosome (XXY). Among the symptoms is an inadequate development of their sex glands (hypogonadism). The effect of lower hormone levels is to diminish their sex drive and to increase their emotional dependency, i.e., make them less assertive and less aggressive. Fortunately, it is a condition that responds to injections of hormones.

Equally instructive are the cases of women who suffer from various types of androgenization, particularly the female androgenital syndrome. A defect of the adrenal glands of genetic females causes the adrenal cortices to synthesize androgens instead of cortisol. They develop external male genitalia and exhibit a higher incidence of typically "male" behavior: tomboyism, rough play, high expenditure of energy. If the condition is not corrected soon after birth, the victims may display even more masculine behavior: lowered interest in children with a correspondingly heightened interest in making a career.[27] A similar effect is observed in female rhesus monkeys whose mothers were injected with testosterone during their pregnancy: the daughters develop behaviorally "along masculine lines." Females given testosterone injections eventually exert dominance not only over other females but over males as well.[28] It seems fair to conclude that some, if not all, of the observable psychological differences between men and women are prescribed genetically and hormonally.

It is hard to imagine the alternative. Men are, virtually everywhere, more dominant and aggressive, women more nurturant and maternal. Even if we say that they are made so by culture, we have to explain how it is that all cultures "choose to emphasize" the same qualities of sexual identity. Besides, all human behavioral patterns are implemented through physiological mechanisms. Feminists and cultural relativists seem to think men are composed of a material body and a nonmaterial soul, and that this soul is free to manipulate its body like a puppet, design cultures, and redefine even itself, all without regard for that inert shell they call the body. This is not to say that all human behavior is biologically determined. Such a statement would be difficult to support, impossible to prove. But it is, we might say, organically mediated, since nothing in this life can be felt, thought, or done without the prompting of brain, nerves, and hormones or without the support of blood and bone.

Psychological difference between the sexes is not limited to hormone-triggered aggressiveness. A wide range of studies have documented a sexual divergence in perception, intellectual abilities, and social aptitudes. Some of the differences have important social consequences. Others, like the differences in perception, are merely intriguing. For example, adult females have more acute hearing than men, and women are generally more receptive to auditory stimulation, men to visual. Female babies are more sensitive to touch and pain and respond more positively to sweets—an affection that can persist throughout the course of life. In this respect, the stereotype of the bonbon devouring movie actress is not completely off the mark. In fact, females are considerably more "mouth-oriented" in a number of ways. Girl babies vocalize more than boys and exhibit more mouth-to-hand activity (as opposed to the more normal habit of bringing the hand to the mouth) and more frequent mouthing during sleep. From the age of one, a girl is more likely to suck her thumb and suck it more often, and as adults, women are far more prone to suffer from eating disorders like anorexia nervosa.[29]

All these details are interesting, some are even instructive. Of greater importance—and greater peril to discuss—are differences in intellectual aptitude. As might have been predicted, men and women do not differ in general levels of intelligence, but in the components of cognition there are significant differences. It has been known for some time that girls in school display greater verbal ability than boys, whereas boys excel in such things as "visual-spatial" ability, mathematics, and analytical reasoning.[30] A series of studies by Benbow and Stanley on "precocious youth" indicates that environmental factors play a part, but that sexual differences per se are important. Even among mathematically talented teenagers taking part in the same special program, boys outscore girls in the math section of the SAT.[31] Some of these phenomena may be attributable to sexual differences in brain lateralization.[32] In general, girls do better in school, but while schoolgirls earn better grades, boys score higher on achievement tests, perhaps because boys like to compete.[33]

Women also excel in the performance of repetitive tasks like the successive subtraction problems that teachers used to assign as punishment. This ability to concentrate on repetitive details has been related to the action of female hormones (estrogens). On the other hand, testosterone has a similar, if less pronounced, effect on males. Donald Broverman and his colleagues for the past twenty years have been performing experiments designed to test what they call the "automatization cognitive style" in men, which they define as a "greater . . . or lesser ability . . . to perform simple, highly practiced repetitive tasks . . . than can be expected from the individual's general level of ability."

They found that strong automatizers tended to be more masculine, dominant men. They were more muscular, typically possessed more body hair, and were more likely to achieve social and economic success. While they did not find higher levels of testosterone in the bloodstream of strong automatizers, they did discover that testosterone injections could improve performance. What is more, those subjects whose testosterone levels remained high over a period of time (indicating a failure to utilize the hormone) did not respond to the injections — an indication that weak automatizers may suffer from an inability to utilize the testosterone that is available to them in the bloodstream.[34]

Hormones are not the only influence. Genetically based differences in the central nervous system (CNS) play a part, as do the life experiences and social environment of individuals. Some differences between the sexes may have a variety of causes. Males are more frequently afflicted with psychiatric disorders in childhood and with developmental problems in their nervous systems. While some male mental health problems have to do with the difficulties in becoming a man, there are clearly biophysical factors. One recent hypothesis traced the source to an inhospitable uterine environment triggered by the male fetus.[35]

It is also important to stress that there is an overlap in intellectual aptitudes and behavior patterns between the sexes. Some women do have better mathematical and analytical abilities than most men — a fact that is put beyond doubt by the careers of many brilliant scholars and scientists, many of them doing research on just this subject of sex differences. This overlapping may be partly a function of the overlap of androgen levels in the womb during the critical period of development of the CNS. Nonetheless, the existence of exceptional individuals and even a fairly low degree of divergence do not invalidate the general conclusion that by nature men and women are adapted psychologically to perform different tasks within different behavioral "styles."

A clearer case for psychological adaptation can be made for the differences in social aptitudes. Men tend to be more sexually active, socially dominant, less responsible, and less emotionally expressive than women. By the first grade, boys have begun to congregate in swarms in which individuals compete for power and prestige. Girls, on the other hand, tend to restrict themselves to small groups of two and three. In general, girls are more likely to seek approval. One study of black schoolchildren (grades 1–6), found that, when social approval and objective success were in conflict, girls opted for approval, boys for success.[36] Girls are more likely to assist in taking care of children and one recent study contributed the obvious but significant observation that females of all ages are more likely to look at a baby in a shopping mall.[37] There is some evidence to suggest that girls may be more fearful than boys. However, it is also true that boys with high I.Q.s (or who will later develop intellectual interests) seem also to be more timid and cautious than their less-gifted peers.[38] Perhaps they are just more likely to learn from their mistakes.

This specialization of emotional and social aptitudes is manifested in a number of universal traits that have been observed in the hundreds of human societies that have been studied. All societies, for example, practice some division of labor by sex. George P. Murdock, after analyzing information on 224 tribes, discovered that in 75 per cent of them women were assigned such tasks as grain grinding, cooking, gathering fuel and vegetables, preserving meat and fish, and weaving; while men were responsible for herding, fishing, lumbering, trapping, mining and quarrying, hunting (98 percent), and catching large sea mammals (99 percent).[39] Some of the variation, which does exist, is partly related to the sexual bias in social arrangements that dictate such things as who is related to whom and where a married couple will reside. There are, in addition, accidents of cultural history that can attach high prestige to what are ordinarily feminine tasks like pottery (as in ancient Greece and China), weaving (Egypt), and cooking (college towns in the United States). Domestic arts that attain the status of a profession or a high art become — predictably — a masculine preserve. While women cook for their families, men become chefs who cultivate a cuisine with rules as arcane as those that mark a religious sect or government office.[40]

Despite a modest degree of cultural variation, the division of labor by sex is quite clearly influenced by innate sexual characteristics. Men perform the strenuous and dangerous tasks that often, as in the case of hunting, require cooperation, while women concentrate on work directly related to the nurture and care of children (to say nothing of the husband). This division of labor, the result of dimorphism, is typically reflected in sexually biased forms of social organization, especially since the male *persona* is more sexually active, less responsible, less nurturant, and less emotionally expressive. To balance these defects, man is more dominant.[41]

The phrase "male dominance," has acquired an ugly ring in recent years. Despite the frequent complaint of feminist writers, there is no evidence that women, as a sex, have ever held a dominant position over men. Stories to the contrary are based either on misconception, fantasy, or actual dishonesty. One of the great benefits of women's studies is that honest feminist scholars have forever exploded the idea that Amazon societies ever existed outside the imagination of poets and painters. Even the cherished old examples of powerful women — in ancient Greek literature and history — have been put to rest by Mary Lefkowitz. These women, it has been shown, in nearly every case, viewed themselves as carrying out the will of their families and in no way considered themselves in a rivalry with the male sex.[42]

Feminist arguments against the universal patterns of division of labor and male dominance take several forms. Some, like Eleanor Leacock, revive the evolutionary theories of L.H. Morgan and Friedrich Engels. Others try to argue from examples of a few decadent tribal societies — whether Bushmen or Hopis — or from societies where the evidence cannot be checked — the Nayar and the Iroquois — that the existence of a few exceptional cases disproves the general principle. However, nearly all of them acknowledge their indebtedness to Margaret Mead. In *Sex and Temperament in Three Savage Societies*, Mead tried to show that sex roles varied so much in her three (carefully selected) societies, that "many, if not all of the personality traits which we have called masculine or feminine are as lightly linked to sex as are the clothing, the manners, and the form of headdress."[43] Mead's own evidence was against her; despite the variations between three particularly repulsive cultures, the men in each of them monopolized high status positions, exercised dominance over women, and assigned high status to whatever had been decreed to be the male occupation. She cited the Tchambuli as a "genuine reversal of the sex attitudes of our own culture" because their men were "less responsible" and "emotionally dependent."[44] Mead certainly did not have an adequate scale on which to measure dependency, but the point of Tchambuli irresponsibility can be granted — especially since male irresponsibility is usually described as a universal trait.

Mead's desire to confirm the theory of cultural relativity has already been demonstrated, and it will not require a great deal of imagination to understand the purpose for writing *Sex and Temperament*. Indeed, she takes it for granted. She begins one of her concluding summaries with "Granting the malleability of human nature" and proceeds to argue against the idea that women actually wish to care for their children because "this is a trait with which women have been more generously endowed by a careful teleological process of evolution."[45] It would be hard to find a scientist who believed that evolution was teleological, i.e., was directed toward some end that had been decreed from the very beginning. That much of her statement was misleading and dishonest. But it would be equally hard to find a scientist who believed that a woman's willingness to bear, nurse, and care for children was only a matter of culture and convenience.

The work of Margaret Mead cannot be taken as a refutation of universal sex roles, but there are other myths. Until recently, some feminist writers were able to take advantage of a certain confusion, in the popular mind, between the terms "matriarchy" and "matriliny." Matriarchy as such, i.e., rule of adult women, has never — so far as we know — existed. Indeed, the title of Steven Goldberg's well-argued polemic, *The Inevitability of Patriarchy* remains — for all the controversy surrounding the book — a reasonable statement of the evidence. However, matriliny, as opposed to matriarchy, is well-attested. In a matrilineal society, descent is traced and property inherited in the female line. In a matrilineal society, a man passes his property and social position not to his son but typically to his sisters' sons. Although it might be supposed that women, under such arrangements, would have more power, Alice Schlegel (herself a feminist anthropologist) has shown that matrilineal societies are on a gradient from one extreme of fraternal domination to the other extreme of marital domination. The nearest approach to female autonomy is in societies where the powers of husband and brother are so nearly equal that they tend to cancel each other out.[46]

Few people today could cite matriliny as evidence for an original matriarchy, but Eleanor Leacock and Karen Sacks have attempted the even more impossible task of resurrecting the political mythology of Friedrich Engels. Leacock argues that primitive societies, before they were contaminated by contact with Europeans, were economically communitarian and sexually egalitarian. This state of primal innocence was destroyed by the development, under European pressure, of private property and social classes. There are two obvious problems with Leacock's (and Engel's) thesis: first, the evidence for the savage Eden is, to say the least, ambiguous; second, it does not explain — as Alice Schlegel has pointed out — the existence of sexual distinctions in societies that are not socially stratified.[47]

Karen Sacks follows the inspiration of Engels, but in a different direction. Women, she insists, make a major contribution to subsistence. In many cultures, the gathering of vegetable food "accounts for the bulk of the diet." Women sometimes take part in game drives and the traditional distinction of economic sex roles — men hunt/women gather — are only social norms and frequently violated. "Biopsychological" explanations are, therefore, invalid and cannot account for the division of labor by sex.[48] The trouble with Sack's argument — and this is a problem that afflicts much feminist scholarship — is that it is tendentious. Women are said to have achieved fame as warriors among the Ojibway, and that is taken as proof that women are as innately aggressive as men and would, if given the chance, make good soldiers. Uncertain anecdotal information is stretched, and a few anomalous cases are inflated to the point that they are equal to the whole vast history of the human race.

A good case in point is the way the feminists write about the Iroquois. The Iroquois are a popular subject for Marxists, largely because they were written about by Lewis H. Morgan — the anthropological godfather of Marx and Engels. They are most commonly taken as a best-case example of a developed society that is sexually egalitarian. Sacks sums up the case for the defense succinctly:

> Iroquois society may have typified the pattern of male and female leadership posi-
> tions prevailing in precolumbian eastern North America. . . . Among the Iroquois
> there was a clear-cut division and balance of authority between the sexes. Men were
> the chiefs, but they were nominated by the women who could impeach them. Women
> were organized under their own formal leaders, the matrons, who were elected to
> represent all women. The matrons organized agricultural labor, supervised house-
> hold management, and acted as the ultimate controllers over decisions of war and
> peace by their power to allocate or withhold food from both war parties and council
> deliberations.[49]

The Iroquois did not, it would seem, simply divide up the responsibilities equitably, but they even reserved a veto power, in matters of state and defense, to the women.

Even without challenging this description, there is no reason to suppose that the Iroquois pattern typified social relations among the Indians of Eastern America. Even so, what sort of people were the Iroquois? Sacks makes them sound like a race of sensitive and caring husbands under the thumb of liber-ated wives. In point of fact, they were military imperialists. Their political policy was, "to expand by adopting and assimilating those tribes who would readily submit and by exterminating the recalcitrants."[50] They practiced, as might be predicted, a rigid division of labor. The women tended fields, managed house-holds, and took care of the children, leaving the men free to hunt, make war, and pursue politics. The unendurable burden placed upon the women's shoulders may have been alleviated somewhat by the slaves brought home from a suc-cessful raiding party. Women did possess great domestic and internal responsi-bilities and, presumably, a high degree of autonomy, precisely because the men thought they had something better to do: conquest.[51]

The historical European parallel is with the Spartans. While the Spartan men were the envy of the ancient world, both for their character and for their mili-tary exploits, the freedom of their women was a scandal. But with a large part of their adult citizens on campaign, the women of necessity were given large responsibilities. No one has ever accused the Spartans — certainly not to their face — of being sexual egalitarians.

The truth is that, despite their relative freedom, Iroquois women did not have a high status in the tribal ideology. Although they did have important religious duties, the men looked down upon them as inferiors and regarded the man/woman relationship as that of master/servant (a confusion of roles Aristotle took pains to refute) and used "woman" as a term of reproach.[52] Even Morgan, who was looking for evidence of primitive matriarchy, was puzzled by the lowly position of women and attributed it to the rigid segregation of the sexes practiced by the Iroquois.

Every feminist has her favorite tribe. With the Marxists, it is the Iriquois, with Alice Schlegel — who is a serious scholar — it is the Hopi, who actually come close to having an egalitarian society. The trouble with the Hopi as evidence is that they are a people suffering acutely from social dissolution. The main distinguishing characteristic of a Hopi man — his life as a warrior — has been taken away, while the self-destructive individualism of the Hopi rules out any rigid form of social or political stratification. Even so, it is not true, as has sometimes been alleged, that Hopi men do not give orders to their wives.[53] They are, after all, men as well as Hopi, although the Hopi women — who are, after all, women — do not always obey.

Most feminist scholars and scientists concede the universality of sex roles and male domination, but they seek to explain it as a predominantly social phenomenon. In a now-famous article, Sherry B. Ortner explains female subordination as a function of her body, whose processes place her in the category of nature in opposition to man, the creator of culture. Despite her careful arguments and manifest intelligence, Ortner dismisses biological arguments on the grounds that they have not been "established to the satisfaction of almost anyone in academic anthropology." Ortner is, however, right in her main contention that the symbolic values of a woman's role in giving birth and nursing a child have come to play a role in the ideology of sex roles.[54]

The division of labor obviously has far-reaching consequences for sexual ideology. Women have traditionally been able to contribute to the subsistence of family and tribe only insofar as such activity did not interfere with their primary duties: bearing and rearing children. A woman's productive activities were limited to tasks that did not take her far from home. While men, free of such heavy responsibility, had both the ability and the need to specialize as defenders and providers, women grew up expecting to take care of children.[55] What a strictly sociological analysis cannot explain is the sexual division of labor in a society like that of the !Kung Bushmen, one that does not discriminate in any discernible way between boy and girl children. Obviously, facts of life serve as the foundation for the cultural and social trends observed by feminist sociologists.

Feminists are right to complain about the low value placed on women's contribution to modern society. In the twentieth century, women have been viewed in their most primitive aspects as playmates and mothers or as would-be competitors. Many feminists had their "consciousness raised" by participating in leftist student movements of the 60's and early 70's:

> They were "earth mothers" during the day, knitting and baking bread and making endless pots of coffee while the men talked Marx, Lenin, and Mao; and "sex kittens" at night, providing the free-sex games that men found so liberating. If they attempted any serious participation in the discussions, they were branded "aggressive" or "sexless" — or worse; if they expressed emotional needs . . . they were called "demanding" or worse.[56]

Stokeley Carmichael summed it up in his statement that the proper position of women in the civil rights movement was "prone." Confronted with an entire generation of spineless males — classic mama's boys, for all their strutting — it is small wonder if young women began to feel themselves oppressed. A woman's life may have been comparatively sterile in the 1950s households portrayed on television, but at least the husbands were good providers who did not leave their wives for a more attractive or younger girl at the office.

In nineteenth century Europe, early feminists did battle against the doctrine of separate spheres, which held that while man's place was out in the world, competing, producing, and conquering, woman's place lay in the home, watching children and sheltered from the coarseness and brutality of modern life. But by 1900 — to say nothing of 1980 — the woman's sphere had shrunk. Domestic tasks became far less demanding, in every sense. They not only required less time and energy but they called for less skill and talent. It is easy in the age of dishwashers and ready-made clothes to regard domestic responsibilities as monotonous and trivial. At the same time, wages for employed women have risen, adding economic and social incentives to look down on domestic labor as degrading.

It was not always so. In other times, women did not only cook the food. They often gathered or grew it. They preserved it and stored it in baskets or earthenware vessels that they had made themselves. The clothes on their backs and on the backs of their husbands and children, they had made with their own hands. If we are tempted to look down our noses at the domestic arts, we have only to look at the revival, especially among highly educated women, of pottery, weaving, and needlework. It is not only in very primitive conditions that women's work can be seen as demanding and fulfilling. It has been remarked on more than once that, while English women have enjoyed more constitutional rights, women actually were more powerful (and seemed happier) in France.

In the past the economic and social significance of women has not always been denigrated. The pupil of Socrates, Xenophon the Athenian, insisted in his *Oeconomicus* that men should choose wives carefully, because man and wife were partners in the household.[57] This partnership in responsibility endured down into recent times in many parts of Europe and the United States. The farm wives of the Middle West and the Southern plantation women were as close to matriarchs as we are ever likely to see. During and after the Civil War, many of the Southern women were forced to take over the running of huge plantations under the worst of circumstances. Their diaries, letters, and memoirs are an eloquent tribute to the powers of women. *The Memoirs of a Lady Rice Planter* by "Patience Pennington" record one heroic struggle to preserve a way of life years after the men had given up on planting rice in the Santee delta.

In most cultures, women have been instrumental in rearing and educating the children of the house. By the nineteenth century, only girls were typically kept at home, and in our own time, the mother is often no more than a "facilitator," an amateur coordinator of professional services provided by teachers, pediatricians, counselors, and recreation specialists.

The dilemma we face today is not how to make women more like men, but how to let women be fully women. This point was grasped by the German sociologist, Georg Simmel, at the turn of the century. What great difference would it make, Simmel asked, if numbers of women had increasing access to education and professional careers? Culture, at least in its public and "objective" manifestations, was an essentially male concern. The modern world depends upon a division of labor and a degree of specialization that reflects the male capacity for dividing himself. Woman's strength, he argued, lay in her refusal to compartmentalize her personality. Being a housewife requires a total immersion in a set of interrelated activities that seem to have no beginning and no end. While some women, if given the opportunity, will succeed in adapting themselves to male culture, the result will hardly be the liberation of women. On the contrary, it will only mean they are free to become artificial men. Simmel called for a heightened awareness of sexual differences and pointed out the many careers, medicine for example, in which the feminine mind would make a distinctive contribution.[58]

How much of Simmel's characterization of women is valid remains to be seen, but it is not entirely out of line with the state of current research. The total fidelity he ascribes to women's nature is a remarkably useful asset for the sex designated by nature for motherhood. Few feminists are willing to consider such arguments, or any argument that defends women as women. Feminists today seem stuck in two ruts, neither of which is likely to lead anywhere. The older generation is still pursuing legal guarantees of equality, a subject that seems to interest ordinary women less and less. Few of them are willing to confront the facts of nature, and those few who do are convinced that nature is their enemy. Simone de Beauvoir, who had written so eloquently of woman's place in nature has now come to regard motherhood as nothing better than a trap.[59] English feminists like Juliette Mitchell and Shulamith Firestone, go a step further and carry Beauvoir's reasoning to its only logical conclusion: rebellion against nature. Nature has destined women to play the part of wife and mother, but what is natural is not legitimate. Firestone writes of "an oppression that goes back beyond recorded history to the animal kingdom itself." The tyranny of the "biological family" can only be overturned if we are willing to promote "the full development of artificial reproduction."[60] Juliette Mitchell recasts this sentiment in a more orderly Marxist mold. "As long as reproduction remained a natural phenomenon . . . women were effectively doomed to social exploitation." Women will only be liberated when they have transformed the structures of production, reproduction, sexuality, and socialization "in which they are integrated."[61]

If the biological family is a form of systematic oppression, then one of the chief instruments of oppression has been the incest taboo. Andrea Dworkin, the leader of the feminist crusade against pornography, does not hesitate to attack a taboo that places "the nuclear family above the human family," and whose destruction will guarantee "the free-flow of natural androgynous eroticism."[62] For some reason, androgyny is the rallying cry of many radical feminists. It is the "new consciousness . . . rising out of the morass of decaying society."[63] It is small wonder that many young women are confused. The traditional role of wife and mother has been attenuated by social and industrial change, her body is transfigured into a pleasure machine for the readers of *Playboy* and for the new race of erotic androgynes. Her only choice of a radical feminist ideology is between the Wendys who believe in Amazons and the lesbian ideologues who would exploit her in the name of sexual solidarity.

Actually, there is another sort of feminist revolution going on, one that Simmel might have endorsed. There is a new awareness among many women writers and scholars that the differences between men and women are nothing to be ashamed of. Much of the research on sexual dimorphism cited earlier in this chapter, was performed by women like Anke Erhardt. Pioneering work on the sex differences of newborns was done by Anneliese Korner. The most important summary of psychological sex differences was compiled by Eleanor Maccoby and Carol Jacklin, whose feminist premises did not prevent them from producing a serious work.

Alice Rossi is in many ways the most interesting of what we might call the new feminists. There was a time when she was orthodox. The author of *Feminists in Politics* and editor of *Feminist Papers*, Rossi was appointed by President Carter to serve as an International Woman's Year Commissioner. In addition to being a feminist, Rossi is also — perhaps to her own sorrow — a genuine scientist and scholar. Her research has led her into dangerous paths and unacceptable conclusions. In her study of college women, she was able to show that mood cycles could be predicted on the basis of the menstrual cycle. Writing later in *Daedalus*, Rossi took up the question of feminist egalitarianism and the opposition to innate sex differences.[64] It is not, she wrote, that genes actually determine what men and women can do, but that "biological contributions shape what is learned and that there are differences in the ease with which the sexes can learn certain things." Rossi eventually came to see that the feminist contempt for "just a housewife" may have more to do with the feminists themselves than with sexist traditions.

Whatever their motives, the radical feminists are doing their best to androgenize the feminine identity. Technology is seen as the key. If babies could only be manufactured and their care managed by the state, women would be free to be just like men. Actually, the technological encroachment into woman's sexual experience is not new. The obstetrics industry, as it has evolved in the twentieth century, forced pregnant women into antiseptic environments designed for the convenience of the (male) physician. She had her legs strapped in the air, as if she were a desperate cornered animal. She was filled with drugs to stop and start contractions — often to suit her obstetrician's schedule — and to numb sensations or induce an artificial euphoria. What had once been a significant, exclusively female experience was gradually transformed into a scientifically controlled and male-dominated experiment in anaesthesia. After the baby was born, women were typically warned against breast-feeding, and if they persisted they were frequently advised not to expect too much. When the baby did not gain weight on schedule — which, since the schedules were based on bottle-fed babies, happened all too regularly — she was advised to abandon the experiment. Physicians, as much as feminists, preferred to ignore the somewhat more complex sexual constitution of women. As Niles Newton explains, men are virtually limited to one sexual act — copulation. She points out that women, on the other hand, receive erotic pleasure not only from coitus but from giving birth and nursing. This pleasure helps to bind a mother to her children and is another piece of evidence to refute any purely socioeconomic explanation of motherhood.[65]

The real feminist revolution of the past twenty years was not conducted by NOW or by the countless ad hoc ERA groups: it was the natural childbirth (or prepared childbirth) movement carried on in large measure by nurses, nurse-midwives, and women obstetricians. Unfortunately, many expectant mothers are probably still being processed through the birth mills. What is more threatening, technology enters ever more into the process. Parents are encouraged to find out the sex of their children in advance and soon may be able to determine it. The technique — amniocentesis — also allows them to discover if the child is likely to be normal, while abortion is held out as the quick fix for the not-quite-normal.

Abortion is, from first to last, an ethical question, but it is one which — as feminists are quick to point out — affects the mother as well as the child. It involves, they say, a woman's right to control her own body. Whatever such a "right" may be has yet to be determined. Even so, the feminists are correct about this: Control over a woman's body is a central issue — although not in the way they understand.

Carol McMillan, in a brilliant exploration of feminist assumptions, makes the case that "contraception and abortion are to women what the tool was to men," i.e., means of controlling nature.[66] The technology of obstetrics, artificial birth control, and abortion, which "explicitly rejects and defiles the natural relation that exists between sex and procreation" is part of a much wider "revolt against the human condition."[67] The Marxist and feminist assault on sexual distinctions will end up by poisoning sexuality itself:

> They abstract it and divorce it from the physical, flesh-and-blood, male-and-female human beings . . . It exists only as an idea. In a feminist Utopia sex is hypostatized into a phantom power which sexless beings pursue but in vain . . . a world of abstract beings seeking abstract pleasure.[68]

The revolt against nature is always made in the name of liberty and always ends in tyranny and death. The ethical dimension of abortion lies outside the scope of an investigation of human nature. There may be circumstances under which infanticide is a necessary and natural response to environmental pressures. However, it is significant that one cost of the sexual revolution is counted in the over 1.5 million unborn babies that are disposed of annually in the United States, a percentage that probably exceeds the infanticide rates of antiquity considerably.

There are other ways to count the cost of sexual equality. Men, unlike women, are not programmed naturally to fulfill their functions in society. The primary male social unit — as defined by nature — is the male group, the club, the hunting band, the "mates." In *Men in Groups* Lionel Tiger has shown, with perhaps too much enthusiasm and eloquence, that men — like other male primates — define themselves in opposition to women. Nearly everyone is familiar with the male initiation ceremonies that persist into modern times as a remnant of simpler societies: the hazing in military academies, the rigors of Marine boot camp, the boys clubs that spring up in neighborhoods — all emphasize maleness and manhood at the expense of the female. It has been plausibly suggested that male initiation rites are most severe in those societies in which fathers do not spend a great deal of time with their sons. The most obvious example are matrilocal tribes in which paternal affection and contact is discouraged.[69] The example of American teenage gangs is also relevant. The dissolution of American urban black families, partly under pressure from a welfare system that discriminates against families, puts unusually great pressure on adolescent boys. These fatherless teenagers are particularly likely to join gangs that provide them with a sense of male identity and masculine solidarity against a world increasingly dominated by mothers, welfare workers, and teachers.

Keeping the average man on the straight and narrow paths of social civility has always posed a problem for women. One of the strongest parts of George Gilder's *Sexual Suicide* is his argument that sexual equality sets the male free to return to a jungle existence. The masculine identity is too fragile to bear competition with women. When women enter a profession, in competition with men, one of two things is likely to happen: either the women are "put in their place" or else the men go away. In the Soviet Union, the men seem to have chosen the former alternative. After the revolution, women were encouraged — as they still are — to work outside the home. The Soviet Constitution proclaimed the loftiest goals of sexual equality. Although the family was "restored" under Stalin as a useful part of the Soviet state, women were still strongly encouraged to play an active part in the economy. The result? In industry and politics, women are generally relegated to the lowest rungs of the ladder. In health care and education, where they predominate numerically, they are typically restricted to low status positions: teachers of young children, nurses, and pediatricians. Nowhere in the industrial West are men so firmly in the saddle.[70]

In the United States and Europe, it is not so simple. In many professions, women are typically (although by no means so exclusively as in the Soviet Union) restricted to unprestigious positions: men are physicians, women nurses; men are principals, women teachers. On the other hand, many male professions have become — as in the Soviet Union — female preserves: elementary school teaching being the clearest example. These are clear signs that the entrance of large numbers of women into a profession has the ultimate effect of driving the men out. This may be happening in the ministry, a profession that has been "feminized" (to use Ann Douglas' terminology) in everything but personnel since the nineteenth century. Since the opening of seminaries to women, they are beginning to predominate, at least numerically. On the other side, anecdotal evidence from relatives and friends suggests that women take education more seriously in girls' schools. Partly, this may be due to the absence of adolescent sexual tensions, but there is also considerable evidence to indicate that young women do not compete well athletically against boys, even when they are matched against less-skilled male players.

As men and women are brought into collision in the marketplace, strange things begin to happen. There is no question that men's attitudes and behavior towards women have been changing. Between 1960 and 1973, the reported cases of rape or attempted rape in the United States rose from a rate of ten per 100,000 population to twenty-four. During 1980, seventy-one out of 100,000 females were reported as rape victims, a considerable increase from the figure of twenty-three reported in the mid 1960s. Part of the influence may be due to an increase in reporting, part to an overall rise in crime rates (a symptom of social dissolutions in general). On the other hand, there is no doubt that not only is rape far more frequent than it was at the beginning of the century, our perception has changed; once a capital crime viewed as monstrous, it is now regarded as somewhere between bad manners and assault.

During this same period, the United States, like Great Britain and most developed countries, witnessed an impressive increase in the amount and the "hardness" of pornography. Feminists like Susan Brownmiller and Andrea Dworkin have quite naturally drawn the conclusion that pornographic films and books, especially those that portray the subjugation and violation of women, are at least partly to blame for the increase. Feminists in Britain launched a program to "reclaim the night" by crusading against smut shops and blue movie theaters. In the United States, more than one community has passed or tried to pass laws that make pornography a violation of the civil rights of women.

Men may be more susceptible to pornography for a very basic reason: sexual dimorphism and differences in sexual "style" both are related to differences in size and numbers of gametes. Human males, with their vast number of small spermata are inclined to polygyny. The counter-pressure toward stable marriage, even monogamy, has been developed by females in search of good fathers. Pornography, however, seems to reawaken polygynous inclinations (never actually asleep in most males) but cannot satisfy the urges that are awakened. Shepher and Reisman suggest that the effect may be frustration, a distrust of women's sexual fidelity, an inability to form friendships with members of the opposite sex, and a generally aggressive and predatory attitude toward women.[71]

Viewed in another light, the male response to pornography may have been adaptive in simple societies: males quickly aroused by visual stimuli may devote themselves more wholeheartedly to the chase. This obviously results in more offspring—so long as the male does not become known as a Don Juan, an unreliable mate, and a bad provider. In a simple society, the women are few and access to them is restricted. Sex is a scarce commodity, like foods high in salt or sugar or protein, and it may be useful to be always on the alert. In a modern industrial society, we are able to satiate our cravings with salty peanuts, sugar, candy, and steak dinners, none of which is terribly wholesome. We are also able to stimulate our sexual appetites with pornography, far beyond our own capacity to satisfy them, sometimes with disastrous consequences for our ability to be part of stable marriage and family.

Although the relationship between pornographic materials and sexual offenses is not entirely clear, it can be shown that certain male personality types—men who combine a certain egocentrism with an impersonal, even antisocial, aggressiveness—are more prone to respond to pornographic stimulation and, what is more, to display a lowered resistance to inflicting pain. Dworkin argues convincingly that certain types of feminists—the liberated sex kittens of *Cosmopolitan*, for example, or Germaine Greer—have contributed to the subjugation of women. "Alliance with the sexual revolution is," she concludes "an alliance with male chauvinism."[72]

Despite the merits of Dworkin's attack on pornography, the fact remains that it is fundamentally inconsistent with her brand of feminism. After all, what is it that the feminists have been telling us all these years if not that women are, in all important points, the same as men? Or, if there are biological differences, it is our moral obligation to eradicate them. If men and women are by right and nature the same, then what is all the fuss about? If women do not enjoy dirty pictures as much as men, it must be a result of culturally imposed inhibitions. One feminist writer does try to come to grips with the dilemma. Beatrice Faust, in asking "Why is there no pornography for women?" begins by declaring that women ought to be free "to choose partners of their own sex, the opposite sex, or both," but ends up confessing that the different attitudes toward sex and pornography by women and men derive from nature and not culture.[73]

Feminists and pornographers have a great deal in common. Both of them assume, at least in public, that men and women are alike in their erotic styles and preferences. For most men, the idea of being raped by a woman is nothing short of ridiculous. He may prefer sex on his own terms, when and with whom he wants "it," but it is a trivial inconvenience to be asked to perform at the drop of a hat. Apart from the associated acts of violence, the mere fact of coerced intercourse would be at the worst unpleasant, an aesthetic affront on the order of free verse. Do the feminists want us to believe that it is the same for women? If it is not, then the whole structure of feminist ideology collapses like a condominium in a high wind.

Then what is left, in the end, for women? Barefoot and pregnant and back in the kitchen again? Are women wrong in finding their lot in the modern world a little less than satisfying? Obviously not. The liberation movement — as misguided as it is — is a symptom of a serious social illness. Women, whose social responsibilities were once broader and deeper than men's, have seen most of their important functions taken over by male-dominated professions. Not only has the bearing of children been turned into an institutionalized medical procedure; every aspect of their rearing is now either controlled or supervised by psychologists and educators.

There is no doubt that the modern devaluation of woman's role is an acute problem in industrial societies; however, it can only be exacerbated by the pretense that a real woman can balance the requirements of a job with the responsibilities of child care. Most women, in fact, do not. A successful career woman is not likely to be a successful mother. For fairly obvious reasons, women dedicated to their careers are less likely to be mothers of large families. Gary S. Becker explains this tendency in terms of economic incentives: the more a woman's work is worth in the marketplace, the less likely is she to invest her energies into additional children.[74] On the other hand, children exert their own pressures. Women are far more likely to leave a job—usually for domestic reasons—than men. The problem of the working mother is reserved for the next chapter, but it may be useful to speculate on the kind of social changes that could result in a real improvement of women's status.

Any such agenda would have to start with a revaluation of domestic life and put new emphasis on the household crafts and arts. In a real sense, this revolution has already begun. In recent years, we have seen a rediscovery of maternity and a new determination among women to reassert control over childbirth. The revival of breast-feeding, initiated primarily by Roman Catholics, has spread to all levels of society, and the home schooling movement has given a great deal of absorbing work to the mothers (mostly evangelical Protestants) of over a million children. The resurgence of domestic crafts, already mentioned, also can be seen as a revival of women's creative life.

Some provision must be made to make professional careers available to women who cannot or will not marry and have children. Some of the most obvious choices lie in mothering surrogates. It is not accidental that so many women are found in education, health care, and social work. The female sex is, as we have seen, better adapted to nurturing than men. More intellectually inclined women might be expected to make use of specifically feminine advantages in language facility. What is often called feminine intuition is nothing more nor less than the tendency of women to induce general principles as a result of experience and observation instead of imposing *a priori* methods of deduction.[75] In many fields, especially the social sciences, where patient observation is more desirable than bold speculation, women put this superiority to good use.

One of women's greatest contributions to modern civilization has arisen from the observably conservative tendencies of wives and mothers. Confronted with a typically masculine bright idea, an invention or a social policy, women are more likely to be suspicious: "Why do you call it a wheel and what's it good for, other than rolling down hills and making a racket?" might have been one of Eve's first questions. Even the wives of the great speculators are often suspicious: Einstein's wife could never understand relativity, Martha Freud was skeptical of psychoanalysis, while Emma Darwin was a devout Christian who learned to take no interest in her husband's work. One argument against women's suffrage was the weight it would give conservative interests. As soon as American women were given the vote, they helped replace the progressive Woodrow Wilson with a midwestern conservative like Warren Harding.

If, as I argue repeatedly in these chapters, the modern world is suffering from an overdose of abstraction, then what is desperately needed at this point is the influence of women. Social and political theorists since the time of Hobbes have spoken generally of "rights" and "duties" and "justice." In his very popular scheme of moral development, Lawrence Kohlberg puts the abstract universalist like Gandhi, a man perfectly content to sacrifice the lives and happiness of millions (including his wife, whom he mercilessly hectored) to the pursuit of their ideas. Carol Gilligan, a feminist educationist, points out that "the blind willingness to sacrifice people to truth . . . has always been the danger of an ethics abstracted from life." Men like Gandhi "stand in implicit contrast to the woman who comes before Solomon and verifies her motherhood by relinquishing truth in order to save the life of her child."[76]

From the very beginning, the feminist push for equal rights has been predicated on the typically male abstractions that have so damaged the social fabric. Even today, Gilligan suggests, women continue to feel "the tension between a morality of rights that dissolves 'natural bonds' in support of individual claims and a morality of responsibility that knits such claims into a fabric of relationship."[77]

G.K. Chesterton once wrote, "There are only three things in the world that women do not understand, and they are liberty, equality, and fraternity." If that is so, we have more reason than ever to thank heaven for little girls. The tragic consequences of feminist ideology are not limited to social disruption and family dissolution. If women begin to harden their hearts in the service of universal love, there is very little hope left either for men or women.

For reasons that will become clear, I do not think that will be the case, as long as women continue to bear children. If we really want to liberate women, we might begin by restructuring our economic and social life — as well as our expectations — in such a way that most families do not feel compelled to send mothers of young children off to work. It is not unreasonable to suppose that many bright women, once their children have reached a certain maturity, would wish to pick up the threads of their academic or professional interests, and it is not necessarily in a society's interest to discourage them. There are, however, serious dangers. The Swedish social democrats, stimulated by Alva Myrdal, tried to structure the economy to accommodate a woman's reentry into the job market. Unfortunately, this led to social policies that have almost destroyed the family in Sweden. The main task of any generation must be to pass on the torch to the next. Any social principle or policy that threatens the viability of a culture must be suspect. Any ideology — whether of liberty or equality — that undermines the one institution charged with the responsibility of rearing and integrating the next generation into society, namely the family, is to be rejected with the firmness that was once reserved for religious heresies.

Notes

1. Wm. Blake Tyrell, *Amazons: A Study in Athenian Mythmaking* (Baltimore: The Johns Hopkins University Press, 1984).
2. Simone de Beauvoir, *Le Deuxième Sexe* (Paris: Gallimard, 1949), 62 ff.

3. M. Kay Martin and Barbara Voorhies, *Female of the Species* (New York: Columbia University Press, 1975), viii.
4. Elizabeth G. Davis, *The First Sex* (New York: Penguin, 1972), 15 ff.
5. Joseph Adelson, "What We Don't Know About Sex Differences," *New Perspectives* IV (Spring 1985), 10.
6. G.R. Elton, "History According to St. Joan," *The American Scholar* (Autumn 1985), 549.
7. Betty Friedan, "Our Revolution is Unique" in Mary Lou Thompson, ed., *Voices of the New Feminism* (Boston: Beacon Press, 1970), 34.
8. Kate Millet, *Sexual Politics* (Garden City, NY: Doubleday, 1970), 24.
9. Shirley Chisholm, "Women Must Rebel" in Mary Lou Thompson, op. cit., 208 ff.
10. Gerda Lerner, *The Creation of Patriarchy* (New York: Oxford University Press, 1986), especially 5 ff. on methods and purpose.
11. For Greek women, Lerner relies on feminist literary critics, Froma I. Zeitlin and Marilyn Arthur, on the usefulness of whose work, cf. Thomas J. Fleming, "Des Dames du Temps Jadis," *The Classical Journal* (October-November 1986), 73–80.
12. Kate Millet, *op. cit.,* 29.
13. Evelyn Reed, *Sexism and Science* (New York and Toronto: Pathfinders Press, 1978), 115: "They say that the matriarchy never existed . . . that women have always been the inferior sex. . . . How do they know these are 'universal' phenomenon if no one can ever penetrate into the facts about [sic] 99 per cent of human life on earth."
14. Ruth Bleier, *Science and Gender: A Critique of Biology and Theories on Women* (New York: Pergamon Press, 1984).
15. Germaine Greer, *The Female Eunuch* (New York: McGraw-Hill, 1970).
16. Steven Gaulin and James Boster, "Cross-Cultural Differences in Sexual Dimorphism: Is There Any Variance to be Explained?," *Ethology and Sociobiology* 6 (1985), 219–25.
17. For basic data, see D.B. Cheek *Human Growth: Body Composition, Cell Growth, Energy, and Intelligence* (Philadelphia: Lea and Febiger, 1968) and Elizabeth S. Watts in Frank Falkner and J.M. Tanner, eds. *Human Growth*, 2nd ed. (New York: Plenum Press, 1986), 159 ff.
18. Stephen M. Bailey, "Absolute and Relative Sex Differences in Body Composition" in Roberta L. Hall, *Sexual Dimorphism in Homo Sapiens: A Question of Size* (New York: Praeger, 1982).
19. Milford H. Wolpoff, "Some Aspects of the Evolution of Early Hominid Sexual Dimorphism," *Current Anthropology* 17 (1976), 579–606.
20. Darryl Gwynne, "Sexual Difference Theory: Mormon Crickets Show Role Reversal in Mate Choice," *Science* 213 (1981), 779–80.
21. Bobby S. Low, "Sexual Selection and Human Ornamentation" in Napoleon A. Chagnon and William Irons, *Evolutionary Biology and Social Behavior: An Anthropological Perspective* (North Scituate, MA: Duxbury Press, 1979).
22. For sexual differentiation, see John Money and Anke Ehrhardt, *Man and Woman, Boy and Girl: The Differentiation and Dimorphism of Gender Identity from Conception to Maturity* (Baltimore: Johns Hopkins University Press, 1972); cf. Jean D. Wilson, Frederick W. George, and James E. Griffin, "The Hormonal Control of Sexual Development," *Science* 211 (1981), 1278–84. The masculinizing effects of hormones in the womb are illustrated by the cases of fetal female rats that are masculinized by the presence of male litter mates and by the free-martin phenomenon in cattle; see Robert Meisel and Ingeborg L. Ward, "Fetal female rats are masculinized by male littermates located caudally in the uterus," *Science* 213 (1981), 239–41.

23. Neil J. MacLusky and Frederick Naftolin, "Sexual Differentiation of the Central Nervous System," *Science* 211 (1981), 1294-1303.

24. MacLusky and Naftolin, *op. cit.,* 1297-98; cf. Bruce S. McEwen, "Neural Gonadal Steroid Actions," *Science* 211 (1981), 1307-08.

25. Money and Ehrhardt, *op. cit.,* 65.

26. Robert T. Robin, June M. Reinisch, Roger F. Haskett, "Postnatal Gonadal Steroid Effects on Human Behavior," *Science* 211 (1981), 1318-24.

27. Money and Ehrhardt, *op. cit.,* 95-100; cf. Anke A. Ehrhardt and Heino F.L. Meyer-Bahlburg, "Effects of Prenatal Sex Hormones on Gender-Related Behavior," *Science* 211 (1981), 1312-18. Discussion of Imperato-McGinley's work in the Dominican Republic has been omitted, because the results are disputed.

28. W. Danforth Joslyn, "Androgen-Induced Social Dominance in Infant Female Rhesus Monkeys," *Journal of Child Psychology and Psychiatry* 14 (1973), 137-45.

29. See Corinne Hutt, *Males and Females* (Baltimore: Penguin, 1972); Anneliese F. Korner, "Some Differences in Newborns with Special Reference to Differences in the Organization of Oral Behavior," *Journal of Child Psychology and Psychiatry* 14 (1973), 19-29; on all related questions the standard (feminist) work remains Eleanor E. Maccoby and Carol N. Jacklin, *The Psychology of Sex Differences* (Stanford: Stanford University Press, 1974).

30. Maccoby and Jacklin, *op. cit.,* 350 ff.

31. Camilla P. Benbow and Julian C. Stanley, "Sex Differences in Mathematical Ability: Fact or Artifact?," *Science* 210 (1980), 1262-64; "Sex Differences in Mathematical Reasoning Ability: More Facts," *Science* 222 (1983), 1029-31.

32. Jeanette McGlone, "Sex Differences in Human Brain Asymmetry: A Critical Survey," *The Behavioral and Brain Sciences* 3 (1980), 215-63, collects evidence to suggest that male brains are more asymmetrically organized.

33. Loren E. Acker, Sharmon Parker, Margaret A. Acker, "Sex Differences in Children's Response to Achievement and Approval," *Child Study Journal* 13 (1983), 165-74.

34. Donald M. Broverman, Edward L. Klaiber, William Vogel, "Gonadal Hormones and Cognitive Functioning" in Jacquelynne E. Parsons, *The Psychobiology of Sex Differences and Sex Roles* (Washington, New York, and London: Hemisphere Books, 1980), 57-75.

35. Thomas Gualtieri and Robert E. Hicks, "An Immunoreactive Theory of Selective Male Affliction," *The Behavioral and Brain Sciences* 8 (1985), 427-41.

36. Beatrice B. Whiting and John W.M. Whiting, *Children of Six Cultures* (Cambridge, MA: Harvard University Press, 1975), 136 ff; cf. B.B. Whiting and C.P. Edwards, "A Cross-Cultural Analysis of Sex Differences in the Behavior of Children Aged Three Through 11," *Journal of Social Psychology* 91 (1973), 171-88.

37. See Acker, Parker, and Acker, *op. cit.*

38. C.L. Robinson, J.S. Lockard, R.M. Adams, "Who Looks at a Baby in Public?," *Ethology and Sociobiology* I (1979), 87-91.

39. Eleanor E. Maccoby, *The Development of Sex Differences* (Stanford: Stanford University Press, 1966), 26 ff.

40. George P. Murdock, *Social Structure* (New York: Macmillan, 1949), 213-14; cf. George P. Murdock and Caterina Provost, "Factors in the Division of Labor by Sex: A Cross-Cultural Analysis" in Herbert B. Barry, III, and Alice Schlegel, eds., *Cross-Cultural Samples and Codes* (Pittsburgh: University of Pittsburgh Press, 1980), 289 ff.

41. See Roy G. D'Andrade in Maccoby and Jacklin, *op. cit.,* 173-203 for a lucid summary.

42. Mary Lefkowitz, *Heroines and Hysterics* (New York: St. Martin's Press, 1981), 1-12.

43. Margaret Mead, *Sex and Temperament in Three Societies*, repr. of 1935 ed. (New York: Dell, 1963), 260 ff.
44. *op. cit.*, 259 f.
45. *op. cit.*, 265.
46. Alice Schlegel, *Male Dominance and Female Autonomy* (New York: HRAF Press, 1972), 7 ff.
47. Alice Schegel, "Toward a Theory of Sexual Stratification" in Alice Schlegel, ed., *Sexual Stratification* (New York: Columbia University Press, 1977), 11 ff.
48. Karen Sacks, "Engels Revisited" in M.Z. Rosaldo and L. Lamphere, eds., *Women Culture and Society* (Stanford: Stanford University Press, 1974), 207–22; cf. Sacks *Sisters and Wives: The Past and Future of Sexual Equality* (Westport, CT: Greenwood Press, 1979).
49. *Sisters and Wives* 83–84.
50. B.H. Quain, "The Iroquois" in Margaret Mead, ed. *Cooperation and Competition Among Primitive Peoples* (New York: McGraw-Hill, 1937), 243.
51. Martha C. Randle, "Iroquois Women" in William Fenton, ed. *Symposium on Local Diversity in Iroquois Culture* (Bureau of American Ethnology, Bulletin 149).
52. Jay Miller, "The Delaware as Women: A Symbolic Solution, *American Ethologist* 1 (1974), 507–14.
53. Mischa Titiev, *The Hopi Indians of Old Oraibi: Change and Continuity* (Ann Arbor: University of Michigan), 27 ff, describes a husband and wife quarrel in which the wife obeys a direct command; cf. Steven Goldberg, "Utopian Yearning Versus Scientific Curiosity," *Society* (September/October 1986), 29–39.
54. Sherry B. Ortner, "Is Female to Male as Nature is to Culture? in Rosaldo and Lamphere, *op. cit.*, 43–66.
55. See Peggy R. Sanday, "Female Status in the Public Domain" in Rosaldo and Lamphere, *op. cit.*, 190–206 for a feminist interpretation.
56. Leah Fritz, *Dreamers & Dealers: An Intimate Appraisal of the Women's Movement* (Boston: Beacon Press, 1979), 25.
57. Ironically, the *economicus* is cited by feminists as an example of ancient sexism.
58. See especially the essays collected in *Georg Simmel: On Woman, Sexuality, and Love*, trans. by Guy Oakes (New Haven: Yale University Press, 1984).
59. Simone de Beauvoir, *The Coming of Age*, trans. by Patrick O'Brian (New York: G.P. Putnam's, 1972).
60. Shulamith Firestone, *The Dialectic of Sex: The Case for Feminist Revolution* (New York: William Morrow, 1979), p. 2. ff, cf. 37 ff.
61. Juliette Mitchell, *Women's Estate* (New York: Pantheon, 1971), 106–07.
62. Andrea Dworkin, *Woman Hating* (New York: E.P. Dutton, 1979), 189 ff.
63. June Singer, *Androgyny: Towards a New Theory of Sexuality* (Garden City, New York: Anchor/Doubleday, 1976), 29 ff.
64. Alice S. Rossi, "A Biosocial Perspective on Parenting," *Daedalus* 106, 2 (1977), 1–32.
65. Niles Newton, "Interrelationships Between Sexual Responsiveness, Birth, and Breast Feeding" in J. Zubin and J. Money, *Contemporary Sexual Behavior: Critical Issues in the 1970s* (Baltimore: Johns Hopkins University Press, 1973), 77–98.
66. Carol McMillan, *Women, Reason, and Nature: Some Philosophical Problems with Feminism* (Princeton, NJ: Princeton University Press, 1982), 128 ff.
67. *op. cit.*, 151–52.
68. *op. cit.*, 155.

69. Roger V. Burton and John W.M. Whiting, "The Absent Father and Cross-Sex Identity" in Zubin & Money, 231–45; cf. Raymond T. Smith, *The Negro Family in British Guiana*. (London: Kegan Paul, 1956), 225 ff.

70. Carol H. Marshall, "The Soviet Family and Law: A Functional Analysis of Change" in *New Scholar* 2 (1970), 49–70; cf. David and Vera Mace, *The Soviet Family* (New York: Doubleday, 1963).

71. Joseph Shepher and Judith Reisman, "Pornography: A Sociobiological Attempt at Understanding," *Ethology and Sociobiology* 6 (1985), 103–14.

72. Andrea Dworkin, *op. cit.*, 82.

73. Beatrice Faust, *Women, Sex, and Pornography: A Controversial and Unique Study* (New York: Macmillan, 1980), 4 ff.

74. Gary S. Becker, *A Treatise on the Family* (Cambridge, MA: Harvard University Press, 1981), 98 ff; cf. Ivy Papps, *For Love or Money: A Preliminary Analysis of the Economics of Marriage and the Family* (London: The Institute of Economic Affairs, 1980), 27 ff.

75. See Carol McMillan, *op. cit.*, 40 ff.

76. Carol Gilligan, *In a Different Voice: Psychological Theory and Women's Development* (Cambridge, MA: Harvard University Press, 1982), 104.

77. *op. cit.*, 132.

5

The Natural Family

Men and women are different. The two sexes display a certain specialization and make an economical use of human resources. Such a difference would have little point if males and females led solitary existences. Women in isolation still would have to bear and rear the children, but they also would be responsible for providing food, shelter, protection, and governance—hardly an efficient arrangement. Fortunately, we live together in conjugal pairs that lead inevitably to the third element of society: children. As the familial ape, man has created an amazing variety of complex social institutions. In the twentieth century, the family as we know it has come under attack from social critics and legislators. The signficance of this attack goes far beyond the particular questions of day-care centers, welfare programs, or alternate "life styles." The heart of the matter is whether the health of a human society depends on the health of the family. If it does, then a consideration of the human family has important consequences, not only for family policies, but for a whole range of issues that are normally discussed as questions of the individual versus the state.

There can be no doubt that the family in Europe and America is undergoing a crisis. This ordeal of the family is generally recognized by both its defenders and detractors. In the view of many, the old ideal of the family was impossibly high: a stable intimate relationship between man and wife, united in permanent union; several children nurtured by a stay-at-home mother and supported by a working father; a loose network of grandparents, aunts, uncles and cousins, most of whom lived nearby and made the world outside the immediate family seem more familiar. Such an ideal may have been only occasionally realized; examples have certainly been getting scarcer with each generation of the past hundred years. And yet, for most of us, it was the image that dominated our social awareness and guided our steps through the paces of marriage, child-rearing, and old age. It was as a world as old as ballads, as true as nursery rhymes. Today, however, it is not simply that people are not living up to the ideal standard: the ideal has itself suffered from the ravages of the twentieth century.

Of course, Americans and Europeans still get married. Indeed, the advice columnists in the newspapers take comfort from the fact that many of us display such an enthusiasm for marriage that we try it more than once. There are a number of indications that our attitude toward family life is changing in fundamental ways: rising rates of divorce, working mothers, and child abuse, coupled with a depressed birth rate. Nearly a fourth of American children under eighteen live with only one parent. In 1970, only 5.2 percent of the female population who had ever married were divorced at the time of the survey. By 1984, that figure had risen to almost 13 percent. Between 1960 and 1982, the number of divorces per 1,000 of population had risen from 2.2 to 5.0. Common estimates suggest that as many as 50 percent of all first marriages will end in divorce. Only a small minority of American families consist of a working father, stay-at-home mother, and one or more children.[1]

Other signs of social dissolution are easier to chronicle but more difficult to reduce to numbers: the proliferation of porn shops, dirty magazines, and massage parlors (and the degree to which they have become acceptable to the respectable middle classes); adolescent prostitution — its increasing popularity; the number of books — often published by respectable university presses — and college sex education courses that advocate open marriages, group marriages, and casual swinging as methods of personal growth. The record of sexual crimes is even less encouraging. In less than twenty years, the incidence of rape per 100,000 population has increased threefold.[2] Since many estimates of unreported rape go as high as four times the number of reported cases, the real figures could be much higher.

Women continue to bear and rear children, but the development of artificial insemination and the increase of illegitimate births — especially in Scandinavian countries, where there is no stigma attached — leads Alice S. Rossi to conclude that "we may be moving through a period during which parenting is being separated from marriage, as sex was separated from marriage in an earlier period."[3]

All these phenomena point to the same conclusion: sexual activity is beginning to be dissociated from the rest of life. This conclusion is reinforced by the increased frequency of child molesting and incest cases. Some of the increase may be due to a growing awareness of the problem and a rising willingness to discuss it and report it. But it is hard to escape the feeling that we have entered into a new era of relations between the sexes. It is not enough to label it as narcissism or permissiveness. Such formulas ignore the crux of the problem, which is that many people no longer regard themselves as essentially members of families (and communities) but as helpless individuals, eager to snatch a little comfort or excitement out of life, no matter what the cost.

One answer to this problem — one that is heard frequently — is that there is no problem. This argument takes the form that the family is merely changing its shape as increasing numbers of people realize that most marriages are not, in fact, made in heaven but on earth. Single parent families and alternative life styles represent only the latest variations on the theme of family life. Levitan and Belous take comfort from studies that show two-thirds of first marriages in the United States last a lifetime, although 40 percent of all marriages end in divorce. Marriage dissolution, their familiar argument runs, was as great a problem in the old days, when early death, not divorce, was the principal cause. Besides, they argue, three-fourths of divorcees under the age of thirty remarry. Marriage, they conclude, is still viewed as the preferred living arrangement.[4]

Other writers, like Alvin Toffler, insist that the family is an institution that has outlived its usefulness. In the new age, the rapid rate of social and technological change has vastly expanded the possibilities for pursuing happiness. In the view of Philip Slater and other Freudians, the family is the source of the neuroticism that arises from oedipal relationships.

How important, how central to human social life, is the family? Murdoch, on the basis of extensive ethnographic notes, regarded the family as universal — a conclusion that has been widely repeated and only rarely challenged. William N. Stephens, who has made an exhaustive cross cultural survey of the family, concedes the existence of a number of borderline cases, where the family's existence can be questioned. Stephens probably is too generous to the opposition. All his ambiguous cases have one thing in common: a scanty and anecdotal ethnographic record. Still, even from his worst-case scenario, Stephens concluded that the family was virtually universal.[5]

There is little complete agreement on what constitutes a family. However, the bare essentials certainly include marriage and parenthood, which represent the two basic principles of kinship: alliance and descent. Kinship is an essentially natural phenomenon, since children can be regarded as a compound, consisting of half of each parent's genotype.

The universality and biological basis of kinship is not the only reason for considering the family a natural institution. The borderline cases are less significant than they might appear. Statistically, they are insignificant. If a dozen or so societies out of several thousand turned out to lack anything resembling the family (which is not the case), the probability of the family still would be greater than 99 percent. The argument is not that it is imposible for anyone to live without family, only that there are very strong pressures against it. Besides, nearly all the borderline cases are societies whose social arrangements have been dictated by extreme conditions or by the decadence and dissolution brought on by contact with more advanced cultures. A familiar example is the weak, "matriarchal" black families of the United States and, especially, the

Caribbean. The elements—a race uprooted from Africa and transported to the New World; the experiences of slavery; extreme poverty; welfare projects that seem designed to destabilize black families and keep them "in their place"—all combine into an unusual pressure against the family. In addition, family norms seem almost to converge in the higher civilizations of China, and Classical antiquity: emphasis on paternal authority, respect for parents, and sexual distinctions.

This is not to say there is not a great variety in the forms of family life. Social science textbooks have acquainted most people with the basic forms of marriage: monogamy (one man/one woman), polygyny (one man/several women). In the nineteenth century, the discovery of the varieties of marriage led to the development of evolutionary theories. These theories were supposed to explain how all the different types had their source in an original, primitive horde. The most influential of these explanations was made by L. H. Morgan, an American student of Indian culture, whose ideas were taken up and popularized by Marx and Engels. In general, these evolutionary theories suppose a primitive condition in which men and women coupled and uncoupled with the zestful promiscuity associated with caged chimpanzees. Afterwards, they practiced—in turn—various forms of group marriage (including incestuous forms), which gave way to polyandry, polygyny, and monogamy.

The trouble with such speculations is that they are not supported by any solid evidence. In fact, group marriage is virtually nonexistent as the dominant arrangement in any culture—"one of the many figments of the Victorian imagination"[6]—while polyandry is so rare as to be "an ethnological curiosity,"[7] confined to four known societies. The classic case of polyandry, the Toda of India, practiced infanticide on girls to maintain the skewed sex ratio on which their peculiar social arrangement depends. All in all, "a mixutre of monogamy and polygyny characterizes about four-fifths of the world's societies. About one fifth are strictly monogamous."[8] The other forms are statistically insignificant. If we were to judge from almost universally observed human tendencies, we could assume man to be, by his heritage, mildly polygynous, like other animals with a similar male/female ratio and degree of dimorphism.

Man is peculiar among higher primates in this habit of family life. Of course, man is not the only primate to have one or another of the elements of family life. As Robin Fox has pointed out, other primates do "recognize" either kinship by descent, i.e. parenthood, or kinship by alliance, i.e. marriage. Alliance is characteristic of various baboons and langurs who live in one-male harems, while among chimpanzees, gorillas, and others, "the adult males form a cohesive unit . . . arranged in a hierarchy . . . not divided from each other by their "family". . . . There is, however, kinship . . . units of uterine kin." In other words, the distinctively human family is a combination of preexisting elements (at least in a rudimentary form): matrilineage and marriage.[9]

For obvious reasons, matrilineage (descent from a common mother) is the only recognized form of primate descent. Indeed, the most basic social fact among primates is the nursing mother. Social anthropologists like Paul Bohannon conclude that the matricentric family is the only essential social institution. In fact, this is true for many other mammals. For primates, the combination of mother and child is the family. Langur mothers are devoted to their babies and jealously protect them from the excessive attentions of other females, even those of higher status.[10] Among the higher primates, ape mothers appear to devote much the same energy and attention to their offspring as human mothers to their children. This care is, at least in part, a function of necessity. The basic trend, in the line that leads from monkeys to men, is toward "prolonging all periods of their early life".[11] This includes gestation and infancy. Most monkeys lose their milk teeth at the end of the year. At that time, they are basically capable of feeding themselves on a regular diet. On the other hand, apes keep their milk teeth for three years, humans for six.

This prolonged infancy is (apart from primates) associated with predatory species, which because of cooperative hunting require a certain degree of social complexity and, consequently, "education." Primates are required to learn even more complicated social behavior and survival techniques than wolves and cats. These social requirements are related in turn to an ever increasing brain size. The need to learn and a larger brain have two important consequences for man. It is a constraint of nature that the primate pelvis can only be extended so far. This means big-brained creatures cannot be born fully mature without causing serious injury, or even death, to their mothers. As a result, the offspring of apes (and men) must be born premature, before their brains have developed too far. This premature birth leads to the need for more concentrated and more extended nursing. The increased reliance on mother's milk — three years among orangutans and some human groups — seems to result in fewer pregnancies, apparently because lactation usually prevents conception. All in all, these changes mean an increase in quality, and quantity, of child care and a decrease in the number of children.

All of these considerations are as true — indeed, truer — of human mothers and their babies as they are of chimpanzees. But, unlike chimpanzees, the human mother is not generally required to provide food for herself and her offspring while she is tending an infant. There is a man, usually "her" man, whose responsibility it is to take care of her and the children (usually their children). This is necessary, because child care is more intense and more prolonged in the case of human infants. Human babies are born so premature that they cannot hold onto their mothers, who would have to leave them to gather food. The retention of milk teeth until the sixth year also triples the number of years a child cannot subsist completely on adult food. All this translates into the need for another member of the species to provide, at least minimally, for the family's needs.

Another distinctive feature of human life is bipedalism — our habit of walking on two legs. This makes an important difference in child care. Primate mothers could not hold onto their babies, even if they wanted to, because their hands are needed for locomotion. However, human mothers can walk and hold onto their babies at the same time. This is all the more necessary, because of the human baby's greater imbecility: it could not hang on, even if it wanted to. Besides, there is little or no body hair to hold onto.[12]

It is one thing to say the human mother needed a man, it is quite another to say how she landed him. Chimpanzees and gorillas are essentially promiscuous; the mother and children are the only unit of kinship. It has been supposed that the transition to the human family is related to the fact that the human female is not subject to the oestrus cycle, which practically compels other primate females to mate at regular intervals. The extravagant sexual behavior of oestrus females is regarded as incompatible with the requirements for constant attendance on children. On the other hand, the human female's menstrual cycle does make her at least moderately susceptible to sexual advances throughout most of the year: the ideal circumstances for a "companionate" marriage.

At all events, it is difficult to imagine that man as man ever passed through a stage of group marriage or general promiscuity. It is hard enough to compel modern husbands to support their wives and children. If sexual favors could be taken indiscriminately from any female member of a group, there would have been small incentive to provide the necessary constant support for women and children. Of course, in a more developed state, a woman's father might assume such a responsibility upon the death or desertion of her husband. But in a state of original promiscuity, a grandfather would be even less likely than a father to provide for his family. All these considerations seem to support Elman Services' idea that "husbandness" precedes fatherhood. There is also the question of maternal responsibility. Child-rearing is an onerous task, which as Malinowski observed "is always individual."

Child care and the sexual division of labor seem to demand a home base. The family household was advantageous, because it allowed the female to specialize in child care and gathering vegetable food close to home, while the husband could hunt and gather at a greater distance. Inside a home, children also could make a significant contribution to domestic labor. In sum, the sexual relationship leads to mutual cooperation, different foraging strategies, exchange of food, and the specific parental roles of mother and father.[13]

It seems then that for as long as he has walked on two legs, man has been a family man, taking care of his wife (or wives) and children. If women benefit from the arrangement, so do men: they live longer, healthier lives and are more likely to stay out of trouble. Marriage is obviously good for the male; it domesticates the hairless primate. In some cases, it may even civilize him. "Once you are married," complained Robert Louis Stevenson, "there is nothing left for you, not even suicide, but to be good."

Universality is not the same thing as uniformity. There is a large, although by no means infinite, set of possible variations on the basic pattern of family life. In addition to the two common types of marriages, there are two other, related, variables: the reckoning of descent and the place of residence. Societies that trace descent from the father (patrilineal) make up almost half of Murdock's ethnographic sample. Those that trace through the mother (matrilineal) constitute about a sixth, while in more than a third of the cases, descent is reckoned through all male and female ancestors on both sides (bilateral), and only a small fraction use double descent, which recognizes only male ancestors in the father's line and females in the mother's. Bilateral descent strikes most Americans as logical and even inevitable, and, in fact, it is found in both industrial societies and among small stateless peoples. While it theoretically includes everyone to whom a person is biologically related, that inclusiveness makes it weak and interferes with the formation of strong alliances. Family arrangements that dictate that the husband move in with the wife's family are called uxorilocal, while those that require residence with the father are patrilocal. For obvious reasons, matrilocal societies also tend to be matrilineal, and so on.[14]

Of the systems of reckoning descent, which is more natural? Such a distinction may not be possible or even useful, but it is worth the effort of speculation. Even to ask the question raises certain other questions. An analysis of the family can be made on more than one level. Economists and political theorists typically treat a family of four (mother, father, son, daughter) as a set of four individuals whose interests often converge. When there is a conflict of interests, these can be assessed by the same methods that would apply to any small group. John Locke, for example, viewed marriage as an ordinary contract, which could be terminated, at no social cost, as soon as the children come of age. Contemporary ethicists like John Rawls and Robert Nozick almost never treat the family as a special case. In the view of most writers on ethics since Hobbes, obligations to family members are no different from any other. If we owe a special obligation to wives and children, it is because we have made a kind of contract with them. There is some merit to this approach. Human beings are distinct individuals, whose interests do not necessarily coincide even with those of parents or children. Potential conflicts among siblings and between generations can be looked at as an essentially genetic competition — as they are by Robert Trivers. Parents, for example, might wish to encourage altruism between sons because it increases their own reproductive success. One or both of the sons, on the other hand, might do better by pursuing his own interests at his brother's expense. In this sense, the mark of Cain upon the human race is not so much our violent propensities as our refusal to be our brother's keeper.[15] Nonetheless, self-sacrificing benevolence remains the norm for relationships within families.

Despite the willingness of many human beings to extend this principle to strangers, altruism is not the dominant mode of most social interactions in which kinship is not recognized. In a real sense, we treat our children as half of ourselves and go to great lengths to advance their interests. Are we justified, then, in describing the family — apart from model-building exercises — as nothing more than a small group?

For many purposes, it may be more appropriate to adopt the perspective of Comte and Durkheim, who regarded the family, rather than the individual, as the proper unit of society. Perhaps the best approach is to regard the family as a sort of system — like an organism. While it is made up of individual parts, which might be in conflict (Richard Dawkins suggests even a creative conflict between the parts of a cell[16]), the whole is greater than the sum of its parts and functions as an organic entity in the larger social systems of which it is a part. This approach has important ethical consequences. If men and women are designed by nature to extend self love to their relations, then we can begin to make sense of Aristotle's declaration that the self-sufficiency on which happiness depends is not "that which is sufficient for a man by himself . . . but also for his parents, children, wife, and generally for his friends and fellow citizens." He is even reluctant to refute the common Greek opinion that a man's happiness is bound up with the good fortune of his descendents — even after he is dead.[17]

If the family is an indispensable intermediary between individuals and society, then it is subject to two sorts of pressures: internal pressures, which arise from the conflicts between members, and external pressures, imposed by social circumstances. From this perspective, the most natural arrangements are those that maximize both the fitness of family members and the family as a group. The mother/child relationship poses no problem. Maternity is the most obvious relationship among all mammals. Chimpanzees and gorillas seem to recognize their mother as a special person long after they have been pushed out of the nest. It was a principle of Roman law that only motherhood was certain; therefore, the Roman father had to acknowledge a child as his own by picking it up in his arms — a custom paralleled in many parts of the world. Matrilineage might reasonably be said to be natural. That was the argument made by the Furies in Aeschylus' *Eumenides*: they had to punish Orestes for killing his mother, while she was guiltless, having only killed her husband.

And yet, what is essentially human about human beings is just this combination of marriage — the recognition of the father — with parenthood. Matriliny may be more natural for chimpanzees, not necessarily for humans. It can introduce tensions into family relations by discouraging familiarity between a father and his children (even to the point of forbidding fathers to reside with

their wife and children) or by pitting a husband against his wife's male relatives in a struggle for power. A father may try to resist the impediments placed
in the way of his "natural affection" and make every effort to cultivate his children's loyalty and arrange to pass on his wealth and social position to his
offspring.

In many matrilineal societies, fathers do contrive to establish the principle
of patrifiliation. Panoff's study of the Maenge of East New Britain is a good
case in point.[18] The families of the matrilineal Maenge could, apparently even
in the time before they were in touch with the West, reside either in the wife's
or husband's village. While tracing descent and property through the female
line, they also (like so many matrilineal peoples) attribute the invention of culture to women. Nonetheless, they still regard woman as, in origin, a mutation
of the male sex. More significantly, they believe the male plays a predominant
role in conception, comparing the female role to that of a vessel merely holding
the embryo—a conception reminiscent of Apollo's counterargument in the *Eumenides*:

> The mother is not the begetter of the child begotten as they call it—merely the nurse
> of the new-sown embryo. The male who mounts is the begetter. The woman keeps
> the offspring as a hostess for a guest. . . .

Panoff has demonstrated a tendency among the Maenge to pass political
authority as much to the son as to a sister's son, despite the institution of
matrilineage.

In what A.I. Richards calls the "Borrowed Husband" matrilineage of Central Africa, marriage is destabilized as a result of the inability of competing
male in-laws to cooperate.[19] The Kaguru of Eastern Tanzania are subject to
a similiar conflict of loyalties. A man possesses political authority on two principles: first, because he is head of a matrilineage that includes his mother, sister,
and sister's children, and second, because he is head of a household, which
in fact belongs to another man's lineage.[20]

The tendency toward patriarchy showed up among the matrilineal plateau
Tonga of Rhodesia, but fathers still were denied jural authority over their sons.
On the other hand, his authority as head of the household prevented the devel-
opment of powerful matriarch clans.[21]

One natural response to this stand-off is to require a father to reside outside
his wife's household. In that event, the sons can be deprived of an appropriate
role model. Burton and Whiting have found a correlation between absent fathers
and particularly severe male initiation ceremonies—a connection that might
indicate that boys have a harder time growing up to be men in the absence
of their fathers. They support this hypothesis by the obvious parallels of soldier's families during the Second World War and urban black neighborhoods,

where fatherless families are the rule rather than the exception.[22] Young black males seem to have a greater difficulty accepting the responsibilities of male adulthood. Their uncertainty is reflected in their participation in teenage gangs, in which maleness is equated with violence and the rejection of all that is identified with the female world.

The evolution of descent systems remains a perplexing problem. Many hunter-gatherer societies are patrilineal, although others have bilateral dual descent systems. The predominance of patriliny has been given a sociobiological explanation. A father maximizes his reproductive success by handing on his social position and, more importantly, his wealth to his sons, who are twice as close to him genetically as his sister's sons. Pierre Van den Berghe supports this hypothesis by pointing out that, as soon as a primitive people acquires sufficient wealth to make a system of inheritance desirable, "the first use to which it was put was reproductive," i.e. buying wives.[23]

If patriliny is more efficient, why would a matrilineal system develop? One of the attractions of older theories that assumed a matriarchal stage of development was their ability to explain the evolution of a more stable and efficient set of arrangements out of those that are less stable and less satisfactory. One clue may be found in some of the drawbacks of matriliny. It has been suggested that the high rate of divorce and adultery associated with many matrilineal peoples might be the cause, rather than the effect, of the descent system. In a strong patriarchal culture, where a father's will was law, there is a degree of certainty about the offspring. Although by Roman law only motherhood was certain, the Roman father — at least in the good old days of the earlier Republic — was reasonably sure he was not lavishing his wealth and energy on a brood of cuckoos. However, where adultery and divorce are common and a man's certainty about this paternity drops below a certain level, he might prefer to bequeath his property to his sister's sons, whose degree of relatedness may be more certain.[24]

Membership in a family is more than a biological fact or a socioeconomic relationship to a household group: it is the most important indication of an individual's position in society. It also determines how he will behave to other individuals. (Most cultures specify certain patterns of behavior for certain relationships: joking, often indecently, with wife's sisters, reverential respect towards father or maternal uncle.) Above all, it will tell him with whom he can mate and have children.

In this sense, the incest taboo can be seen to establish the fundamental parameters of all family and social relations. A member of a family or descent group is always forbidden to take a mate — and usually forbidden to have sexual relations — within the forbidden degree of relatedness. It is possible that the extent to which we apply the incest taboo is in proportion to the extent to which we acknowledge kinship. In the United States, a family connection is not recognized much beyond the nuclear family and only rarely beyond descent from a common set of grandparents. Among the members of that third generation — first cousins — marriage is generally frowned upon and is often against the law. Nonetheless, marriage between first cousins is not unknown. On the other hand, neither marriage nor sexual relations are permitted between brother and sister or parent and child. At the other end of the spectrum are tribal societies in which members of an entire lineage or clan are forbidden to intermarry, a prohibition that sometimes extends to members of age grades — people born within a certain period of time or initiated in the same ceremony.

Many social scientists have seen the incest taboo as a primary cultural invention that drove a permanent wedge between man and nature. Freud's Oedipus theory, in which a primal father is overthrown by his sons who take possession of their mother, is only a graphic and fairy-tale representation of the same view.

Man, it is argued, is as naturally promiscuous as other animals. Without a stringent taboo, he would mate within the family, precisely because familiarity breeds desire. Incestuous breeding is genetically restrictive, to say the least, because it limits the range of potentially beneficial variations. In addition, inbreeding would discourage the development of larger social structures, which are almost universally related to exogamy. Put simply, families or clans cement alliances and construct a broader social organization by exchanging daughters — although it is rarely a simple swap. Durkheim led the way for this sociological interpretation of incest by rejecting the idea of an instinctive aversion and linking the taboo to the origin of social evolution: "We seen in exogamy a prohibition of incest."[25]

This theory of social utility could allow Marxist and other social revolutionaries to regard the incest taboo — and the family it protects — as a social mechanism invented by man in history. As a mere cultural invention, it would be, no matter how useful, convenient fiction, to be abandoned once it had outlived its utility. If this were so, it is surprising that such an archaic invention was not, like kingship, tossed aside long ago. Before proceeding with such a social revolution, we should be sure of our premises: first, that mammals do not avoid incestuous relations, and second, that among men familiarity does in fact breed desire instead of contempt.

At first sight, animals in barnyards and zoos seem to confirm the purely sociological interpretation. But domesticated animals have been specially bred for certain purposes, which can override the most natural instincts. Anyone who has tried to raise a few chickens is aware of the value of a "broody" hen, the rare bird that will sit on a nest and hatch the eggs. The observation of caged animals is hardly a better guide to natural behavior, especially in matters of sex. The only proper basis for evaluation is the behavior of animals in the wild. Norbert Bischof, who has made such a study, concluded that "in the whole animal world with very few exceptions no species is known in which under natural conditions inbreeding occurs to any considerable degree." In some species, incest is virtually impossible because of the isolation of the sexes. Sexually mature animals either live alone or only the females stay with their mother, thus reducing the chance of incest. Among harem-forming species, the males are driven out of the group to associate with other males until they can acquire females. The daughters are abducted by young males or taken over by apprentices to the leader of the harem. Among monogamous species, "detachment of adolescents is . . . mostly enforced by aggressive behavior of the same-sexed parent." Chimpanzees engage in indiscriminate sex play with siblings until they are old enough to mate, at which time the female begins to repulse her brothers.[26]

This surfeit response is not restricted to chimpanzees. Westermarck, over sixty years ago, argued that the incest taboo was a natural development of this tendency.[27] It has been observed several times, that genetically unrelated young men and women who are reared together as children — as on an Israeli kibbutz — do not typically find each other sexually attractive. In the more traditional Middle East of Lebanon, where marriage with father's brother's daughter is a social norm, such marriages produce fewer children and are more likely to end in divorce.[28] The Sim-pua marriages of Taiwan are another case in point. A young girl is adopted by her future husband's family and is reared to be the perfect wife. Like many social experiments, it works better in theory than in practice. It too, is marked by serious strains, lower fertility, and higher rates of divorce and adultery. Such marriages generally are regarded with disfavor by everyone except the arranging parents.[29] The problem common to these marriage forms is the premarital familiarity of husband and wife.

The aversion to sexual relations between brother and sister is not entirely mysterious. Michael Ruse and E.O. Wilson sum up prevailing sociobiological theory.

> Lowered genetic fitness due to inbreeding led to the evolution of the juvenile selection; the inhibition experienced as sexual maturity led to prohibitions and cautionary myths against incest or (in many societies) merely a shared feeling that the practice is inappropriate. Formal incest taboos are the cultural reinforcement of the automatic inhibition, an example of the way culture is shaped by biology.[30]

If there were no inherent bias against or in favor of it, we should expect brothers to mate with their sisters about 50 percent of the time, but in fact the observable cross-cultural bias against incest appears to be about 99 percent. Despite the scare-stories that 10 percent of American families are afflicted with incestuous relations, actual or attempted coitus in which one of the siblings is thirteen years or older, would seem to be far less frequent. Pierre Van den Berghe reviewed the relevant data and concluded that, in Western societies, postpubertal coitus between individuals more closely related than first cousins "is an event encountered in the life history of at most one person in 100, probably less than in 1,000."[31] This does not mean no one ever has sexual relations with his sister, even in societies in which the penalty for incest is death. "Natural inhibitions and propensities do not determine but only motivate behavior. We can live at odds with ourselves, and this danger makes us inclined to narrow down the newly gained fullness of scope to within bearable boundaries by means of collectively created norms."[32]

The interesting fact to observe is this: While mammals ordinarily avoid inbreeding, human beings at a very early time in their history devised a prohibition against incestuous union. This prohibition in the higher civilizations of Europe and the Orient includes all forms of erotic behavior. Civilization, rather than repressing the primitive, develops and formalizes it.

In the broadest terms, therefore, we might be justified in speaking of a natural family as a monogamous to mildly polygynous group defined by incest-avoidance, with a strong pressure on fathers to protect and assist their own children, and investing the males of the family with at least nominal control over its activities. To appreciate the range of activities carried on by the most primitive families, it is useful to turn to Julian Steward's observations on the Shoshone.

> Virtually all cultural activities were carried out by the family in comparative isolation from other families. . . . It is perhaps difficult to imagine that a family, alone and unaided, could obtain virtually all the food it consumed; manufacture all its clothing, household goods, and other articles, rear and train its children without assistance; take care of its sick except in time of crisis; be self-sufficient in its religious activities; and, except on special occasions, manage its own recreation. . . .[33]

Although Steward was describing an unusual ecological adaptation to special circumstances, the extreme autonomy of the Shoshone family must be something like the condition of the primordial human family, since it is, in general outline, supported by the pattern of so many "primitive" communities.

The history of civilization is in many ways a long transition, across several millennia, from the autonomous family to the deracinated individualism of the modern state. "In the beginning," the family, which extended for several generations, functioned economically as a unit of production as well as of consumption. It was charged with all the responsibilities we now associate with the operations of government. It maintained order, educated children, provided social security. It made war. The development of wider social and political forms of organization did not, at first, challenge the autonomy of the family. Within its homestead, which it was prepared to defend, the family reigned supreme. Among the Nuer, so painstakingly described by Evans-Pritchard, there is no external mechanism of social control that can routinely intrude upon a family's business. As a rule of thumb, it can be stated that whatever powers are not assumed by the state are exercised by family, clan, and tribe.

The most vital powers of the family are concerned with the obligations and authorities that support its primary functions. In general, the primitive family exerts a jural authority over all its members. In practice, this means mature men exercise authority over children and women. In one cross-cultural sample, 66.7 percent of the societies held the explicit view that husbands should and do dominate their wives.[34] In only 3.2 percent of the cases was there evidence of wife dominance. Children are expected to obey their parents, wives their husbands. The Polynesian Tikopia indulged their children outrageously, but to strike a father was regarded as an act of sacrilege. A son guilty of such a crime was expected to commit suicide.[35] On the other side, the more responsible parties are required to care for their children and to give them the instruction that will enable them eventually to take their place in society as adults. Grown children are expected to care for aged parents.

Among civilized communities of the preindustrial West, the principles of kinship and family autonomy yielded ground only grudgingly to the state. Greek children were legally obliged to ensure the proper care of their parents in old age. It was an obligation taken very seriously. At Athens, aspiring office-holders were asked if they treated their parents well. To a great extent, membership in a family was the primary basis for social and political identity. It is true that reformers like Cleisthenes tried to break up the political power of the large clans in Attica. Even so, the individual was not liberated from his family. As late as the fourth century, B.C., a man with sons could not make a will, that is, he could not alienate property from the family. The family remained the economic unit of production and sons typically followed their fathers' vocation. Children and wives remained legally subordinate to parents and husbands. In the liberated age of the Sophists, Aristophanes took for granted a certain respect for motherhood. In *The Clouds*, a father listens patiently to all his son's new learning until the relativist student threatens to beat his mother. The father's response is to burn down the school. As Athenian society expanded the economic and political spheres and, especially during wartime, imposed heavy obligations on adult males, the nuclear family came to represent a domestic refuge from public life, the role it is designed to play in any period of crisis.

The evolution of Roman family law, in general, bears out Sir Henry Sumner Maine's contention that it represents the change from family status to legal contract. In the early days, it is assumed that a girl was transferred from her father's to her husband's authority. No woman, until the late Empire, was ever completely independent. She remained under her father's authority if she were single or if she married without a transfer of authority. Failing a father, a guardian was appointed. By the end of the Empire, the forces of social disintegration had brought about a gradual emancipation of women and children from the authority of the *paterfamilias*. The transition, far from complete, was arrested and reversed, and barbarian Europe exhibited a level of social development more typical of the mythological period than anything known from classical literature.

Most contemporary discussions of family history begin with the end of the Middle Ages — a limitation that often imposes a set of ethnocentric blinders on the historian. Scholars like Philipe Aries and Lawrence Stone are forever discovering that some aspect of family life — conjugal intimacy or affection for children — was invented during the sixteenth or seventeenth century. Until then, they argue, children were mistreated or exploited sexually. Such generalizations could not be made by historians who knew much of the age of the Antonines. Indeed, John Demos has provided convincing evidence to the contrary: that it is precisely in modern times that child abuse has become a serious problem.[36] Nonetheless, the past 500 years have wrought overwhelming changes in the lives of Western families.

Many of the changes are related to the liberation of the individual — a gradual and uneven process in Europe and the United States. At times, it has even seemed the family was reasserting its control, but such revivals usually turn out to be a strengthening of the nuclear family at the expense of extended kinship. The gradual withering of family functions encompasses nearly every phase of human existence: child-rearing and education, economic activities, health and welfare, self-defense, and recreation. A general list of such categories inevitably sounds like a string of ministerial portfolios or cabinet departments, not without reason, since the state ultimately has assumed the functions of the family.

In modern times, the first phase of the family's decline looked like a revival. The rise of the state in the Renaissance was accomplished at the expense of other social institutions. The newly assertive monarchs and their advisers viewed all concentrations of power (except their own) with distrust.[37] The church, guilds, noble families, and powerful clans all came under sustained attack. The theorists of absolutism, like Jean Bodin and Thomas Hobbes, were adamant in their opposition to such rival centers of power and loyalty. As the new modern states began to make war on the extended family, the only alternative was the nuclear family. There were, of course, many other factors in the emergence of the modern nuclear family — economic as well as religious — but there is, nonetheless, a marked relationship between the rise of the state and the shrinking of kinship into the conjugal household.

Generalizations are difficult in so complex a set of evolutionary changes. England advanced very rapidly — as did New England later — while progress in France was a good deal slower. Peter Laslett has shown that the multigenerational household was never a norm in England and the United States.[38] Significant as it is, Laslett's research should not be taken (as it usually is) as a proof that extended families were not important in preindustrial England.

In some cases, the older generation lived around the corner or even on the property. Most widows in the United States resided, until recently, with one of their children. Even in eighteenth century Britain and North America, there was a good chance of a child being socialized in a household with many relatives, especially if the family was well-off.[39] The broad picture of massive change remains valid.

This social evolution is reflected in a number of legal changes. In conditions of primitive life, the head of a family is not typically the owner of the land in the modern sense; he is more of a life tenant. He cannot alienate it from his natural heirs, either by gift or by will. Such an attitude prevailed to a large extent at the end of the Middle Ages: family property was entailed, that is to say its transfer was restricted to the heirs. By the mid-sixteenth century in England, it had become relatively easy to break or ignore entailment and pass on property — or even sell it — at will. This and other legal changes strengthened the hand of the head of the house and diminished the influence of the extended family, for whom and with whom real property formerly had been held. By degrees, the influence of kin and community eroded, leaving the nuclear family free and self-sufficient.

At the same time, other changes were taking place that would undermine the nuclear family itself and liberate the individual from its shackles. In a general way, the individual has only been on his own in the most advanced stages of civilization. Father and mother may compete with each other for power within the family and with their own brothers, sisters, aunts, and uncles, but such decisions as whom to marry, what career to pursue, were only occasionally made by individuals. In the seventeenth and eighteenth centuries, families — usually, but not necessarily, the father — decided on the marriage of sons and daughters and on what the sons were going to do to make a living.

Within the nuclear family, the case was clear cut. Marriage, in the tradition of English common law, made man and wife of one flesh. This meant not only that divorce was virtually out of the question, but that the wife's property and income were under the control of her husband. Although such a custom was liable to abuse — drunken spendthrift husbands who sold their wives' jewels, leased their property for three lifetimes, and left the ladies to starve without recourse — it was based on a reasonable recognition of what the marriage bond meant. Of course, in earlier times, a woman had brothers and uncles who felt a good deal of responsibility for her welfare. In more primitive areas, like the Scottish highlands or the rural American South, it was not always safe to abuse a man's sister or daughter. One of the severest social strains in the nineteenth century South was between brothers-in-law. Whatever the real motives, men often alleged that the origin of the quarrel lay in the mistreatment of a sister. In this respect at least, a woman may have been better off in more backward parts of the modern world.

The nineteenth century witnessed the decay of most of these legal sanctions of patriarchal authority. Divorce laws in the United States were slowly liberalized. The grounds on which a wife could sue were expanded. Previously, impotence and, occasionally, the most grotesque forms of abuse, had been the ordinary basis for a petition of divorce. The fact that a husband had squandered his wife's property, introduced a concubine into the house, and subjected his spouse to regular beatings were not usually sufficient grounds. When there was a divorce, the children remained in the father's custody. By the end of the century, divorce was much easier to obtain, eventually on the grounds of incompatibility alone. A plea of incompatibility — so frequent in modern no-fault divorce proceedings — was not in origin a cynical effort to cover adultery or the change of heart that results from a mid-life crisis. The idea of marriage had changed in modern times. What had been a union that ensured the procreation of children and deflected illicit lust became, in addition, an institution for "mutual society, help, and comfort" (as the Prayerbook of 1549 expressed it). Marriage was gradually turned from a practical expression of community needs into a private fulfillment of personal desires. Inevitably, the law took account of such a revolution and allowed the divorce of unsociable, unhelpful, and uncomfortable partners. In some states, divorce is even granted in response to a plea from one partner.

In other ways, a husband lost his hold on family members. Control over a wife's and children's earnings was eventually disallowed; at the same time, a man was no longer liable for crimes committed by his wife. Women gradually were given power over their own property as they became, for the first time, legal persons. The right to vote, granted in 1920, was only a confirmation of the fact that the old-fashioned marriage had been virtually dissolved into a utilitarian partnership of competing individuals. Nonetheless, a whole array of legal protections for family status has endured: community property, inheritance rights in cases of intestate succession, the right to sue on the basis of wrongful death of a family member.

The decline of family functions in the twentieth century is an old story.[40] Without going into excessive detail, a few of the more obvious changes can be pointed to: the almost complete triumph of school attendance laws, which transferred educational responsibilities absolutely from the parents to the state; the decision (made comparatively late in the United States) to make the state the primary guarantor of welfare and security for the aged. Perhaps the most profound change was economic. To express it in familiar Marxist terms: the family was no longer a unit of production, but a unit of consumption. Consider the most basic economic fact of domestic life: eating. In rural America, grain and vegetables had to be planted and harvested, game killed, cows milked, pigs and chickens raised, fattened, slaughtered and dressed — all before anyone could think of eating. In addition, most food had to be preserved — salted, dried, (later canned), or pickled — and stored. By the middle of the twentieth century, most food could be bought ready to cook. Gardening and hunting now were taken up as amusements. But even as a place of consumption, the use of the home declined as more and more families learned to make use of restaurants and fast food chains. Eating out became another form of recreation, which, like sports, movies, and social club activities, would be engaged in outside the home. In *Late Capitalism*, Marxist critic Ernest Mandel points to:

> The growing market for precooked meals and tinned foods, ready-made clothes and vacuum cleaners, and the increasing demand for all kinds of electrical household appliances. . . .

Mandel concludes that, as Europe and America turn into service economies, "the material basis of the individual family disappears in the sphere of consumption."[41]

It would be an oversimplification to say that the state — or capitalism — has actually usurped all these familiy functions. In most cases, legislators and "professionals" were only doing their best to address a very real problem. The economic and political freedoms that go along with industrial capitalism had many unpredicted side-effects: not only were nuclear families now free to travel in the pursuit of economic gain, but children — especially large numbers of them — became a burden on the small household. Where once aunts and grandmothers were at hand to assist, a mother — often a working mother — was now expected to shoulder the entire responsibility.

The most fundamental household task is the socialization of children. Of course, the institutions of community life have always exerted a considerable pressure on this process through initiation rituals, admonitions of older men and women, even specialized instruction in certain skills, like hunting or making pottery. In more advanced cultures, a special class of teachers arises — although most serious education remains in the form of apprenticeship. A Roman boy of Caesar's time was sent to schools to learn grammar, literature, and eventually rhetoric, but his most advanced training was to be had by studying under famous jurists or orators. The Emperor Vespasian endowed the first chair of higher learning, but Roman education always remained a patchwork of family indoctrination, private tutors, and community schools. Only the rich — down to the mid-nineteenth century — could affort to shunt their children off to the tender mercies of the professionals.

By the beginning of the twentieth century, a pattern of development had emerged: compulsory education from the age of six or seven to sixteen or eighteen. Such laws were based on the assumption that parents either did not know what was good for the child or did not know how to go about providing it. The early twentieth century also saw the rise of professional elitism among caretakers — physicians, teachers, and counsellors — whose propaganda in large measure convinced parents that the care and rearing of children had to be guided by professionals. At first, middle-class women were only urged "to study their children." But by the 1920s, a host of experts were warning against the ill effects of maternal care. Behaviorist John B. Watson led the chorus: "Mother love," he declared, "is a dangerous instrument." Everything became a matter of scheduling and training. As Janet Margolin notes of these developments, Watson was simply applying the latest theories of "scientific" business management to children.[42] While the 40s and 50s (the golden age of Dr. Spock) witnessed a remission in strictness, permissive attitudes did not prevent Watson's chief disciple from raising his children in a modified "Skinner box." But by the 60s, American social workers and psychologists were pushing for social parenting and had persuaded Congress to give tax-incentives for day care. By the 1970s, this trend had so far developed that a baby could look forward to several years of day-care/nursery school before entering kindergarten. After twelve years of elementary school, come four years of college and perhaps several years of postgraduate training. After an interim thirty-five to forty years of productive independence, he will once again enjoy the blessings of professional services at retirement villages and nursing homes. In the end, he will pass on, painless and numbed, in a hospice for the terminally ill.

This loss of functions was at least partly responsible for a reconsideration of the family's place in society. It increasingly came to be regarded as a sanctuary, a domestic refuge from an impersonal world. Ann Douglas places this development in the context of the feminization of American society: as woman's economic role was diminished, she was increasingly expected to provide a "place where children stayed before they began to work, and where her husband rested from his labors."[43] From a more exclusively masculine perspective, G.K. Chesterton insisted that a man's home was the only place in which he could be free "to alter arrangements suddenly, make an experiment, or indulge a whim." Even Marxists, like Horkheimer, who had their own axes to grind, admitted that the home and hearth offered a retreat from a world in which people were reduced to an impersonal status (*verdinglichung*), although he too, like Hegel, considered domestic life to be essentially feminine.[44]

Even this attenuated function of domestic sanctuary has begun to crumble. Christopher Lasch points out that, despite our confidence in the inviolability of the nuclear family, "In reality, the modern world intrudes at every point and obliterates its privacy. . . . Increasingly, the same forces that have impoverished work and civic life invade the private realm and its last stronghold, the family."[45]

It is easy to overstate the problem. Privacy, for example, is not necessarily a cardinal virtue enjoyed by families in all periods. On the contrary, it is a relatively modern invention. As historians of the family have shown, individual and family privacy—like the ideal of conjugal affection—is to some extent a modern phenomenon, brought on by the ideals of the Reformation and the economic realities of bourgeois existence. In old-fashioned agrarian societies, the community also invaded not only the privacy of families but influenced and directed their most intimate and significant decisions: birth, marriage, and death were circumscribed by rituals that reinforced the social controls of the village. Deviations from social orthodoxy were punished in a variety of sometimes cruel and unusual ways. And yet, these implicit social controls of kin and neighbors are of a different order from the explicit powers assumed now by the state or imagined by social visionaries.

In recent times, the most elementary principles of domestic life have come under attack. It is no longer a question of competition between the family and other institutions of community life. Contemporary critics of the family would either subordinate all of its essential functions to the state or do away with it.

Alice S. Rossi noted the shift in emphasis of family theory.[46] The new model for family studies includes rejection of traditional sex roles and replacement of parental functions by institutions. This radical program was devised to accommodate the reality of family to the propaganda of the sexual revolution. The new sexual freedom meant women were to take up the predatory habits of men, seizing pleasure where they find it, regardless of the consequences or the cost. The trouble is, as Rossi observes, what will become of the children? If women, as well as men, divide their time between the work place and singles bars, who will look after the kids?

Most of the sexual revolutionaries did not trouble their heads about the consequences. The O'Neills, celebrities in the field, redefined marriage as "an open and honest relationship between two people, based on equal freedom and identity of both partners." Love, in their world, becomes "sex without jealousy," monogamy an unnatural trap.[47] The Smiths (another reassuringly conjugal pair of sexual utopians), in their introduction to *Beyond Monogamy*, speak grandly of the sexual "eufunction," which will be facilitated by sex clubs and sex therapy programs. Another contributor to the same volume is content to analyze the consequences of open marriage on a cost/benefit model—again without serious consideration of any little third parties.[48]

Unfortunately, the prospects for group marriage or swinging are not all that encouraging. The Constantines studied twenty-six group marriages and found that 58 percent lasted less than a year and only two survived more than four years. The more people involved, the less likely they are to stay together. More significantly, these complex mating arrangements tend to resolve themselves into pairs.[49] In communal households—several family groups and individuals— the children are subjected to conflicting pressures from the adults. Without any clear lines of authority or firm standards, the children begin to exhibit "the

Cinderella effect"—the conviction that everyone expects them to do opposite things simultaneously.[50]

The problems of communal households are predictable and serious. Many of them cropped up on the Israeli kibbutzim that practiced group parenting (although not group marriage) and a roughly egalitarian distribution of labor. The women have come to specialize in more traditionally domestic tasks and are demanding the recognition of a mother's primary responsibility for the care of her own children. Group marriage and communal households, for all their drawbacks, are a serious attempt to come to grips with the problem of child rearing. Most other proposed solutions read like a Robert Heinlein novel in which sexual freedom is the first and only principle of life. Under those circumstances, parental freedom will be the inevitable result of sexual freedom, and mothers and fathers will be free to "parent" or not, according to their whims. If such parental freedom will not work in the relatively stable setting of group marriage or utopian communes, what are the alternatives?

The most creative feminist agenda outlined a number of possibilities. We could establish a priestly class of parents, who will be paid to practice monogamy, bear children, and provide a stable home life. Such a class could be drawn from old-fashioned Catholics, Southern Baptists, and Mormons. This notion has two obvious drawbacks: first, it concedes the point that old-fashioned religious households are better for children; second, as Long suggests, the Moral Majority already has enough occasion for looking down its nose at the erotic minorities. If a parental priesthood won't work, then perhaps an international child exchange with overpopulated/underdeveloped countries. Or, why not a class of technocratic professionals in charge of breeding and rearing? If this summons up too many bad memories of *Brave New World*, we can always try a National Child Service that pairs off one adult with one child in a unilineal descent system.[51]

In fact, the only reasonable alternative to families is the standard answer: a professional class of child development experts. While few theorists (much less parents) are willing to turn over all responsibilities to such institutions, there is no doubt of their increasing popularity. It is often argued in newspapers and popular books and magazines that day care is good for children: it enhances their intellectual development and accelerates the socialization process.

Research on the effects of day care on children is largely inconclusive. Much of it seems designed to prove the case for day care or early schooling. Typical of such research are widely quoted studies of the effect of special intensive tutoring given to young black children of poor families. Not surprisingly, their academic and social performance showed an improvement over the norm. What this suggests for more normal families is not at all clear. It will be many years before we can assess the effects of day care with any degree of accuracy. However, the most thorough review of the evidence suggests that "infant day care, at least, may lead to insecure attachment to mothers during infancy and, later on, "heightened aggressiveness and noncompliance during the preschool and early school-age years." The effects seem particularly marked on boys.[52] (Of greater immediate concern may be the high rates of serious diseases that have been discovered.)[53]

This conclusion is not surprising when we recall that females of mammalian species, including the primates, are hormonally (and probably neurally) programmed to be more nurturant and more inclined to care for the helpless than males, who are either aloof or even hostile at the sight of impotence.

The males of some species, like the Japanese *Macaca fuscata*, exhibit special attachment to the young. This is probably true of humans, but the strength of such attachment is nothing like the bonding of mother to child and of child to mother—a bonding that is said to take place soon after birth.

Human children, like other primate offspring, exhibit a need for a central caretaker, a mother or an adequate mother surrogate. Even children in day-care centers, where they have been taught to regard the caretakers as providers of safety and comfort, in a crisis will typically run to their mothers when she is present.

Maternal deprivation can lead to serious emotional problems. Bowlby, in his famous postwar studies, showed that infants under six months suffer from emaciation and despondency if they are removed from their mother. He suggested that the vulnerability decreased with age, but that it was still very serious at three to five and of considerable consequence at up to eight years.[54] Bowlby's conclusions have been attacked, but his general results have been confirmed by studies and observations of both human and primate offspring. Young chimpanzees, separated from their mothers, fall into despair. The mothers' death typically leads to death of the orphan, even if it is adopted by others. Studies of pig-tailed macaque infants have demonstrated the occurrence of both psychological and physiological changes when infants are removed from their mothers for ten days.[55] Human children, on the other hand, who are afflicted with serious emotional disorders, are frequently found to have suffered the loss or frequent separation from parents or other important "love-objects."[56] Another study supports, at least in part, the hypothesis that "the quality of the early mother-infant attachment relationship predicts later social-emotional functioning.[57]

There is little prospect of the family being replaced by alternative social forms or by state institutions. Earlier experimental societies have tried to find ways around the conjugal household. Albert Ellis, in *Group Marriage* makes the predictable suggestion that we look to the example of religious communities like the Shakers, who rejected sex entirely, and Oneida Perfectionists, who practiced an exotic combination of complex marriage and coitus reservatus. However, the secret to the very partial success of these sexual innovators was their repression of conjugal intimacy and their complete control of any aspect of personal life that might threaten the stability of the community.[58]

The modern state actually depends on the family to do the hard job of preparing children for their life as citizens. Even the Soviet Union eventually gave up its war on the family once it had destroyed all the old extended networks of kin and community. While the old-fashioned extended family "is the most profound and effective counter agency against domination by external authority . . . inherently antagonistic to the super-state," the Soviet authorities are able to use the attenuated nuclear family as a "training-ground for submission."[59] To what extent this is true in the United States remains to be seen. For some time, there has been an uneasy alliance between the family and the state, an alliance that depends on the family's recognition of the state's right to regulate, control, and limit the exercise of authority within the family. As we have seen, familial powers have been reduced to a bare minimum in the United States—and to less than a minimum in Sweden.

The mention of Sweden raises the specter of family policy at the national level. Such policies can cover the whole of domestic life: from the big picture of population growth and income distribution down to the smallest details of sex education and discipline. Family policy in the United States, is still a patchwork of state, local, and federal laws; however, since the 1970s, there has been continuous discussion of a more comprehensive plan. Most proposals include sweeping economic programs—income redistribution and full employment—but their main agenda is usually devoted to the creation of a national network of "integrated family support services," day-care centers, and sex education programs.

In calling for new programs and powers, social critics frequently point to problems like child abuse and adolescent suicide. The usefulness of these issues for social planners is obvious: the victimization of the helpless cries out for legislative and judicial protection. In many ways, the rise of the abuse "problem" and the cries for reform parallel the earlier development of the delinquency problem and the creation of an enormous industry dedicated to saving children. In both cases, a medical model is used; the role of government is viewed as therapeutic.[60] While reported cases of abuse have increased dramatically in recent years, this may be partly the result of a growing willingness to discuss the issue. If the extent of the problem is clouded in uncertainty, the causes are even more obscure. For one thing, many writers do not distinguish between actual abuse and cases of routine corporal punishment. For another, sweeping generalizations are made without reference to historical or individual variation.

The rights of parents increasingly are being overridden by child abuse legislation. The American legal tradition, rooted in common law, used to uphold the parents' right to bring up their children as they saw fit.[61] A number of legal developments in Britain and the United States weakened this right: compulsory school attendance laws that usurped the parents' right to decide on the proper education, Elizabethan Poor Laws (widely imitated in the United States) that allowed parish church wardens to indenture or apprentice the children of the poor, and the elaboration of the *parens patriae* concept, which made the state responsible for children's welfare.[62] All fifty states now have child abuse "reporting" laws, most of them requiring physicians, teachers, and social workers to report suspected cases of abuse to authorities. Most of those laws do away with traditional legal protections like the privileged relationships of physician and patient, husband and wife. Worse, they do away with the old English presumption of innocence: on the slightest suspicion, parents can see their children taken and placed in foster care.[63]

Whether child abuse is actually increasing is a debated point, although it is hard to believe that the estimated 200,000 annual cases of sexual molestation do not represent an increase. What does seem clear is this: the children at greatest risk are not those in normal, two-parent families; on the contrary, when all other variables of class and maternal age are controlled for, "preschoolers in stepparent-natural parent homes . . . are estimated to be *40 times* as likely to become abuse statistics as like-aged children living with two natural parents."[64] The routine explanation, that abused children grow up into unstable adults more likely to get divorces and abuse children, is inadequate. In one study of ten abuse cases in Pennsylvania, in which there were children of a previous marriage, it was observed that only the stepchildren were abused and not the natural children.[65]

Child abuse is not the only risk imposed by divorce. Children of single-parent and stepparent-natural parent families are more likely to run away from home or be arrested for crime. In general, children living in intact families are less susceptible to antisocial peer pressures or to engage in deviant behavior.[66] It has been noted repeatedly that boys separated from their fathers are more susceptible to adolescent depression and are more likely to become hoodlums. Girls also suffer from divorce in a number of ways. The absence of a father, for example, is correlated with low self-esteem, difficulties in interacting with males, and increased sexual activity.[67] Family instability also contributes to child and adolescent suicide, and, indeed, is correlated with generally high rates of suicide.

Self-destruction is the most puzzling act of which any organism is capable. Apart from a rare case of altruistic sacrifice, suicide confers no apparent advantages upon either the victim or his relatives. When someone kills himself, especially an adolescent, it is a clear sign that something has gone wrong; when increasingly large numbers do it, there is some kind of social problem. Although the rates of adolescent suicide are no longer increasing, they remain at an alarmingly high level. To some extent, adolescent suicide rates can be correlated with the percentage of youth in the population,[68] but since suicides are attempted many times more often than they are completed, there must be something seriously wrong with the way some of our children are growing up.[69]

There are a number of factors that can be correlated with suicide rates: family disintegration (in one local study of adolescents, both parents were present in only half of the cases of suicide attempts); women in the labor force, especially in the white middle class; gender-equality; and nonparticipation in a religious community.[70] While Durkheim's classic study of suicide now appears hopelessly flawed, his insight, that it had something to do with religion, remains valid. It is not a question of Catholicism vs. Protestantism, as Durkheim believed, but of religious commitment.

Stephen Stack, in a cross-national analysis, found that, even after controlling for female equality and industrial development (both contributing factors), "the greater the religiosity, the less the suicide rate." In the United States the correlation is closest for young adults — "the group with the greatest decline in church attendance."[71] Married people are less likely to commit suicide than singles or divorcees, and people with children less than the childless.[72]

Children are victims of divorce in even more obvious ways. Neither stepparents nor grandparents can be expected to contribute economically to the same degree as parents. If a father is given custody (in only about 10 percent of the cases), this not only consigns the children to the tender mercies of hired help, but payment for child care is a serious economic drain on the family's resources.

In the more typical case of maternal custody, the absent husband is freed of the immediate pressures to support his children. Even when courts declare an adequate figure for child support payments, there is no guarantee that the father will abide by the decision. Fewer than half fully comply.

In general, the economic prospects for American children of divorced parents are considerably less bright. Lenore Weitzman estimates that "on the average, divorced women and minor children in their households experience a 73 percent decline in their standard of living in the first year after divorce." While husbands are better off economically (their standard of living rises 42% in the first year), they experience a host of other problems, including abnormally high rates of mental illness.[73] Obviously, it is desirable for married couples to stay together, particularly if they have children. And yet, state after state has followed California's lead in making provision for no-fault divorces. Every year, over a million marriages in America are dissolved in divorce. If the trend continues, a majority of Americans will be involved in a divorce. This will mean, in essence, that men and women will have to learn not to trust each other. If rumors of the California singles scene are anywhere near accurate, a Hobbesian war of everyone (male) against everyone (female) has already begun.

Despite the overwhelming evidence in support of the traditional family as the most wholesome environment for rearing children, progressive family critics are generally in agreement that problems of abuse, teen pregnancy, and juvenile delinquency can only be addressed by government, preferably at the national level. The Swedish solution is by now notorious. In 1979, Sweden amended its Child and Parent Code to prohibit any form of corporal punishment — no matter how mild or transitory — or psychological abuse, such as sending the child to his room or reading his mail.

There are few public advocates of Swedish policies in the United States, but a number of tentative moves have been made in that direction. Several Senate bills have been introduced, which would set up a comprehensive day care program throughout the United States. Sweden has had such a program since the 1960s. Some states have designed very ambitious child care legislation. Increasingly, the courts, as well as state legislators, have begun to treat children as individuals with rights. The Supreme Court declared (*In re Gault*) that minors may not be denied Fourteenth Amendment rights, and, in 1985 (*New Jersey v. T.L.O.*), the court argued that public school officials do not act in *loco parentis* but as representatives of the state, not merely as surrogates for the parents. North Carolina now guarantees the rights of children to be reared free of racial, religious, and sexual preferences and provides for "aggressive outreach" to parents who refuse to make sex education and contraceptives available to their children. In fact, the greatest activity is in the area of sexual education and the sexual freedom of children.

Most of the initiatives have been made by semiprivate organizations, i.e. organizations that are technically nongovernmental, but which receive massive tax support and influence the drafting of legislation and the implementation of policies — groups like Planned Parenthood and its offshoots, the National Education Association, and most prominently, the Sex Information and Education Council of the United States (SIECUS). SIECUS advocates "free access to full and accurate information on all aspects of sexuality," which they define as "a basic right for . . . children as well as adults."

Not surprisingly, Planned Parenthood's Alan Guttmacher Institute released a 1985 report on teenage pregnancy, blaming the problem on inadequate education in use of contraceptives. The authors contrast the situation in the United States with Sweden, where contraception and sex education have kept the birth rate (legitimate as well as illegitimate) well below replacement levels.

All these groups and government agencies assume that the primary responsibility for child care, education, and socialization is not the family but the state. The corollary to this assumption is that the state, through public schools and health and welfare agencies, should be the instrument of revolutionary social changes that will reduce the family to a convenient economic unit or a legal fiction like corporations.

In one sense, children and adolescents are slowly being converted from an integral part of families into something resembling a minority pressure group.

The same process can be seen even more vividly in the case of the elderly. The conventional picture drawn by groups like the Gray Panthers is not pretty. After years of hard work and dedication to their families, the nation's elderly are consigned to a squalid condition; living off food stamps in a rented room and abandoned by ungrateful children, they have only the government to turn to. Modern society is infected with "ageism," and younger generations view old age as "aesthetic pollution" and deny the elderly their fair share of government resources:[74]

The old consensus on aging, based on the so-called modernization theory, blamed the problems on industrialization, which broke up the old multigenerational household. Social changes gradually marginalized the once honorable elderly into a position where they were forced to rely on Social Security and other forms of state assistance.

Unfortunately, modernization theory does not seem to explain everything. Cross-cultural studies indicate that old age is not routinely valued per se: it is the wealth, power, and special skills possessed by some old people that confer high status on them.[75] Even so, there is no question that it seems less desirable to be old in the 1980s than in the 1780s. Consider the ways in which people lie about their age. Like Jack Benny, many people continue to report their age as thirty-nine or forty-nine long after they have turned that corner. This tendency to report ourselves as younger than we are accounts for the statistically disproportionate number of people whose official age is thirty-nine or forty-nine. In eighteenth century America, however, the reverse was true, and the excess numbers were forty-one and fifty-one. Social historian Brian Grattan concludes that "the view Americans took toward age was utterly different in the late eighteenth century."[76]

As it turns out, the elderly (over 65) do not generally regard themselves as a victimized class.[77] Economically, they are reasonably well-off: 70 percent own homes (most of them paid for); 14 percent are below the poverty line (as opposed to 11.4 percent in the general population), but most of the poor over 65 were poor all their life.[78] The real problems of being old — apart from illness and the prospect of death — are related to the rapid process of disengagement. In their classic study of old age, Cumming and Henry suggested that, as Americans grow old, they go through "a process of adaptation to the conditions of later life" that includes a "reduced sense of commitment," a general feeling of satisfaction, a freedom from restrictive social norms.[79] All of this can be true, but not if people, upon reaching sixty-five, express their freedom by moving to retirement communities, where they are "disengaged" from the family and friends.

In 1900, about sixty percent of the elderly lived with one of their children, but by 1970 that figure was down to 18 percent.[80] Americans are proud of their independence, and many never enjoy actually living with a married son or daughter. On the other hand, our sense of immortality and continuity is bound up with our descendants. Separation from them (and from productive work) is a kind of death.

None of this discontinuity and violent disengagement was necessary or inevitable. Industrialized nations have deliberately adopted policies like Social Security, which drive a wedge between the generations and set them into competition for increasingly scarce government dollars. This is not to say governments should abandon their obligations or shrink from offering retirement insurance. But Social Security now constitutes a scheme of income redistribution from families rearing children to grandparents. This situation exerts a strong negative pressure on population growth, which translates into fewer taxpayers paying higher costs for Social Security.[81] The case of the elderly is exactly parallel with that of the children. Where the state comes to assume the primary obligation for support and care, nobody wins.

In one sense, the Marxists and Freudians are correct: civilization does have its discontents. The bourgeois family is expected to do too little and too much. It exercises too little control over economic production and child-rearing but has an almost unbearably great responsibility for giving shape and substance to our lives. Our high expectations for domestic bliss almost inevitably go unfulfilled, but the imperfections of married life do not go far in explaining the high divorce rates of recent times. On the contrary, we are now faced with an expectation of divorce, rather than marital happiness. Experiments with prenuptial contracts are only a symptom of how little faith men and women have in each other and in the institution of marriage.

Civilized men and women pay a price for their comforts and security and political stability. They give up the "right" to be irresponsible. A civilization like ours is something like a colonial empire — it can be maintained only if a great many people are willing to make sacrifices for it. This means a certain subordination of natural inclinations. We cannot afford the free-and-easy child-rearing practices of a simple egalitarian society.

> In evolutionary perspective one can argue that much of the meaning of 'socialization' derives from a mismatch between the preadaptation of babies and the 'Western' views on what a mother should do.[82]

However, much of our family trouble is not so much the fault of civilization as of deliberate policies undertaken by Western governments. The state is, after all, the invention of families and not the other way around. For several centuries, the state has committed itself to whittling away at the powers and functions of the family, while demanding ever higher standards of performance. Most parents no longer can rear their children as they like, and if they pick up bad habits at school or the day-care center, even spanking may no longer be used as a routine remedy.

Human nature is resilient. Perhaps we can learn to live with high rates of divorce and the permissive sexual code that has developed in many parts of urban Europe and the United States. Some possible survival strategies might emerge under the pressures of the new moral code and state intervention in the family. For men, family life may no longer be as attractive as it once was. As sex becomes liberated from responsibility, there is no selfish reason to assume (much less maintain) the burden of supporting a wife and children. Among American blacks, many men have apparently already come to this conclusion. There may also be incentives to homosexuality: an individualistic moral code that treats everyone as potential sex partners and the competition with women that has resulted from the feminist movement.

Men will not be the only ones susceptible to these pressures. Women are doing their best to break down the double standard in sexual morality, but they increasingly will be compelled to shoulder the responsibility for child care. If they have succeeded in holding on to a male provider, they will be careful not to drive him off by presenting him with either too many children or a brood of cuckoos. Abortion seems the easiest way out. One study of white middle-class women in Los Angeles found confirmation of this trend: the earlier these women had engaged in sex, the more likely they were to be promiscuous and the fewer children they were likely to have. In addition, married women who committed adultery were far more likely to have an abortion.[83]

Children who have grown up in households where divorce, child abuse, and abortion are regarded as normal, are obviously not well-equipped to create stable families of their own. Some of them will, because they have seen the future and know it doesn't work. Others will be unable. Most of us, after all, do our best to recreate the families we grew up in. Many people, especially in strict religious communities, continue to maintain the old-fashioned family values they inherited. As Southern Baptists and Mormons continue to rear children remarkably like their grandparents in an increasingly alien world, a cultural collision of some sort seems inevitable. What, for example, will be the reaction of traditional parents, when their daughter brings home a fiance from San Diego — the child of divorce and remarriage who has witnessed his mother's and father's infidelities? Old-fashioned parents may begin to rethink this modern custom of marriage for love and bring back some form of arranged marriage. At the very least, they will teach their children to look for the symptoms of instability — that is, assuming they are interested in the happiness and reproductive success of their offspring. One hears stories of socially conservative mothers telling their daughters to postpone marriage and pursue a career because men are no longer trustworthy. On the surface, it is hard to quarrel with their reasoning.

Considerations like these may lead some people to question the basis of our individualistic thinking. To be fair, family "experts" who run cost-benefit analyses on swinging or the economists and libertarians who reduce the family to a set of competing indiviudals are only taking modernism to its logical conclusion. But man is not by nature or in history an individual. The individual is not even, properly speaking, an element of social analysis. Rather than explaining our social life, the principle of individualism tends to dissolve it. Human nature is social, and our sociability is a reflection of the fact that we are born into families whose basic structural elements have not been decided by law or consented to by free individuals: they were decreed by nature. The patterns of family life evolve, shift gears, change directions, and the transmutations of the basic elements are so varied and sometimes take such fantastic forms that we are tempted to say, "This people does not recognize the family." However, the world has a never before seen flourishing and productive societies committing themselves to undermining these fundamental principles of our social life: taboo on sexual relations within family, maternal care, paternal authority, the basic division of labor between the sexes, the primary household responsibilities of the family for rearing children, and caring for the elderly and infirm. Destroy this foundation, and you wreck the entire social and political edifice erected upon these natural principles.

Notes

1. For figures on divorce, see tables in *Statistical Abstract of the United States* 1986 (Washington: U.S. Government Printing Office), 37, 45, 79.
2. See *Crime in the United States* (Washington: Federal Bureau of Investigation, 1980).
3. Alice S. Rossi, "Gender and Parenthood," *American Sciological Review* 49 (1984), 4.
4. Sar A. Levitan and Richard S. Belous, *What's Happening to the American Family?* (Baltimore: Johns Hopkins University Press, 1980), 21 ff.
5. William N. Stephens, *The Family in Cross-Cultural Perspective* (New York: Holt, Rinehart, and Winston, 1963), 8 ff.
6. Paul Bohannon, *Social Anthropology* (New York: Holt, Rinehart, and Winston, 1963), 72.
7. G.P. Murdock, *Social Structures*, 25.
8. Stephens, *op. cit.*, 34.
9. Robin Fox, "Primate Kin and Human Kinship" in Robin Fox, ed. *Biosocial Anthropology*, (New York: Wiley, 1975) 11 ff.
10. Phyllis Jay, "The Common Langur of North India" in Irven Devore, ed. *Primate Behavior: Field Studies of Monkeys and Apes* (New York: Holt, Rinehart and Winston, 1965), 221.
11. Adolph H. Schultz, "Some Factors Influencing the Social Life of Primates in General and of Early Man in Particular," in Sherwood L. Washburn, *Social Life of Early Man*.
12. Sherwood L. Washburn and Irven Devore, "Social Behavior of Baboons and Early Man" in *Social Life of Early Man*, 96 ff.

13. Duane Quiatt and Jack Kelso, "Household Economics and Hominid Origins," *Current Anthropology* 26 (1985), 207–11.
14. G.P. Murdock, *Social Structure*, 23 ff.
15. Robert L. Trivers, "Parent-Offspring Conflict," *American Zoologist* 14 (1974), 249–64; cf. Robert L. Trivers and D.E. Willard, "Natural Selection of Parental Ability to Vary the Sex Ratio of Offspring," *Science* 179 (1973), 90–92. Gary Becker applies an economic analysis to the same set of problems and concludes that altruism predominates in family relationships. See *A Treatise on the Family*, 172 ff.
16. Richard Dawkins, *The Extended Phenotype*: The gene as the unit of selection (Oxford: Oxford University Press, 1982), 209–27.
17. *Nicomachen Ethics*, I.9, 1100a.
18. Michael Panoff, "Patrifiliation as Ideology and Practice in a Matrilineal Society," *Ethnology* 12 (1976), 175–88.
19. A.I. Richards, "Some Types of Family Structure Amongst the Central Bantu" in Meyer Fortes and E.E. Evans Pritchard, eds. *African Political Systems* (London: Oxford University Press, 1940), 246 ff.
20. T.O. Beidelman, *The Kaguru: A Matrilineal People of East Africa* (New York: Holt, Rinehart and Winston, 1971), 43 ff.
21. Elizabeth Colson, *Marriage and the Family Among the Plateau Tonga of Northern Rhodesia* (Manchester: University of Manchester Press, 1958), 345 ff; cf.
22. Roger V. Burton and John W.M. Whiting, "The Absent Father and Cross-Sex Identity" in Zubin and Money, 231–45.
23. Pierre L. Van den Berghe, *Human Family Systems: An Evolutionary View* (New York: Elsevier, 1979), 101.
24. See John Hartung, "On Natural Selection and the Inheritance of Wealth," *Current Anthropology* 17, (year?) 607–22.
25. Emile Durkheim, *Incest: The Nature and Origin of Taboo*, trans. by Edward Sagarin (New York: Lyle Stuart, 1963), 65 ff.
26. Norbert Bischof, "Comparative Ethology of Incest Avoidance" in Robin Fox, *Biosocial Anthropology*, 42 ff.
27. Edward A. Westermarck, *The History of Human Marriage* 5th ed. (London: Macmillan, 1921), I, 164.
28. Justine McCabe, "FBD Marriage: Further Support for the Westermarck Hypothesis of the Incest Taboo?," *American Anthropologist* 85 (1983), 50–69.
29. Arthur P. Wolf and Chieh-Shan Huang, *Marriage and Adoption in China, 1845-1945* (Stanford: Stanford University Press, 1980).
30. Michael Ruse and Edward O. Wilson, "Moral Philosophy as Applied Science: A Darwinian Approach to the Foundation of Ethics," *Philosophy* (in Press 1985).
31. Pierre L. Van den Berghe, "Human Inbreeding Avoidance: Culture in Nature," *The Behavioral and Brain Sciences* 6 (1983), 94.
32. Bischof, *op. cit.*, 62.
33. Julian Steward, *Theory of Culture Change: The Methodology of Multilinear Evolution* (Urbana: University of Illinois Press, 1976), 102.
34. Martin K. Whyte, "Cross-Cultural Codes Dealing with the Relative Status of Women" in Barry and Schlegel, *Cross-Cultural Samples and Codes*, 349.
35. Raymond Firth, *We the Tikopia* (New York: George Allen Unwin, 1936), 140 ff.
36. John Demos, *Past, Present, and Personal: The Family and the Life Course in Historical Perspective* (Oxford: Oxford University Press, 1986).
37. See, for example, Lawrence Stone, *The Family, Sex, and Marriage in England, 1500-1800* (New York: Harper & Row, 1977), 123 ff.

38. Peter Laslett, "Size and Structure of the Household in England Over Three Centuries," *Population Studies* 23 (1969), 199 ff.

39. For a sensible discussion of the complexity of family history, see Edward Shorter, *The Making of the Modern Family* (New York: Basic Books, 1975), 45 ff; For a thorough but ideological analysis of Europe, see Michael Mitterauer and Reinhard Sieder, *The European Family: Patriarchy to Partnership from the Middle Ages to the Present*, trans. by Karls Oosterveen and Manfred Harzinger (Chicago: University of Chicago Press, 1982). To complicate the picture still further, the extended family persisted in some English industrialized areas where it proved economically advantageous; cf. Michael Anderson, "Family, Household, and the Industrial Revolution" in Michael Gordon, ed., *The American Family in Social Historic Perspective* (New York: St. Martins Press, 1973), 59-75.

40. For a classic discussion, see W.F. Ogburn and M.F. Nimkoff, *Technology and the Changing Family* (Boston: Houghton Mifflin, 1955); cf. Carle Zimmerman, *Family and Civilization* (New York: Harper and Row, 1947).

41. W.F. Ogburn and M.F. Nimkoff, *op. cit*, 391.

42. Janet Margolin, *Mothers and Such: Views of American Women and Why They Changed* (Berkeley: University of California Press, 1985).

43. Ann Douglas, *The Feminization of American Culture* (New York: Alfred Knopf, 1977), 48.

44. Max Horkheimer, "Autoritat und Familie" in *Kritische Theorie: Eine Dokumentation* (Frankfurt: S. Fischer, 1968), 277-360.

45. Christopher Lasch, *Haven in a Heartless World: The Family Besieged* (New York: Basic Books, 1977), XVII.

46. Alice S. Rossi, "A Biosocial Perspective on Parenting," *Daedalus* 106 (1977), 1-32.

47. Nena and George O'Neill, *Open Marriage: A New Life Style for Couples* (New York: Evans, 1972), 40-41.

48. Janet R. Smith and Lynn G. Smith, *Beyond Monogamy: Recent Studies of Sexual Alternatives in Marriage* (Baltimore: Johns Hopkins University Press, 1974), 7 ff.

49. Larry L. and Joan M. Constantine, *Group Marriage* (New York: Macmillan, 1973).

50. Rosabeth Moss Kanter, Dennis Jaffe, D. Kelly Weisberg, "Coupling, Parenting, and the Presence of Others: Intimate Relationships in Communal Households," *Family Coordinator* 24 (1975), 433-52.

51. Judith Long, "Beyond Equality of the Sexes," *Family Coordinator* 24 (1975), 465-72.

52. Jay Belsky and Russell Isabella, "The 'Effects' of Infant Day Care on Social and Emotional Development" to appear in M. Wolraich and D. Routh, eds. *Advances in Developmental and Behavioral Pediatrics* 6 Vol. 9 (Greenwich, CT: JAI Press).

53. Robert F. Pass, et. al., "Young Children as a Probable Source of Maternal and Congenital Cytomegalovirus Infection," *The New England Journal of Medicine* 316, no. 22 (28 May 1987), 1366-70.

54. John Bowlby, *Attachment and Loss*, Vol. I (London: Hogarth Press, 1969).

55. Martin Reite, Robert Short, Ronny Seiler, J. Donald Pauley, "Attachment, Loss, and Depression," *Journal of Child Psychology and Psychiatry* 22 (1981), 141-69.

56. Donald H. McKnew and Leon Cytryn, "Historical Background in Children with Affective Disorders," *American Journal of Psychiatry* 130 (1973), 1278-85.

57. Michael Lewis, Candice Feiring, Carolynn McGuffog, John Jaskir, "Predicting Psychopathology in Six-Year-Olds from Early Social Relations," *Child Development* 55 (1984), 123-36.

58. Lewis A. Coser, "The Sexual Requisites of Utopia," repr. in Rose Laub Coser, *The Family: Its Structure and Functions*, 2nd ed. (New York: St. Martin Press, 1974), 532 ff.

59. Carol H. Marshall, "The Soviet Family and Law: A Functional Analysis of Change" in *New Scholar* 2 (1970), 57.

60. See Anthony Platt, *The Child Savers: The Invention of Delinquency* (Chicago: University of Chicago Press, 1969).

61. Elaine C. Duncan, "Recognition and Protection of the Family's Interests in Child Abuse Proceedings," *Journal of Family Law* 13 (1973–74), 803–18.

62. Jeanne M. Giovannoni and Rosina M. Becerra, *Defining Child Abuse* (New York: The Free Press, 1979), 36 ff.

63. Mason P. Thomas, Jr., "Child Abuse and Neglect; Part I: Historical Overview, Legal Matrix, and Social Perspectives," *North Carolina Law Review* 50 (1972), 204 ff.; cf. Allan Carlson, "The Child-Savers Ride Again," *Persuasion at Work* (August 1985).

64. Martin Daly and Margo Wilson, "Child Abuse and Other Risks of Not Living With Both Parents," *Ethology and Sociobiology* 6 (1985), 197–210.

65. Joy L. Lightcap, Jeffrey A. Kurland, Robert L. Burgess, "Child Abuse: A Test of Some Predictions from Evolutionary Theory," *Ethology and Sociobiology* 3 (1982), 61–67.

66. Laurence Steinberg, "Single Parents, Stepparents, and the Susceptibility of Adolescents to Antisocial Peer Pressure," *Child Development* 58 (1987), 271–75.

67. Mavis E. Hetherington, "Effects of Father Absence on Personality Development in Adolescent Daughters," *Developmental Psychology* (1972), 313–26.

68. See the best construction put upon the figures in Daniel Offer, Eric Ostrov, Kenneth I. Howard, *The Adolescent: A Psychological Self-Portrait* (New York: Basic Books, 1981), 123–24.

69. *Centers for Disease Control: Youth Suicide in the United States, 1970–1980* (Atlanta: Department of Health and Human Services, 1986), 4; cf. Barry D. Garfinkel, Art Froese, Jane Hood, "Suicide Attempts in Children and Adolescents," *American Journal of Psychiatry* 139 (1982), 1257–61.

70. John F. Newman, "Women in the Labor Force and Suicide," *Social Problems* 21 (1973), 220–30; Joseph Harry, "Parasuicide, Gender, and Gender Deviance," *Journal of Health and Social Behavior* 24 (Dec. 1983), 350–61.

71. Steven Stack, "The Effect of Religious Commitment on Suicide: A Cross-National Analysis," *Journal of Health and Social Behavior* 24 (Dec. 1983), 363 ff.

72. Nick Danigelis and Whitney Pope, "Durkheim's Theory of Suicide as Applied to the Family: An Empirical Test," *Social Forces* 57 (June 1979), 1081–1106.

73. Lenore J. Weitzman, *The Divorce Revolution: The Unexpected Social and Economic Consequences for Women and Children in America* (New York: The Free Press, 1985), xii.

74. See Rochelle Jones, *The Other Generation: The New Power of Older People* (Englewood Cliffs, NJ: Prentice-Hall, Inc., 1977), 79 ff.

75. Corinne N. Nydegger, "Family Ties of the Aged in Cross-Cultural Perspective," in Beth B. Hess and Elizabeth W. Markson, *Growing Old in America: New Perspectives on Old Age*, 3rd ed. (New Brunswick, NJ: Transaction Books, 1985), 71–85.

76. Brian Grattan, "Factories, Attitudes, and the New Deal: The History of Old Age" in Hess and Markson, 28–44.

77. Eva Kahana, Jersey Liang, Barbara Felton, Thomas Fairchild, Zev Harel, "Perspectives of Aged on Victimization, 'Ageism', and Their Problems in Urban Society," *The Gerontologist* 17 (1977), 121 ff.

78. Beth B. Hess, "America's Elderly: A Demographic Overview" in Hess and Markson, 3–22.
79. Elaine Cummings and William E. Henry, *Growing Old: The Process of Disengagement* (New York: Basic Books, 1961), especially 168 ff.
80. Gary R. Lee, "Marriage and Aging" in Hess and Markson, 361–68.
81. See Allan Carlson, "The Time Bomb Within Social Security," *Persuasion at Work* (Sept. 1985); cf. William Graebner, *A History of Retirement: The Meaning and Function of An American Institution, 1875–1978* (New Haven: Yale University Press, 1980), especially 186 ff; for negative correlation of Social Security benefits and fertility, see Charles F. Hohm, Fred J. Galloway, Carl G. Hanson, Daniel A. Biner, "A Reappraisal of the Social Security-Fertility Hypothesis: A Bidirectional Approach," *The Social Science Journal* 23, 2 (1986), 149–63.
82. Nicholas Blurton Jones, "Ethology, Anthropology, and Childhood" in Robin Fox, *Bisocial Anthropology* (publication info. needed), 75 ff.
83. Susan M. Essock-Vitale and Michael T. McGuire, "Women's Lives Viewed from an Evolutionary Perspective, I: Sexual Histories, Reproductive Success, and Demographic Characteristics of a Random Sample of American Women," *Ethology and Sociobiology* 6 (1985), 137–54.

6

In the Beginning

Man is a family man. That is one starting point for any sensible discussion of politics. Since we are not a solitary species, our social and political institutions are not made up of individuals but of families and communities. Man is, in Rousseau's phrase, "everywhere in chains" that bind him in a social order with some of his fellows and against others. Was he ever free? Augustine thought that Adam and Eve, before the Fall, were not subject to authority, but (as St. Thomas, among others, pointed out) already in Eden wives were subject to husbands, children (if they were born) to parents, and the whole human race to God.

More hinges on the discussion than might appear. It is not only political theories of natural rights and the social contract that are derived from an original state of anarchy. It is impossible to speak of such everyday policy issues as conscription, tuition tax credits, or gun control, without introducing the state's legitimacy (or lack of it) into the argument. And with the problem of legitimacy comes the problem of origins — inevitably, since it is on man's primitive origins that every discussion seems to turn.

Why this should be so is not at all evident. After all, there are many sides to this question of political legitimacy. Max Weber suggested several sources for the aura of legitimacy that surrounds most lawful regimes: tradition, emotional attitudes, rational beliefs, and legal arguments.[1] A monarchist may rely on tradition, for example, to buttress his loyalty to the king, while the various fascist parties made much of pageantry and rhetorical extravagance in their efforts to sway the emotions of a crowd. American constitutionalists, especially those of the strict constructionist variety, use rational and legal arguments to defend or attack the basic principles and policies of the federal government — often on the grounds that this or that action is illegitimate.

Weber's analysis has been influential but not, perhaps, as helpful as it at first appears. Traditional, rational, and legal defenses of a regime are all rooted

135

in pre- or sub-rational prejudices that predispose certain people to accept certain kinds of argument. What is sacred or self-evident about the rules of logic, for example? Most of the world's population continues to get by without acknowledging the principle of contradiction, and the "primitive mind," analyzed so brilliantly by Levy-Bruhl, is well represented in advanced societies. As for tradition, it was under attack even in Weber's time, while legal arguments—worst of all—depend on pieces of paper and the opinions of lawyers. Defenders of constitutions are a little like naive fundamentalists who, when they are asked why they believe the Bible is infallible, invariably reply, "Because it says so." Weber might have said that legitimate sovereignty rested upon the inclination of people to accept it and let it go at that.

It is not very comfortable to consider legitimate political authority as resting on no firmer foundation than prejudice. Even more disquieting, the nature of authority itself is a matter of considerable controversy. One of the wisest of modern political writers, Bertrand de Jouvenel, described authority as "the faculty of gaining another man's assent" or—in more political terms—as "the ability of a man to get his own proposals adopted."[2] For Jouvenel, authority is essentially implicit and dependent upon loyalty rather than coercion. When the authority of a regime declines, it is compelled to assume and exert a greater degree of naked force. The police state or authoritarian regime, is, in effect, a government that has lost most of its authority.

How do we go about gaining another man's assent? The most ordinary approach is to appeal to his rational self-interest. Many writers, especially those who have been influenced by the doctrine of utility, reduce authority—and, indeed, nearly all political relations—to a question of rational self-interest. On this view, we are obliged to obey the government only so long as it is consistent with our own interest. Any consideration of self-interest, in turn, implies the appeal to reason, because only a rational man is able to weigh consequences: "When there are good reasons for doing or believing something, such action or thought acquires a quality which is otherwise lacking." That "quality" is authority.[3]

But is it? When we assent to the government, or when a child obeys his mother, is this obedience really based on reason or self-interest? Wouldn't this argument exclude children and the subrational? Wouldn't it imply that the very rational were more inclined to acknowledge authority—an implication that is, surely, contradicted by experience. For most of us, I suspect, the quality of authority is such that it overrides any rational perception of what is, in a specific case, good for us. This is a serious problem for liberal political theory, which rests (in all its various forms) on the rational decision-making of self-interested individuals. Carole Pateman points out that utilitarian arguments may succeed in establishing a basis for obedience (i.e., we'll be better off), but they fail to provide "mechanisms of mediation between the demands of self-interest and the claim of the state."[4] In going from what a government requires to what a citizen ought to do, some notion of accepted tradition or social norm is required. Brian Barry describes the activation of such civil commitments as "cashing in on some norm" already subscribed to by both parties.[5] But whether we refer to norms, commitments, or authority, there is something that has the same savor of inevitability as the customs of the Australian Walbiri, whose "law" is ascribed to the mythical dreamtime and is thus "beyond critical questioning and conscious change."[6]

Obedience to authority may be, as Hume suggests, ultimately derived from a sense of our own self-interest but, as he goes on to observe, "men may be bound by conscience to submit to a tyrannical government against their own and the public interest."[7] (Of course, a man may rebel against authority, but that is another matter.) We pay our taxes, even though we may believe the money is used unwisely or even against our interests. It is not simply that we fear the long arm of the government tax collector (although that may enter into it). If we obey the law out of respect for authority, that authority somehow transcends — not just our desires but our reason itself. There are some questions, we feel (that is, those who respect authority) it is not up to us to decide. We may believe the government is mistaken in its policies, but we do not question its right to pursue, at least up to a point, its unwise course of action. The anarchist Michael Taylor succeeds in expressing the paradoxical quality of authority: "An exercise of authority gets a person to do something he would not otherwise have done, but . . . he will then do it because he wants to."[8]

The question is, why do we acquiesce? One answer, frequently proposed, treats laws as the rules of the game, but this approach can lead to absurd or dangerous conclusions. Some writers have pushed the comparison to the point of suggesting that we are free at any point to pick up our marbles and go home. This line of thought must lie behind the acts of painless civil disobedience that became so common in the 1960s. Do I disapprove of a policy? Then I am free to break any law to bring my case to the people. The *reductio ad absurdum* of this argument was offered by the armed robbers and muggers who suddenly discovered that they were "political prisoners," because their crimes had been committed as a protest against an unjust or racist society. A less obvious problem, but just as serious, with this argument is that it does not really get at the quality of authority. The point is, we do not feel free to change the rules or abandon the game when it suits our purpose.

A far more reasonable version of the rules argument is used by John Rawls, who argues that the rule of law is rules plus coercive force. We obey the law, quite properly, because its rules are just and because we live in a society where others expect us to play by the rules. In addition, by living in a society and benefiting from its rules and institutions, we give up our right to disregard them—the position advanced by Socrates when he refused to escape from a sentence of death.[9]

There is some merit in Rawls' version of the old contract argument. Consider the simple case of traffic laws. Custom and law dictate that in the United States people drive on the right side of the road, stop for a red light, and go on a green. An individualist who suddenly changed his mind and decided to drive on the left or go on a red, would endanger the lives of other drivers and pedestrians. He is all the more unjustified in his whimsical decision in that his own safety had been preserved by the rules of the road he has decided to defy.

The exercise of authority seems to imply the possibility of coercion, but would we go so far as to say with John Austin that law, at least, always takes the form of a command from a sovereign? (This notion has profoundly influenced American jurisprudence, which has come to regard the essence of laws to be the fact that they are upheld by judges.) There is a crucial distinction that can be made, between a moral decision based on reason and acts of obedience that are subject to coercion. Clearly, one quality of law is its ability to have its judgments enforced. But if the authority of law is based on its right to demand obedience, where does that right derive from? Laws may be written in the imperative mood, but we still are left with the old problem: what is the quality of legal authority that inclines our heart to obey the law?

The older legal writers agreed that the essence of the nation state was the fact that, within its borders, it could pass and enforce any law it liked, an idea that has its roots at least as far back as Bodin and Hobbes. A nationalist approach to law is not inevitably despotic. Under the absolutist monarchs of the seventeenth and eighteenth centuries, sovereign authority was subject to internal checks from, for example, the estates of the realm. But in modern states, there can be no restraint on the will of the people: *vox populi, vox dei*. For democratic absolutists, sovereignty is the "superior or final authority in a community, that its rules override the rules of any other association."[10] There can be, presumably, no appeal to a higher or more ultimate set of rules: neither private conscience nor the Pope can supersede the power of the tyrannical majority. If taken to its conclusion, democratic absolutism implies the right of the state to do anything it likes, so long as it is backed by the majority. Racial or religious minorities would have no legal protection, and the highest political morality would be that of the concentration camp guard who only follows orders.

There are two aspects of legitimacy that ought to be kept separate: the sovereign power of a regime and the expression or exercise of that power. It is conceivable that an authority could be legitimate and yet demand things that are immoral, make commands that are illegitimate. (This possibility is the only sensible basis for conscientious objection or civil disobedience.). We might illustrate the question with the all-too-familiar problem of a mugging. A hoodlum may coerce me to do his bidding, but as soon as he has left the scene of the crime, I shall invoke the forces of law and order. The ideas of justice, reason, or utility simply do not apply: I may be a robber baron or have inherited my money from the exploiters of honest labor. Perhaps the thief's family suffered at the hands of my grandfather Morgan or Gould. Perhaps he intends to give the money to an orphan's home. It might even be argued that he is not only compelled by his own conscience but is also acting in my best interest by drawing my attention to a higher morality.

Any of these suggestions can be puffed up to the size of political ideology by Stalinists, National Socialists, and the street-fighting clergymen who embrace political extremism. None of them has been able to confer legitimacy on the naked use of force. On the other hand, suppose the hoodlum, instead of demanding my money, insisted — at knife-point — on my saving his accomplice from drowning. The rescue is itself a moral and perhaps even "legitimate" act, although the demand is without any shadow of authority. However, what if a legitimate state should demand — as the "Thirty Tyrants" commanded Socrates — to expropriate another man's property; would I be justified in resisting? What if the government were not, as it was in Athens under the Thirty, an oligarchy but a functioning democracy?

If we adopted Bruce Ackerman's argument for liberalism, we would be unable to resist any of the mugger's reasonable claims. Ackerman's first principle of social justice is, "Whenever anybody questions the legitimacy of another's power, the power holder must respond not by suppressing the question but by giving a reason that explains why he is more entitled to the resource than the questioner is."[11] Even with all the restrictions that Ackerman loads onto his principle (specifically, consistency and neutrality), the position is untenable, not only because it is in conflict with ordinary experience, but because it leads him to endorse euthanasia and infanticide.

Most people, confronted with an immoral demand from a legitimate government, would bring up the question of human rights. But if a defender of natural rights (e.g. property rights) like John Locke or Robert Nozick, is asked the source of these rights, he is practically compelled to take refuge in one or another version of the state of nature myth. In which case, "rights" presumably are things Adam and Eve picked up off the ground in Eden and handed down to all their descendants. However, there is an older argument, one that has fallen out of favor, not of natural rights but natural law. It used to be believed that the legitimacy of positive laws derived from the higher principles of the natural law, which is, as Blackstone declared, "binding over all the globe, in all countries, and at all times; no human laws are of any validity, if contrary to this natural law."[12] The great merit of natural law lay in its usefulness: it provided a ground of fact for legality. It was not the whim of the sovereign that made law; God and nature ultimately were responsible. The distinctive element of natural law (apart, that is, from divine will) which conferred legitimacy was the fact that it was regarded both as prior to positive law and as a source for law residing in the nature of the universe and of man.

Legitimacy, in this natural law sense, is usually taken to mean a kind of morally privileged position. My possession of property or power is regarded as legitimate if, at the very least, my claim is better than another's — all else being equal. In this limited sense, legitimacy resembles the territorial space staked by certain animals. In many species, individuals seem to recognize the "legitimacy" of another's territory. An invader loses heart in a contest the closer he gets to the possessor's home base. Established right among humans functions in much the same way, and possession is, as we used to say, "nine points of the law."

But how is the legitimate right established in the first place? Consider the ordinary use of "legitimate" in English. In Latin, it means no more than lawful, but its first English use, from which all others seem derivative, refers to the legal status of children born in wedlock (the only sense recognized by Dr. Johnson). In this sense, institutions are legitimate, just as children are, if and only if they can trace their origins back to an act or condition which confers an aura of rightness. "The apple does not fall far from the tree," we say of children or of obvious family traits that they "come by it honest." Defenders of religious sects, social classes, and commercial enterprises make much of their superior antiquity or of being the "original," no matter how ludicrous their claim to superiority. There are those who take pride in being descended from one of the fanatic ne'er-do-wells that sailed on the *Mayflower*; Baptists (i.e. Anabaptists) often speak of being founded by John the Baptist (who was not even a Christian!); and in Philadelphia there are two seafood restaurants of the same name, both claiming to be the original — one because it is in the original building, the other because it is owned by descendants of the original family.

This habit of mind, which might properly be called aetiological, owes something to the Greeks, who devoted a great deal of attention to the search for *aitia*, originating causes. To the Greek (and later the Roman) mind, the first question to be asked about an institution or a custom or even a nation was: Who was the first? Who founded Cyrene? Who invented the lyre? Who discovered bee-keeping? What god caused the quarrel between Achilles and Agamemnon?

Territorial disputes and questions of precedence could be resolved by quotations from Homer (even in Roman law, Homer was cited as evidence), and the founder of a city was paid semidivine honors. This cultural predisposition finds philosophical expression. The Greek word for element or first principle (*arche*) means beginning, and a major methodological principle of Aristotle's philosophy is the *entelechy*, a process of development from beginning to fulfillment in which the end is implied by the beginning. It is a way of thinking that we have never abandoned. We speak of the sources of tradition or legitimacy, using the metaphor of springs from which a river flows. The great passionate debates in science are nearly all over the origin of things. Did the universe begin with a great bang? Did life begin in a primeval soup on earth or did the genetic code arrive from other worlds? What are the origins of the human species? There is no other reason why Darwin's theories should have made such a stir. He did not say that man was "only a monkey shaved." But, by tracing the ancestry of man back to a "hairy, tailed quadruped, probably arboreal in its habits," rather than to Adam and Eve in the Garden, he seemed to be depriving man himself of his legitimate status.

It is hard to imagine it could be otherwise. As soon as we begin to search for cause and effect relationships, at least in human affairs, we are assuming that the effect can be explained by the cause, that is, by origins. If the cause is tainted, so is the effect. Good does not ordinarily come from evil, (except as the fulfillment of a divine intent). In politics, the legitimacy of regimes is routinely justified by a reference to origins. Monarchists, for example, use a number of arguments: legal, utilitarian, historical, and religious, but all have to do with origins. The English monarchy of the seventeenth century was legitimate because: a) William the Conqueror was the legal heir of Edward the Confessor and passed his sovereignty down to his legitimate heirs, the Stuarts (with a few interruptions, e.g. the usurpations of Henry IV and Henry VII that mark the beginning and end of the Wars of the Roses); and b) the Anglo-Saxon kings — and William — had won their crowns by right of conquest; and — most decisively — c) kings owe their power to God, a power that can be traced from the patriarchs of the Old Testament. Divine right was particularly useful after the Wars of the Roses and the marriages of Henry VIII obscured the legal issue. But the main point is that both monarchy in general and the English monarchy in particular owed their legitimacy to their origins: the will of God and the career of William the Bastard.

Republican opponents of royal absolutism in the seventeenth century had a similar interest in early English history and in the state of early human society. Parliamentary legalists like Sir Edward Coke searched the old records for proofs that the king's power was limited by his councils. At the end of the century, the chief parliamentary propagandist, John Locke, pieced together his own myth of natural rights and the social contract as an answer to Hobbes' and Filmer's royal absolutism: government was based on the consent of the people, because originally free men had got together and decided to subject themselves to authority.

It would be hard to find a political system that did not base its claims to legitimacy on its origins — real or imaginary. Marxists, for example, repudiate the legality of the modern state by discovering that its origins lie in class division, repression, and coercion. The Marxist state—both its ideal and the makeshift dictatorship of the proletariat—are legitimate because it is founded upon the overthrow of the bourgeoisie and the restoration of the original condition of human equality. From all this, it seems reasonable to conclude that the legitimacy of the social order itself, of civil order, must be sought in its origins. In fact, this has been the method adopted by political philosophers almost from the beginning.

The most basic question is this: How did man come to govern himself? Was he ever free and wild? If he was, what were the conditions under which he surrendered his freedom? Do those conditions continue to have some bearing on the social and political life of modern men? No political questions have ever been more seriously debated. Plato, Aristotle, Cicero, St. Thomas, Grotius, Hobbes, Locke, Rousseau, and most recently John Rawls are among the philosophers who have taken part in the debate. From the beginnings of political anthropology, the subject of civil origins was at the center, in the work of L. H. Morgan, Sir Henry Sumner Maine, and E. B. Tylor, and in one way or another it continues to exercise a fascination for social and political anthropologists, as well as political theorists.

It would be more than tedious to rehearse all that has been written on the subject or to try to categorize all the various theories under certain headings like conquest, contract, irrigation, evolution. For one thing, not all the theorists are talking about the same thing: while older writers devoted themselves to the basic subject of how and why we subject ourselves to political authority, most moderns are more concerned with the origin of the state, which is usually regarded as a specific type of political organization. There is an equally serious problem with sorting out the theories in neat categories: many of them overlap. The theory of Hobbes, for example, is usually taken as an example of a social contract: Once upon a time, brutish men lived in a state of nature, which was the same thing as a state of war. Eventually, the brutes saw the disadvantages of their situation, and so they banded together, gave up much of their natural liberties, and subjected themselves to a ruler. Modern society is, therefore, based on that original, one-sided agreement. However, there are other elements in Hobbes' theory; force, for example. It is the lawless violence of human nature that makes the state necessary, and Hobbes seemed to have regarded the state as an institution, which—for all practical purposes—had a monopoly on the use of coercive force.

It seems more natural, therefore, to look at the possible elements that would go into the making of a reasonable theory and to note, incidentally, a few of the more influential speculations. What are these elements? It should be obvious, from what we know about human aggression, that force or power will have to be taken account of, as will man's social nature, which involves at least the appearance of free will and the ability to make agreements. Finally, no historical theory could be of much use, if it did not take into account the evolution of social and political institutions. If we use the conventional language of political theory, we might settle on power, contract, and evolution as our three elements.

Power

Man is an animal prone to quarreling, jealous of his own rights, which he is ever eager to increase at the expense of others. On a subway or at the New York Stock Exchange, he seems to deserve the epithets some of the ancients used, over and over, in describing his primitive nature: "disorderly and bestial." Plato's uncle Critias described primitive man as "a servant to force, when there was no reward for the good, no punishment for the wicked." Laws and religion had to be invented in order to restrain our natural propensities. Unlike most theorists, Critias had the chance to put his world view into practice. As a leader of the "Thirty Tyrants" at Athens, he ruled without regard for law or custom; and his ambition was the establishment of absolute rule by the "best," that is, the well-born and brave. He would probably have endorsed the speculation of the later historian Polybius, that the rule of the strongest was the first form of government.

Power does not have to be amoral or even human. It might come from God. In fact, most Christian thinking on the subject derives from Paul's declaration that there is no power that is not from God. Since the Fall, man's wickedness has always needed the correction of kings and magistrates. The association of power with our fallen state can lead to the conclusion that government is the work of sin and the devil. However, the more familiar conception is Bossuet's assertion of the divine right of kings: God has given the kings of the earth the divine mission of curbing our quarrelsome nature.

Christian theories illustrate both temptations offered by power theories. If man is so wicked and dissolute that he needs to be kicked in line — the view of Hobbes, Machiavelli, and most dictators — then Halifax was right to compare a nation to "a great galley where the masters must be whipping with little intermission." On the other hand, if government is really nothing more than the exercise of force, perhaps it is the work of the devil, perhaps we were better off — as Burke playfully suggested — when we lived in the natural state. That is certainly the Marxist view, as elaborated by Marx's collaborator Friedrich Engels. Engels picked up the speculations of the American pioneering anthropologist L. H. Morgan, and traced the states of human social evolution from a primitive, sexually promiscuous communism to the modern state, based on monogamy, class oppression, and private property.

Even though Engels probably took his theory very lightly, it has had enormous influence. In fact, there is a reasonable core to the notion of primiitve equality, despite its misuse by Hobbes, Rousseau, and Engels. The simplest societies are more egalitarian than the modern state. Echoing Engels (and Adam Ferguson), Morton Fried argues that the most primitive human social organization is "one in which there are as many positions of prestige in any age-sex grade as there are persons capable of exercising power." Eventually, societies develop rank and status along with the other accoutrements of private property. Even in the state of equality, males still dominated over females – although less so than in later times – and adults exercised authority over children.[13] There are, however, several problems with Fried's thesis. First, he mistakenly thought the higher primates were egalitarian and that his views were confirmed by the example of nonviolent and unassertive chimpanzees. Second, it is not at all clear that the most egalitarian societies – Mbuti Pygmies and !Kung Bushmen, for example – are really primitive in the sense of "original." They are just as likely to be freaks as fossils. Third, many hunting-gathering tribes are not so egalitarian as Fried would like them to be. It would be difficult, if not impossible, to exclude completely the evidence (summarized in Chapter 3) that man is, like most primates, a creature that seeks a position of command over his fellows or that man is at least as inclined to hierarchy as he is to equality.

The use of force or violence is rarely unilateral. More often it is a question of conflict. Although conflict can result in the permanent triumph of one side against another, it can also play a more positive role in holding groups together. As Adam Ferguson observed, men are as often united "from a principle of fear" as from "a principle of affection."[14] Conflict between groups very obviously draws each of them closer together against the enemy.

In a case study of developing hierarchy in Buraland (Northern Nigeria) Ronald Cohen points out the effect of aggressive neighbors on state-formation. A stateless society has three possible responses to an expansionist neighbor: they can be incorporated (or subjugated); they may run away; or they may "organize themselves more thoroughly to withstand the power of the new state."[15] Less obvious, perhaps, is the positive contribution made by competition within groups. Any society, if it is to be dynamic and concrete, must contain (as Georg Simmel insisted) "some quantitative ratio of harmony and disharmony, of association and competition."[16] Conflict can even bring together individuals and groups that otherwise might have remained apart. One characteristic of a more complex organization is the creation of alliances and structures that cut across the lines of social organization established by kinship. Apart from political hierarchy itself, secret societies in Africa and the United States (e.g. The Masons) can be formed to give mutual assistance to members, regardless of family connection. Outsiders inevitably view these associations as conspiratorial and may work to suppress them.

To what extent might conflict have played a part in the formation of the earliest societies? Walter Burkert suggests, perhaps somewhat fancifully, that the human sense of community developed out of collective aggression in ritual societies of men who cooperated in the hunt.[17] Much of the early writing on human sociobiology focused on the role of male competition for power. In studies by Goodall, Bauer, and most recently Frans De Waal, chimpanzee males are described in almost anthropomorphic terms: they form coalitions, use mock (and ritualized) aggression to intimidate rivals and even appeal for the support from influential females. Lionel Tiger outlines a still broader pattern for human males that "bond in a variety of situations involving power, force, crucial or dangerous work, and relations with the gods."[18] Young men do not usually inherit positions of influence automatically. Even the most rigid caste societies are open to competition between equals. As a consequence, human society almost always has the appearance of a parade: younger men (in the rear) struggling with each other for the chance to work their way toward the front, while at the head of the line old men are either dropping back voluntarily or are being pushed, unceremoniously, to the rear. Male competition can take many forms, some of them exotic. Influential Indians in the American Northwest used to vie with each other in contempt for wealth. Prestige was measured by how much a man could give away or even destroy. American academics sometimes compete strenuously for petty promotions and salary increases that would bring a smile to the face of a restaurant manager. This male competition is not only a fact of life: it is one of the principal bases of every form of social organization.

However things might have been "in the beginning," the individualist societies of Europe and America depend very heavily on competition as a principle of cohesion. Marx and other critics of capitalism like George Fitzhugh saw competition in the nineteenth century as socially disruptive—as it undoubtedly was—but they overlooked the possibility that it could stimulate more friendly forms of rivalry. Perhaps Walter Bagehot and the other social Darwinists were right to emphasize "the uses of conflict" in promoting the progress of nations. Only a society open to disagreement and rivalry will have the opportunity to choose between alternatives. What is more, it is possible to strive and compete for excellences that benefit the whole community. Tocqueville noticed the prominence of volunteer organizations in American life. In many parts of the country, they still contribute to the general welfare. Although it would be wrong to discount the ethical motives that prompt the volunteer firemen, or door-to-door solicitors for the Heart Fund and United Way, what gives these organizations their tone is the competitive spirit. They always speak of reaching goals and outdoing previous performances. They infiltrate business through representatives who subtly egg on employees to do their share and not let the company's image down. Without this competition, they could hardly be so successful.

Even societies that are united by kinship and common religion have ways of institutionalizing rivalry between the various levels of social organization. It seems clear, therefore, that almost from the very beginning, some men were united together against other men and that within any society rivalry and competition for power and authority play an important role in establishing and maintaining the social order.

Agreement

Man cannot live by himself. Left to his own devices, an individual would be hard put to provide for his material needs, let alone to satisfy his passions. In isolation, most of us would fare no better than poor old Ben Gunn on Treasure Island. This insight into human insufficiency, as old as Plato and Aristotle, is at the heart of every theory of social contract. It is an easy, although unjustifiable conclusion that the only universal law is the satisfaction of needs and that human society depends upon our ability to make nonaggression pacts with each other. That is substantially the view advanced by Epicurus and his many unacknowledged disciples. The Latin poet Lucretius gives the fullest and most familiar form of the myth: Men lived originally in a brutish state of lawless violence and sexual promiscuity, but sexual attachments and the arrival of children softened their savage manners and induced men to swear oaths and to commend their wives and children to each other's protection.[19]

The language of agreement was not completely unfamiliar to Christian thought.[20] In the Medieval and Renaissance struggle between Pope and Emperor, supporters of Rome found it convenient to revive the idea: authority might come from God, but the community agrees to invest it in an individual. In the eyes of Jesuits like Suarez, the political community — the state — was nothing more than an association for mutual aid.[21] By the end of the Middle Ages, the Church had come to represent the act of political union as a social contract between the people and their rulers.[22] But it was a Dutch Protestant, Hugo Grotius, who gave the theory its classic expression: Man lived originally in a state of primitive communism; however, this unsatisfactory condition of day-to-day subsistence gave way to private property as men learned to work and save. But property could only be secured on the basis of agreements. The rights of sovereignty, like property rights, also depend upon agreements made by people. Although the sovereign power comes from and can revert back to the people, it can also be alienated permanently — again, by a covenant — to one ruler and his heirs.[23]

Grotius' theory was shot through with ambiguities, especially for anyone who tried to apply it, but it is easy to see "why it should have been taken up by the theoreticians of absolutism."[24] Among the most prominent absolutists was Thomas Hobbes. Although Hobbes' influence has been enormous, he actually contributed little that was new to the contract theory, apart from a pessimistic view of human nature that is as old as Critias or the author of *Ecclesiastes*.

John Locke and other anti-royal writers found it more convenient to look on the brighter side. Hobbes had insisted that men were equal in the natural state and that this equality led to aggression and fear. Locke, on the other hand, regarded the natural state as merely inconvenient. To remedy the defects that arose from "every man's being judge in his own case," men came together and agreed to surrender as much of their natural rights as would ensure their security. If government came into being out of popular consent, then its authority continues to rest on the rule of the majority.[25]

The most dramatic contribution to the theory was made by Rousseau. Skeptical of any view of the social contract that might justify the alienation of natural rights, Rousseau portrayed man's natural state as an idyllic independence. In his "Discourse on Inequality," he agrees to "lay aside the facts" in giving an account of the natural state. Neither marriage nor property is natural; man's only innate characteristics are free will, perfectibility, and compassion for others. In the *Social Contract*, Rousseau (like Locke) concedes the naturalness of the family as an institution for rearing children — but no more. In Rousseau's Eden, men did not need government, because there was no injustice, but as the population grew, so did complexity and the need for regulation.

As a theory of social evolution, the social contract can only be regarded as an historical curiosity. As Sir Robert Filmer, writing even before Locke, was able to point out, no group of men has ever been found to agree unanimously on so important a point, and — as Locke was aware — no mere majority could compel a minority to alienate their natural liberties. But even if we follow John Rawls and set aside the pseudohistorical element of the contract, a serious difficulty remains: it is altogether too abstract. The principle of utility, what each man thinks is good for himself (or even for all mankind), is used as a sort of crowbar to pry apart all the natural bonds between husbands and wives, parents and children, and members of a community. Even in modern times, when we have done our best to realize Hobbes' state of nature as a state of war, when men and women are urged and sometimes compelled to turn over feeble parents or defective children to the state, when we are driven from place to place in search of employment, we still try to create real communities out of sterile planned neighborhoods and regimented workplaces. Our migrations are a little like the wanderings of the Trojan prince, Aeneas. More than once, he tried to found a little Ilium, where he could live upon the memories of a happier time. How unlikely it is that such a species as ours could ever have existed, especially in its natural state, as a set of atomized, self-seeking individualists.

Sociobiological theory has helped to elucidate at least one aspect of human cooperation: kinship. Since we have a genetic interest in those who are related to us, it is natural for us to contribute to the welfare of our offspring and siblings, even if we have to make some sacrifice of our own immediate interest. In a "primitive" village population of 100 to 200 people, a certain level of generalized altruism also makes sense, since in most cases we are probably more related to our neighbors than we are to anyone living beyond our borders.

Whether or not the human propensity to cooperate is derived from kin-based altruism is uncertain. We are not, however, singular in this tendency. Many primates engage in social grooming. Grooming behavior is not primarily cosmetic or even hygienic in primates. In some species, it is "the most frequent kind of social action." Some of it is between maternal care-givers; in other circumstances, it takes place between males. Frequently, high-status males are appeased and placated by their inferiors. Grooming between the sexes always increases in the mating season. Grooming can be successfully solicited, and this simian behavior underlies a pattern that is close to the human: the request for food or other objects. Since grooming and food transfer create networks of exchange, the human phenomenon of wealth and economic exchange may well be rooted in precisely such simian patterns of behavior. In this context, the old adage "I'll scratch your back if you'll scratch mine" takes on the character of the natural law.

The implications of such ethological data for economic theory are enormous. In the first place, exchange can be plausibly viewed as an essentially behavioral relationship, independent of objects. Second, exchange can be interpreted as a much more complex affair than a profit-loss transfer, since grooming and food transfer can be conducted in more than one context; e.g., maternal nurturing of children or coercion of inferiors.[26]

Social exchange, then, may arise from the altruistic relationship between parents and child as well as from the aggressive competition for favors. In recent years, the most common method for studying the price and payoffs of competition and cooperation has been through game theory. The favorite game has been the prisoner's dilemma: two criminals are caught for a minor offense. Both will surely be punished unless one of them decides to plea bargain by accusing the other of a more serious crime. If both "cooperate" (i.e. refuse to talk) they receive a moderate reward in the form of a light sentence. If one talks, then he receives a great reward (i.e. goes free) and the other a more serious punishment. If both talk, both lose.

The trouble with most game theory was that it remained theoretical, until Robert Axelrod conducted a prisoner's dilemma tournament. In two rounds of competition, scientists and game players were asked to design a program. In both rounds the clear winner was TIT FOR TAT — the simplest of all. TIT FOR TAT specified only two rules:

1) begin by cooperating
2) repeat the opponent's previous move.

In other words, begin with the expectation of cooperation. If the other player is "loyal," continue to cooperate. If he tries to improve his score by defecting, punish him by following suit until he changes his ways, then forgive him immediately.

Other strategies beat TIT FOR TAT in a head-to-head contest, but over the long haul of the tournament, it racked up the highest score. In fact, all successful strategies included the same basic elements: cooperation, swift retaliation, and forgiveness. When the competition was played out over hundreds of generations, only the cooperative strategies survived. In a chapter co-written with geneticist William D. Hamilton, Axelrod outlines a possible evolutionary scheme for cooperation: Cooperating groups are better able to secure benefits. Genetic kinship provides a possible mechanism for cooperative genes to emerge. Once that happens, even a small number of cooperators could take over a non-cooperative population, while the reverse is impossible.[27] However far cooperation can be extended, it is clear that familial relations provide the setting in which most of us learn to get along with others and extend a helping hand. The affectionate behavior of husbands and wives, parents and children, extends far into the broader social nexus and forms a countervailing pressure to the force of male competition.

Evolution

Cooperation pays off, in the long and short run, and the evolution of altruism and reciprocity can be plausibly explained. However, cooperation is not the same thing as the state. For this, a broader and longer evolutionary theory is necessary.

Evolutionary theories are an inevitable feature of modern intellectual life. Nature, we are taught from the cradle, does everything by degrees. It is only natural that we should think of man as having passed through various stages of social development. There are enough theories of social evolution to fill a volume in just cataloging them. Obviously, most accounts of social origins have to rely on an evolutionary component. In the contract theories of Epicurus, Hobbes, and Locke, man is described as evolving from a bestial state — whether innocent or savage. Social Darwinists, on the other hand, laid great stress on the competitive skills that certain individuals developed in their struggle to survive.

Most of these theories suffer from a number of serious flaws. They are almost always based, it goes without saying, on conjecture and wishful thinking: a philosopher can use the state of nature as a mirror to his own picture of reality.

What is more serious, they violate the principle of continuity by introducing great gaps into the history of the human race. In the beginning, they always seem to argue, man lived in one way, until he crossed some magic equator by making covenants or making war. The break, in either case, is as decisive as the expulsion of Adam and Eve from the Garden.

In most evolutionary theories in biology, qualitative changes are the result of a gradual accumulation of quantitative changes, added up over millenia (punctuated, perhaps, by infrequent periods of rapid change as organisms are forced by altered conditions to pass through a bottleneck). But in the theories of social evolution advanced by Rousseau and Engels, each stage is marked by clear and decisive breaks, watched over by angels with fiery swords.

Let us assume we actually know very little about human social evolution and concentrate instead on what we do know about the human species. We are not, so far as it is possible to tell, a solitary species. Despite the wide variety of social systems in the world, men are typically found living in families and those families most often are parts of large collectivities. If we should harbour any suspicions that we once did live alone, a quick glance at the habits of chimpanzees and gorillas should be enough to reassure us.

To the extent that man is man, he lives in families. Creatures living in a prefamilial state, therefore, do not fall within the range of the discussion. The oldest evolutionary theories actually did take account of this fact of familiality. In the *Politics*, Aristotle applied two types of argument to the problem of social evolution. First, he followed Plato in pointing out that, as individuals, human beings are insufficient to provide for their own needs. While families come much closer to the ideal in this respect, man only fulfills his nature by reaching a perfect state of self-sufficiency (*autarky*) in political society. "Man," he observed, "is born for citizenship." Even the happiness of an individual is incomplete if it does not extend to family and friends.[28]

In his second argument, Aristotle concentrated not on the reason for social development, but on the states. In his view, colored strongly by his perception of Greek history, civil society evolved out of the family household by way of the village. The fulfillment of the process was the *polis*, or city state. In some respects, Aristotle's vision of social evolution is not so much a theory as an observation. Schematic as it is, it touches on the essentials: family, community, and state. Although the details vary from culture to culture, the components of social organization are to some extent the same. Aristotle, like Plato, cited the patriarchal Cyclopes in the *Odyssey* as an example of the most primitive stage of civilization, in which each man ruled his wives and children. In one sense, the pattern is universal: male dominance and the household as the most basic social unit. But in another sense, the details are misleading: Obviously, in a matrilineal society, a man is more likely to exert power over his sister and her children.

If kinship is the basis (or, at least, a basis) for society, some other forces must be at work in establishing forms of association that go beyond genetic relatedness. Sir Henry Sumner Maine introduced the important insight that the peoples "destined for civilization" passed through a transition from social organization based on kinship to one based on territory.

> From the moment when a tribal community settles down finally upon a definite space of land, the land begins to be the basis of society in place of kinship.[29]

In Maine's view, the evolution of civilization passes through the stages of family, gens (a tribe with common descent), and country.

Maine's simple stages have been refined and recast into a systematic theory of social evolution by Elman R. Service, who outlined the observable stages of political development in a series of influential works.[30] In Service's account, there are three basic stages of development:

1) Egalitarian societies, where status is determined primarily by age, sex, and individual ability; whose leadership is generally implicit and conflicts among relatives are settled within families and interfamilial disputes are resolved by informal means — self-help, negotiation, ritual, etc.
2) Chiefdoms, in which the informal authority of leaders has been institutionalized and in which, typically, kinship is structured and ranked according to relative birth order of the founders and members of descent groups. This more highly ordered descent system is more in the direction of social status and points to the emergence of inequality; social and political norms can be enforced and disputes resolved by the agency of the chief.
3) States, in which political power is established along lines that cut across kinship. Families and clans still may be quite influential, but rulers like Shaka the Zulu or Cleisthenes the Athenian work to create allegiances that transcend the family, i.e. the army or voting groups.

Service's account has not gone unchallenged, but it is a useful scheme that draws together an immense amount of cross-cultural data. If we were, like Plato in the *Republic*, to draw up a plausible account — a myth — of social evolution, it would have to include a set of stages something like Service's. We should also have to spell out the pressures under which societies become more complex.

The most obvious pressure is population. The increase of population density (not population increase per se) makes territory of greater significance, facilitates the development of trade and barter, and practically compels families and clans to discover regular means of resolving their (now more frequent) disputes. Sheer numbers result in qualitative change. The dynamics of small groups are usually quite different from those of larger entities. A family business with a dozen employees, all on a first name basis, does not operate along the same lines as a multinational corporation. With expanding size comes a greater need for direction and for the institutionalization of leadership.[31]

Another pressure is competition. The presence of an external threat (often from a better organized society) can make unification an urgent necessity. A relatively unorganized society, when faced with the threat of a better organized neighbor, can either "get big or get out." Those that choose the latter either will flee to less desirable land (this presumably explains why the Eskimos and Bushmen live where they do) or fission themselves into such small groups that they are hard to track down and subjugate, or both. If they fail, they face incorporation, often as a servile class, into a growing state.[32]

The circumstances, of course, will vary enormously, and it is a mistake to lay down a universal pattern of development. Some early kings may be relatively benign; others, like Shaka the Zulu or the rulers of ancient Mesopotamia, have been appallingly brutal in their drive to consolidate power. New technologies often play a significant role. The consolidation of royal power in Hawaii could not have been accomplished without the firearms introduced by Europeans. Details vary.

Most universalist theories of evolution are little more than reflections of an author's hobby horse or the special perspective of his discipline. Wittfogel's hydraulic (i.e. irrigation) theory is a good example. Wittfogel, an ex-Leninist, wanted to explain the wrong turn taken by the U.S.S.R. toward "oriental despotism" and discovered large-scale agriculture as the key to the state. Extensive irrigation works require an intricate coordination of human labor. This, in turn, seems to demand a systematic political organization.[33]

Unfortunately, not all states emerged under these circumstances. The mistake lies in the way the problem is stated. Subordination and hierarchy do not have to be explained away as historical inventions. If inequality is a troublesome proposition, it is one that has always been with us, because differences in skill, intelligence, beauty, strength, and even luck will always play a part. In the course of social evolution, the results of good luck become institutionalized, but these hypertrophic social adaptations of hierarchy, status, law, and bureaucracy are not necessarily less "natural" than the duels, feuds, secessions, and rabbling that serve the same functions in stateless societies.

For Aristotle, the state is not only natural; it is "prior" to all other social institutions, because it is the fulfillment of our nature, which seeks self-sufficiency. In this sense, civilization would be more normal than a primitive band society. While Aristotle's teleology finds few modern supporters, his argument is worth a second look. After all, behavior does vary in response to the changing availability of resources. In this sense, at least, a species may be programmed to seek self-sufficiency.

Consider the simple example of hummingbirds that feed on nectar. The social behavior of these birds makes a valuable study, because they furnish evidence to prove or disprove the hypothesis that territorial behavior occurs when the fitness benefits exceed costs. The evidence is relatively easy to measure, since it is a question of the caloric benefit of nectar (which translates ultimately into fitness benefits) versus the calories expended in territorial aggression and defense. While territorial behavior in birds is typically associated with direct competition for mates (or for resources necessary to acquire mates), many species of hummingbird also compete for territory at other times. Simple cost-benefit interpretation stipulates "that one behavioral form have a higher net benefit than the other." In fact, hummingbirds do begin to spend energy on territorial defense at the point that aggression pays.[34]

In human societies, a similar model predicts territoriality wherever resources are sufficiently abundant and predictable that the cost of defense is outweighed by the benefits of possession. However, while in some circumstances, even sparse and unpredictable resources are worth some energy investment, on the other hand, an unlimited resource may need no defense at all. Under some conditions, human beings (among other species) do without territory or the more complex social organization sometimes required to establish and maintain control over a resource. Mbuti! pygmies, as well as chimpanzees, respond differently to abundance and scarcity.

When food-gathering can be more efficiently managed in larger groups that exploit a comparatively small area, social life must be more rigidly ordered. In this light, social "evolution" is not just a metaphor drawn from natural selection, since the link between the evolutions of species and of social organizations is population density. In devising his theory of natural selection, Darwin was inspired by Thomas Malthus' observations on the tendency of populations to increase faster than the food supply. This meant that in the inevitable struggle for survival, superior individuals — with sharper teeth or faster speed — would win out over the less able. The result would be more descendants. A similar process is at work in social evolution, as groups compete against each other for control of resources. Chimpanzees (again like many human societies) band together more densely and with stricter hierarchy in the presence of rival groups.

Competition between groups invites the application of Gause's principle of competitive exclusion to the human situation. Two species occupying the same ecological niche cannot coexist forever. Garrett Hardin states the principle in four words: "Complete competitions cannot coexist," because one species will outbreed the other. Eventually, one must triumph at the expense of the other.[35] Robert Carneiro suggests that the same principle might apply to rival human societies, especially since the members of each group will typically be more closely related to their own people than to the other. Competition, which results inevitably in expansion and conquest, has reduced the hundreds of thousands of autonomous neolithic societies down to a mere 150 or so.[36]

Social organization, like all cultural products, is the product of an evolutionary process that has resulted in the specific characteristics of *Homo sapiens*. In the most plausible theory that has been so far advanced, Lumsden and Wilson argue for a coevolutionary process of genes and culture: Genes prescribe rules of mental development, while the mind, in turn, absorbs existing cultural forms, which are altered, generation by generation, "by the summed decisions and innovations of all members of the society." Since some individuals are genetically better adapted to survive and reproduce in their culture, their more successful traits (genetically prescribed) spread through the population.[37]

To what extent this process is still operative remains a guess. One criticism of the gene-culture theory accuses Lumsden and Wilson of reducing the significance of culture and of attributing differences in human groups to genetic variation. Obviously, some differences must be genetically based, but cultural diffusion of successful innovations cannot be ruled out. Cultural variants may also have a life of their own and may also be subject to the laws of natural selection.[38]

In using such language, we begin to approach a central theorem of the social sciences: that in man, cultural evolution has replaced biological evolution. To what extent culture has a life of its own is still open to debate. What cannot be doubted is: a) the genetic basis and adaptive significance of human culture and b) the application of the selection process to cultural evolution, both in the form of gene-culture interaction and in the spread of successful institutions and innovations.

The exact mechanisms remain obscure, but Lumsden and Wilson must be on the right track in their recent emphasis on cognitive development. Semantic memory, they argue, organizes impressions into meaningful clusters. Where such clustering is cross-cultural, they can be attributed to human nature. Since culture is an artifact of cognitive processes, then cultural variation and evolution should be consistent with our mental organization when variations in behavior begin to manifest themselves. Their acceptance or rejection will be guided not only by their utility, but also by their "fit" with human cognition. A new custom that increased food production, but which depends on incest or matriarchy, probably would be rejected. Evolution is, after all, an historical process, and a species sums up the representative experience of its development. Because of the historical constraints on adaptation, successful species are not necessarily those which adapt best to their environment. One recent theory of evolution is stated as "the survival of the adequate."[39] Social evolution is no different.

In several important respects, then, the potential complexity of human social organization is a function of the organization of the mind, the availability of resources, population density, and the presence of competitors. For one reason or another, these circumstances are not always present. But when they are, as is more typically the case, then we are "programmed" — like hummingbirds and chimpanzees — to respond appropriately by developing higher levels of organization. The state may not be inevitable, but it is the predictable outcome of necessary circumstances — necessary, because the success of the human species depended upon the reproductive success of individuals. What Aristotle regarded as an inherent impetus to find self-sufficiency in the state is more like a code or strategy for successful use of resources in competition with other human groups and other species. To describe the !Kung or Mbuti as a more natural society than ours is, therefore, to stigmatize the human race as a natural failure and to treat the extraordinary reproductive success of advanced civilizations as a fluke.

Natura non facit saltum ("nature does not make leaps") was a guiding principle in the development of evolutionary theory, whether or not it admits of the exceptions that have been proposed. Even those sudden leaps forward that are proposed in the theory of punctuated equilibrium do not constitute discontinuities: Stability is the norm both for a species and for a community. And *Homo sapiens* has proved to be disconcertingly stable for 3,000,000 years.[40] If, by analogy, we were to suppose periods of great cultural creativity, that would not damage the case for continuity. Technological discoveries (like the chariot) are rapidly diffused by those who can exploit them. Certain types of political organization may well have radiated outward from creative centers in Mesopotamia and the Indus Valley. Conquest, colonization, and trade all may be vehicles of social innovations, once they have taken place. The powers inherent in law, social status, and the state may often be used for purposes we find morally repugnant, but neither the problems nor the methods of social regulation are inventions of power-seekers.

Man in a state of nature is as much a political and social creature as he is in modern civilization:

> If we are asked, therefore, where the state of nature is to be found? We may answer, It is here, and it matters not whether we are understood to speak of the island of Great Britain, or the Cape of Good Hope, or the Straits of Magellan.[41]

If man has any "natural rights," they derive not from any presumed primal state of independence. "Man has never been free," Joseph de Maistre declared in response to Rousseau. Our rights must come not from nature but from our nature, human nature, and that natural law that is the behavioral code of the human species.

Since these assertions are controversial, they need proof, or at least evidence to back them up. That evidence can only be drawn from the human record — historical and ethnographic. Rather than repeating Aristotle's arguments, the error of the Middle Ages, we should follow in his footsteps.

When Aristotle set out to discuss the varieties of political life, he did not lock himself up in a study and talk in abstract terms. He was too good a naturalist for that. Instead, he sent his students far afield to take notes on the constitutions of the Greek city-states. What is more, he even received information about the arrangements of non-Greek states, like Phoenician Carthage. To make a start at settling this business of man's political nature, we should do the same. Man lives in families, so far so good, but there are other questions that must be addressed: To what extent do families and communities actually exercise the powers we associate with the state? Even if political authority is in principle part of our legitimate inheritance, how necessary is it to our well-being? Are there natural limits that can help us to declare that some acts constitute tyranny, while others amount to treason? This much we know or seem to know: that legitimacy of social institutions depends, in the minds of most men, on their origins; and that the family and competitive male groups are the two poles around which individuals are drawn as they create and sustain the complex social organism we call the state.

Notes

1. Max Weber, *The Theory of Social and Economic Organization*, trans. by A.M. Henderson and Talcott H. Parsons (New York: Free Press, 1964), 124 ff.
2. Bertrand de Jouvenel, *Du Pouvoir: histoire naturelle de sa croissance* (Geneva: Editions du Cheval aile, 1945), chapter 1.
3. Carl J. Friedrich, ed., *Authority* (Cambridge, MA: Harvard University Press, 1958), 30. Friedrich is no utilitarian, but his rationalist approach leads to similar conclusions.
4. Carole Pateman, *The Problem of Political Obligation: A Critical Analysis of Liberal Theory* (London: John Wiley, 1979), 165.
5. Brian B. Barry, ed., *Power and Political Theory: Some European Perspectives* (London: John Wiley, 1976), p. 68 ff.
6. M.J. Meggitt, *Desert People: A Study of the Walbiri Aborigines of Central Australia* (Sydney: Argus and Robertson, 1962), 251.
7. *A Treatise of Human Nature*, III. 8, 9.
8. Michael Taylor, *Community, Anarchy, and Liberty* (Cambridge: Cambridge University Press, 1982), 23.
9. John Rawls, *A Theory of Justice* (Cambridge, MA: Harvard University Press, 1971), 235 ff.
10. D.D. Raphael, *Problems of Political Philosophy* (New York: Praeger,1970), 51 ff.
11. Bruce A. Ackerman, *Social Justice in the Liberal State* (New Haven: Yale University Press, 1980), 4 ff.
12. Sir William Blackstone, *Commentaries on the Laws of England,* Introduction II. 41.
13. Morton H. Fried, *The Evolution of Political Society: An Essay in Political Anthropology* (New York: Random House, 1967).
14. Adam Ferguson, *An Essay on the History of Civil Society*, repr. from 1st ed. of 1768 (Edinburgh: Duncan Forbes, 1966), 24 ff.
15. Ronald Cohen, "The Natural History of Hierarchy: A Case Study" in T.R. Burns and W. Buckley, eds. *Power and Control: Social Structures and Their Transformation* (London: Sage, 1976), 185 ff.

16. Georg Simmel, *Conflict* (Glencoe, NY: Free Press).
17. Walter Burkert, *Homo Necans: The Anthropology of Ancient Greek Sacrificial Ritual and Myth*, (Berkeley: University of California Press, 1983).
18. *Men in Groups*, 112.
19. *De rerum natura* V, 925–1160.
20. cf. Augustine, *Confessions*, III, 8.
21. *De Legibus* III. II. 4.
22. For general discussion see Otto Von Giercke, *Political Theories of the Middle Age*, trans. by Frederick William Maitland (Cambridge: Cambridge University Press, 1900).
23. *De Iure Belli et Pacis*, I. II. 1.
24. Richard Tuck, *Natural Rights Theories: Their Origin and Development* (Cambridge: Cambridge University Press, 1979), 79.
25. *The Second Treatise on Civil Government*, Ch. II.
26. Peter C. Reynolds. *op. cit.*, 171 ff.
27. Robert Axelrod, *The Evolution of Cooperation* (New York: Basic Books, 1984).
28. See especially *Politics* I, 1252a–53a; cf. Wolfgang Kullman, "Der Mensch als Politisches Lebewesen Bei Aristoteles," *Hermes* 108 (1980), 419–43.
29. Henry S. Maine, *Lectures on the Early History of Institutions* (New York: Henry Holt, 1888), 72; cf. also his *Ancient Law*.
30. Elman R. Service, *Origins of the State and Civilization: The Process of Cultural Evolution* (New York: Norton, 1975); cf. *Primitive Social Organization: An Evolutionary Perspective* 2nd ed. (New York: Random House, 1971).
31. Henry T. Wright, "Toward an Explanation of the Origin of the State" in Ronald Cohen and Elman R. Service, eds., *Origins of the State: The Anthropology of Political Evolution* (Philadelphia: Institute for the Study of Human Issues, 1978), 49–68. On the difference between small and large group dynamics, see Mancur Olson, *The Logic of Collective Action: Public Goods and the Theory of Goods* (Cambridge, MA: Harvard University Press, 1965).
32. See Ronald Cohen in Cohen and Service, *op. cit.*, 141–60.
33. Karl A. Wittfogel, *Oriental Despotism: A Comparative Study of Total Power* (New Haven: Yale University Press, 1957).
34. Larry L. Wolf, "Aggressive Social Organization in Nectarivorous Birds," *American Zoologist* 186 (1978), 765–78; cf. Gary Stiles, "Time, Energy, and Territoriality of the Anna Hummingbird (Calypte anna)," *Science* 173 (1971), 818–21; Frank B. Gill and Larry L. Wolf, "Economics of Feeding Territoriality in the Golden-Winged Sunbird," *Ecology* 56 (1975), 333–45.
35. Garrett Hardin, "The Competitive Exclusion Principle," *Science* 131 (1960), 92–97.
36. Robert L. Carneiro, "Political Expansion as an Expression of the Principle of Competitive Exclusion" in Cohen and Service, *op. cit.*, 205–23.
37. See *Promethean Fire*, 19 ff. for summary.
38. For this argument — overstated — see Robert Boyd and Peter J. Richerson, *Culture and the Evolutionary Process* (Chicago: University of Chicago Press, 1985).
39. Daniel R. Brooks and E.O. Wilson, *Evolution as Entropy: Toward a Unified Theory of Biology* (Chicago: University of Chicago Press, 1986).
40. For this discussion of punctuated equilibrium and its irrelevance for human evolution, see Niles Eldredge, *Time Frames: The Rethinking of Darwinian Evolution* (New York: Simon & Schuster, 1985), 125 ff.
41. Adam Ferguson, *op. cit.*, 12.

7

Order Without Law

"Man was born free, and everywhere he is in chains." Rousseau's defiant proclamation has had the effect of a tune heard in the streets. Cheap and sentimental as it is, we cannot seem to get it out of our minds. Regicides have danced, and revolutionary armies have marched to its cadences. Two hundred years later, we find ourselves, liberals and conservatives, radicals and reactionaries, humming the tune of natural rights: man in his natural state is a free individual; for his convenience and protection, he invented civil government, to which he surrendered just so much of his natural freedom as was necessary to maintain life and secure liberty. Whether we look on the dark side of the social contract — like Hobbes — or on the bright side — like Rousseau, Locke, and the Spanish Jesuits — it still seems clear that every manifestation of civil order, including the state, is an artificial contrivance to which we owe allegiance only so long as it suits our purposes.

Of course, much depends on the reference of that "our." If we interpret it to mean *us as individuals*, we are libertarians or anarchists; if *us as representatives* of the society, we are some species of republicans; if *us as the oppressed classes*, we are socialists and probably Marxists. Still, hardly anyone in the mainstream of political discussion is prepared to repudiate the vision of the social contract.

It goes without saying that many philosophers and political theorists have refused to be taken in. Aristotelians, monarchists like James VI and I and Sir Robert Filmer, and counterrevolutionaries like Joseph de Maistre all argued against what they saw as the fallacies in the theory. Utilitarians — and most people who treat social relations in the abstract — more or less ignore it. Even so, the social contract cannot be kept down. Kant took it up and made it respectable; more recently, John Rawls has given it a new lease on life as the "original position" of equality, which is, theoretically, the human condition. But in the long run, it has not mattered a great deal whether the contract was in or out of fashion, since it has remained the dominant political myth of Europe and America. It is as much the basis of American individualism as of Soviet socialism. It influenced Lincoln as much as Engels and Marx.

The clearest image projected by the contract myth is the vision of man the individual, free to choose his own way of life, at liberty to create social structures out of natural necessities. We are still repeating Epicurus' argument that language and all the forms of civil society were created in response to the need for sustenance and security. In his argument for a minimal state, Robert Nozick takes it for granted that protection of individuals (against theft, murder, fraud, etc.) is an obviously necessary function of the state, while other functions (moral regulation, benevolence) must be justified.[1] But this would be valid only if it could be shown that the state's first powers are related to protection or that it is even possible, in practice, to distinguish between regulation of violence and the regulation of morals. Nozick's line of reasoning seems to assume that in the "state of nature," human behavior was not socially controlled or, at least, not to the same extent it is in civil societies.

State of nature theories are tempting, because they seem to confirm certain cherished ideals of liberal political philosophy — the notion of rights. Most Americans first confront the idea of natural rights in the "Declaration of Independence":

> We hold these truths to be self-evident: that all men are created equal, that they are endowed by their Creator with certain inalienable Rights, that among those are Life, Liberty, and the pursuit of Happiness. That to secure these rights, Governments are instituted among Men, deriving their just powers from the consent of the governed. . . .

Jefferson and his colleagues did not have to mine Locke's *Second Treatise on Civil Government* for these ideas: they were in the air breathed by everyone in 1776.

The subject of rights is complex and has taxed the ingenuity of historians and philosophers alike. In the purest, libertarian form, however, the doctrine is simple: Human beings are individuals born with the right to pursue their own interests and to defend themselves against those who would attack their persons or property. On the other hand, if we emphasize the right to happiness or equal opportunities, we may end up like John Rawls, advocating a government-sponsored redistribution of income and property or like Bruce Ackerman, repudiating any claim to property rights unless such claims can be proved to be superior to any challenger.

These suggestions are horrifying to a libertarian who regards individual rights as an irreducible first principle. But both views, no matter how opposite on the surface, derive from the same underlying conception of man as an individual

creature endowed with rights. Since these rights are presumed to have something to do with our natural state, it only seems reasonable to wonder if there
is any evidence for such a state. A very simple question seems to pose itself:
Has man ever existed as an individual free of social regulation? Is it even possible, to say nothing of desirable?

Almost from the beginning, Western writers have entertained their readers
with tales of simple societies without laws or government. Homer's Cyclopes,
when they weren't eating strangers, were patriarchal pastoralists: each man
governed his wives and children—a realistic ethnographic description, which
influenced both Plato and Aristotle. However, most reports of primitive simplicity are more like Montaigne's glowing account in his essay "Of Cannibals":

> These people are wild, just as we call wild the fruits that Nature has produced by
> herself and in her normal course. . . . The laws of Nature still rule them. . . . They
> have . . . no name for magistrate or for political superiority, no custom of servitude,
> no riches or poverty, no contracts, no successions, no partitions, no occupations but
> leisure ones. . . .

Montaigne's American idyll did not survive contact with the native Americans,
but civilized man finds it difficult to part with his cherished illusions. In the
early 1970s, Eden was rediscovered in the Philippines. The "gentle Tasaday"
were a Stone Age tribe who seemed to live up to the dreams of Rousseau and
Montaigne. Every imaginable institution of our culture—the Smithsonian, the
Encyclopedia Britannica, National Geographic—leaped on the Tasaday band-
wagon. I recall a college student from Miami University using the Tasaday as
a rejoinder to the Greeks' more Delphic view of human nature. Without reading
the reports, I answered as any sensible man would, that the reports were either
based on superficial research or, more probably, a hoax. And a hoax it seems
to have been, carelessly contrived by a former official of the Marcos regime.[2]

The Tasaday are only an extreme example of our gullibility. There is a host
of peoples that have been mentioned as candidates for true primitive simplicity—cultures without violence, authority, or inequality: in Africa, the Hot-
tentots, Pygmies, and Bushmen; in America, the Hopi and Eskimo; and in
the Western Pacific, the Andaman Islanders and Australian Aborigines—to
mention only a few of the more obvious. In the most convincing of these
examples—the Eskimos, Bushmen, and Pygmies—we are dealing, in general,
with marginal cultures on the verge of extinction. The Bushmen and Eskimos,
for example, have found themselves living in areas that can only be described
as ecological extremes. The Bushmen, like the Pygmies, have lost out in competition with more powerful Bantu tribes and are reduced to a condition resembling serfdom. It is no wonder that they no longer make war—they always lose.

Nonetheless, they cling to memories of other, more heroic times. They have all suffered from contact with Europeans.

Even so, people must live even under the most extreme conditions and most marginal circumstances, and if they are to live, they need food and shelter, which require, in turn, some measure of cooperation. To that extent, Epicurus was correct. They also will need to find some means of resolving disputes. Even angels, so we are told, once quarreled over precedence. Tribes without rulers, government, or law, conduct themselves pretty much as people do everywhere. An American farmer in the nineteenth century had recourse to the mechanisms of government only on the rarest of occasions, and even today his descendants can lead their lives without ever calling upon a policeman or a congressman to maintain the public order, because they can rely on a wide variety of informal social controls, which can be used to maintain order either in a stateless society or in the modern state. Family structures and child-rearing practices contribute a great deal to the social order, as do the networks of gossip that constitute public opinion. Religious mechanisms of ritual and taboo also may be considered communal in nature, insofar as they work to suppress individual assertiveness. The defense of honor, on the other hand, whether it takes the form of self-help or group action, is more a function of male competition and assertiveness. Taken together, all these forces may keep the public order in the state's absence or, where political government has been established, they still may shoulder the greater part of the burden. Some areas of social regulation are essentially domestic or communal.

The Family

There is no longer much doubt about the universality of marriage and the family. Despite a diversity of marriage forms, patterns of residence, and descent systems, there are certain features that are virtually invariable. Marriage, for example, is almost always a legitimate bond between one man and one or more women. The family is, among other things, an economic unit in which labor is divided up by sex — a division that reflects the sexual dimorphism of the human species. Men are almost always responsible for hunting and fishing, while women specialize in the care of children, the gathering, preparing, and storing of food, and the making of clothing. In the terms made familiar by Talcot Parsons, man's role is instrumental, woman's affective. The power relationships in the family are equally clear and universal: Men dominate over women, adults over children, parents over offspring. In effect, the authority of the household is vested in its senior males.

In some societies, it is difficult to trace lines of authority much beyond the household. The Bushmen of the Kalahari, the Hazda of Tanzania, the Mbuti Pygmies not only lack the elements of law and the state, but they fail to recognize any formal organization of band or tribe. Numbers of families simply band together for some indefinite time and disband for any number of reasons: a quarrel may have arisen or better opportunities may lie elsewhere.

To a Westerner, the whole thing looks less like a social organization than a progressive dinner. Even Australian aboriginal societies that have a firmer view of their social identity are still without the mechanisms of formal government. Still, "The absence of individuals or groups . . . with permanent and clearly defined legislative and judicial function does not mean that social interaction is chaotic. There are explicit social rules, which, by and large, everybody obeys; and the people freely characterize each other's behavior insofar as it conforms to the rules or deviates from them."[3]

In such stateless societies, land — such as it exists — is largely a matter between families. Within the household, or even the clan, affairs are settled by the dominant members. As Lucy Mair observes of African societies, "We can take it that the inhabitants of a single homestead always recognize the authority of their senior male,"[4] although this authority may have no more coercive force than the vague power an American father has over a teenage son.

Other cultures — and this is certainly more typical of primitive societies — extend the principle of kinship into a larger social order. Among these are several African peoples made famous by ethnographers: the Nuer, the Dinka, the Tiv, and the Gusii. These and similar peoples have a social organization based on kinship, but it does not provide mechanisms for political decisions or for adjudication of disputes. In this connection, M.G. Smith distinguishes between kinship per se and lineage, which has a political character. Stateless societies, he suggests, do have government, but it is rather more a political process than an administrative structure.[5] The Nuer, to which Evans-Pritchard devoted so many years, can be taken as a typical example. They "have no government, and the state might be described as ordered anarchy." The Nuer do have a traditional code for compensating injuries, but "there is no authority with power to adjudicate on such matters or to enforce a verdict." Their social structure is segmented from the tribal level down to the village, hamlet, homestead, and hut. At nearly every level, a dispute may break out between sections. The ease with which they are resolved depends upon the level: "Social cohesion increases as the size of the community narrows." Between tribes, the only recourse would seem to be war, but within a village, personal feuds are not tolerated for very long. The obligation to pay compensation for an injury or to make peace is largely a function of acknowledged kinship, since among the Nuer — as among many peoples — the family is the only undisputed social and jural entity.[6]

Within a Nuer family, power resides in the hands of older males, typically a father or eldest son. The Nuer are a particularly good example of family self-government, because they exhibit, at the ideological level, all the characteristics of patriarchy, but in the ordinary round of daily experiences, this patriarchal power is exercised only implicity, if at all. In theory, a father owns all the property – including any livestock he may have given to a grown son. He has the *patria potestas* – the authority to beat, exile (divorce, in the case of a wife), or kill his dependents. Similarly, the Gusii homestead is described as "an internally self-governing unit," in which "the head was supposed to be obeyed in everything."[7]

In practice, Nuer fathers are loving and indulgent. Evans-Pritchard never saw a man strike his wife – it is disgraceful to be known as a wife beater. But if a father is ungenerous or unjust, his adult sons may not answer back or express disapproval. Their only recourse is to go and live with maternal relatives, but a permanent rupture is unthinkable. Normally, a father's ultimate sanction against rebellious sons is exile. In a culture where social identity depends on kinship, expulsion from the household – and the family – is tantamount to a sentence of outlawry. Any man may injure or kill the exile without fear of vengeance or demands for compensation. It is better for a man to be dead – to have joined the ancestors – than to be deprived of kindred, living and dead. Such considerations led MacIver to identify government with the family: "Wherever the family exists – and it exists everywhere in human society – government already exists."[8] If we substitute social order for government, his declaration is not an overstatement.

Even among the more well-developed social structures of Bantu-speaking African tribes, an original kinship structure "can still be recognized as the framework of their political system."[9] In the kingdom of Ankole (Uganda), "a certain amount of judicial and political power was left . . . to the extended families,"[10] and the punishment for murder was left up to the victim's clan. In the nearby well-organized Kingdom of Basoga, "the lineage principle was incorporated in the state organization" – although there were serious conflicts;[11] and in the highly organized Zulu state, kinship seniority was a principle of rank independent of political power.[12]

But it is not only in Africa that we find social organization either a function or an outgrowth of the family. The family is almost universally an essential social unit. As Hoebel says of the Ifugao (Philippines), "An Ifugao's family is his nation."[13] Family loyalty is reinforced, typically by the collective responsibility of family and kin for a family member. They are liable to share in his punishment and obliged to assist him in getting revenge.

In the modern West, the family retained considerable power until recently. Not much more than a hundred years ago, a husband could be punished for his wife's misdeeds – if it could be proved he knew of them – on the grounds he had the power to prevent them. But he could probably not be brought to justice for beating either his wife or abusing his children. Even in the United States of the 1980s, where the state assumes responsibility for the education and safety of children and the welfare of the elderly, and where the law has driven a wedge between husbands and wives by the guarantee of "equal rights," even here families probably play a greater role in maintaining order than either courts or legislatures.

The most obvious way in which families contribute to social order is by rearing, and therefore indoctrinating, children. If a child is brought up to honor and value the things that his parents — and their generation — honor and value, then by the time he comes of age, there will be little need for harsher corrective measures. The Hopi may be the most familiar example of a people relying on indoctrination as a primary means of social control. Hopi children, almost from the moment of birth, began to be socialized. They were never isolated, never forced to find satisfaction within themselves. Although they were weaned — emotionally — from their mother to the household, they were never weaned from the household itself. They were given elaborate instruction in religious doctrines and rituals whose object was to mold them into a "socially minded" individual. Community solidarity was instilled into the children even to the point of punishing the whole group for the wrongdoing of one. The constant theme of Hopi education seems to have been the superiority of the community to the individual and the overwhelming importance of kinship. Children were given a deliberate instruction in the obligations owed to community and kindred, especially respect for elders. When they misbehaved, the most effective punishment was the withdrawal of the emotional support that characterized everyday Hopi life. When fissures developed within a Hopi community, the only solution was separation.[14]

Public Opinion

When a Hopi in a village had a grievance, one recourse was to proclaim his case — literally — from the rooftops, in a chant. By informing the community of what he had suffered, he improved his chances for redress. This public address system also served as a deterrent to future injuries.[15] In all these family-centered societies, relations between (and within) families are shaped to a great extent by public opinion. In primitive conditions of extended families living in clusters of huts, real privacy is out of the question. If a man beats his wife or practices a vice, it eventually will come to the attention of his neighbors. Turnbull's characterization of the pygmy might well be generalized: "The two attitudes which disturb the pygmy most are contempt and ridicule."[16]

Among many stateless peoples, conflicts between households can be settled by appeals to community sentiment. Village elders with no legal or coercive power are able to arrange a peace precisely because they are backed up by the will of the community. It would be a mistake to underestimate the effectiveness of this "moral force," since "public ridicule may feel quite as coercive as imprisonment or destruction of property."[17]

Our Western and American individualism, however, comes out very strongly in the frequently heard professions of contempt for public opinion. We tell our herd-minded adolescents to be themselves, regardless of what others may think, and we encourage ourselves not to worry about keeping up with the Joneses, because it is our inner sense of self-worth that counts — our conscience rather than any public estimation of who or what we are. How much we really believe these exhortations — much less act upon them — is a matter for debate, but it is clear that for most of our history, mankind has been content to subject itself to the tyranny of public opinion.

Our sense of worth or, to use the older word, our honor depends very much on what others think. Honor is not an abstraction like truth or morality. Not only is it felt viscerally, but is is conferred by visible and palpable things. Achilles flew into a rage when Agamemnon deprived him of Briseis, not because he was "in love" with the girl, but because she was his prize, a living symbol of the esteem in which he was held by the other Achaeans.

Different societies prize different virtues. Americans value a certain open-handed friendliness and informality, which many of their different ancestors — Scots, Germans, Swedes, and Poles — would have scorned as marks of cowardice. The ways in which societies distribute rewards and allocate prestige are also means of social control. Homer's Achaeans valued courage and martial prowess. They reinforced these values by rewarding heroes like Achilles and Diomedes and punishing cowards like the ignoble Thersites. William J. Goode expresses this phenomenon in the terms of social exchange:

> People are willing to comply with others' wishes or needs in return for compliance with theirs, or for rewards from still other people for their actions. That is, the specific link between individual actions and the larger needs of the society is created by all the ways by which individuals are persuaded or forced to do what others want, in return for which they get cooperation and help from others.[18]

The sum total of these interactions constitutes a prestige system that governs social behavior from the cradle to the grave. It does not require medals and parades or a state pension, and while it may reinforce its claims by threats, coercion, and force, public opinion is rooted in cooperation. When an individual violates the code, a society's first line of defense is to make him conscious of his deviation — as in the Hopi grievance chants.

To be effective, shame does not necessarily require the paraphernalia of a scarlet letter, the stocks, or ducking stools. It can be triggered by the slightest symbolic gestures, which shows that everyone is aware of a transgression. Redfield reports such cases as the Orokaiva (of New Guinea): When a man finds his coconuts have been stolen, he ties a piece of husk to a stick to make the thief feel shame when he comes by. Among the Sunda, punishment for liars consists of heaps of twigs piled up, piece by piece, by people walking by the scene of the dishonesty. A more familiar (at least to Americans) method of spreading the scandal is gossip. Of course, gossip is supposed to be kept secret, but anyone who lives in a small town knows that it quickly becomes public enough to get back to the subjects. Scandal-mongering may be as contemptible an occupation as moralists have made it out to be; however, we should not overlook its vital function as a means of reinforcing community norms.

Jean Briggs, who spent two years among the Utku Eskimos, remarked on the incessant stream of gossip directed against bad temper, stinginess, and childish behavior.[19] Although such gossip may not succeed in punishing the guilty or correcting their behavior, it does forcefully bring the moral lessons home to others in the community. The Eskimos, like the Bushmen, are very sensitive to criticism, even in their homes, and envious disapproval can be a powerful disincentive to anyone ambitious for distinction or power. Elizabeth Marshall Thomas, who lived among several groups of Bushmen, observed of a successful headman that he gave away everything he had in order to defuse any envy that might be felt for his prestige.

Informal social pressures also played a large role in shaping the life of the Cheyenne. From infancy, a Cheyenne was taught self-control and respect for the elders. Relationships with relatives were conducted according to prescribed patterns.[20] The social norms were further engrained in games and sports. During adolescence, the boys were constantly praised and admonished by their older relatives. Serious crimes were punished by various means, usually with the backing of the chiefs. Murderers typically were banished for five to ten years during which they were regarded as polluted. One dramatic instance is illustrative.

Little Wolf was the Cheyenne chief who had led a band of 300 on the famous long march memorialized in the book (and film) *Cheyenne Autumn*.[21] Twenty years earlier, he had warned Starving Elk to keep away from his wife and at the end of the march the chief killed his enemy in a fit of rage. Little Wolf withdrew from the camp and, although many Cheyenne came to join him, he stayed away for twelve years, like a more resolute Achilles. Even when the other chiefs repeatedly begged him to attend a council meeting to arrange for their successors, he held out. E. Adamson Hoebel concludes his account with this:

> To him the murderer's stigma stuck . . . and because of it he could not touch his lip to the pipe with other men. From the fatal day on, he did not eat from other men's bowls. The greatest man of all the Cheyennes, the head of his people . . . was yet a man apart. Custom and the law make it so.[22]

The power of public opinion has not gone completely unobserved in the United States. A long line of commentators on the American South, at least as far back as Burke and most recently William Wyatt-Brown[23] have remarked on the degree to which Southerners were guided by the principles of honor and shame. With the advent and growth of media of communication, it has become more possible to speak of a national sense of shame. Certainly, the press has made serious attempts to inspire a sense of disgrace in the American people, most notably over the Watergate scandal, the tragedy of Vietnam, and the Iranian hostage crisis, which inspired so many penitential rituals (including several attempts at the ritual sacrifice of scapegoats). But these are political obsessions that have divided us. The recovery of unity and a sense of shared purpose and common identity often may require supernatural sanctions.

Ritual and Taboo

The social regulation of the Seneca Indians reinforced the effect of public opinion with fear of the supernatural—"oral tradition supported by a sense of duty, a fear of gossip, and a dread of retaliatory witchcraft."[24] The integrative function of religious rituals has been recognized since the days of Durkheim and even before in Robertson Smith's *The Religion of the Semites*. Communal acts of worship and expiation have the effect of affirming the bonds between families and individuals. In small communities, any number of petty jealousies and disagreements may threaten to unravel the social fabric. Unity can be restored by a general participation in a common ritual or festival. The Mixtecan Indians of Oaxaca State, Mexico, have few, if any mechanisms to enforce the moral law or ensure order. Aggressive outbreaks are rare, but fissures sometimes develop. Social solidarity, however, is affirmed by the almost ceremonial drinking bouts that take place at fiestas. The failure or refusal to take part marks a man and reduces his status. Like the Hopi, the Mixtecans rely on a system of childhood indoctrination that emphasizes emotional self-control. Also like the Hopi, ritual serves as a unifying force.[25]

In some cultures ritual may pervade nearly every aspect of social life. The Tsembaga of New Guinea have a low level of political organization. Among them, war remains essentially a private affair. However, as described by Roy A. Rappaport, their ritual cycles play a dominant role in regulating not only affairs within the tribe but also the relationships between the Tsembaga with their neighbors and with the nonhuman environment:

> . . . this regulation helps to maintain the biotic communities existing within their territories, redistributes land among people and people over land, and limits the frequency of fighting. In the absence of authoritative political statuses or offices, the ritual cycle likewise provides a means of mobilizing allies when warfare may be undertaken. It also provides a mechanism for redistributing local pig surpluses. . . .

Rappaport may have overdone the ecological emphasis in his analysis of the Tsembaga, but his description makes it clear that both war and the resolution of hostilities are matters to be settled largely by means of ritual.[26]

Religious rituals translate the social order into a realm beyond experience. In most simpler societies, this order is based on kinship: the family, the clan, the tribe, all of which may have their own rituals and supernatural sanctions. At any level of social organization, supernatural powers can play a part in easing tensions and maintaining harmony. One frequent source of conflict in any society, one that is potentially explosive, is what came to be known — as the Baby Boom generation reached adolescence — as the "Generation Gap." Ancestor worship is one obvious means of elevating familial authority to a status beyond challenge or dispute. Meyer Fortes applied the Roman idea of *pietas* to the Tallensi, for whom it is a "cultural value" that serves "to regulate the potentiality of schism between successive generations." As an "apotheosis of parental authority," the dead ancestors are able to reward and punish their living descendants for keeping — or failing to keep — the rules. Death, disease, and misfortune all can be attributed to the ancestors' displeasure with children who disobey their parents. The African Tallensi (like the Tikopia of the South Pacific described by Raymond Firth) make constant reference to the ancestors in their conversation and speak of them as if they continued to influence affairs.[27] On the other hand, a fear of filial mistreatment after death (neglect of nourishment or rituals, etc.) can restrain parents as it seems to among the Ibo of Nigeria.[28] In the United States the cult of *pietas* and family honor remained until recently a powerful influence on behavior south of the Ohio River.

There are more powers to be feared than just dead relatives. The living may wittingly or unwittingly possess certain powers of sorcery or witchcraft that are unleashed in response to social transgressions of various kinds. The fault does not have to be an overt injury. Simple envy is often sufficient to draw forth the sorcerer's power. In Latin, it is in practice difficult to distinguish between the two senses of *invidere*: "to envy" and "to look on with the evil eye." But envy is not merely a personal resentment. In many cultures, it operates as a major obstacle to ambition. It is particularly effective when accompanied by supernatural sanctions. Among the Tangu, for example, the household heads seek to forge alliance with other families and build up their powers as "managers," but the managers' ambitions are limited by the fear of sorcery, a fear that is all the more effective since it cannot be tested or refuted.[29]

Because the operation of supernatural powers is invisible, they can be invoked to punish crimes that otherwise would go unpunished, offenses that lie outside the scope of other forms of social regulation. In a family-centered society, it can be very difficult to punish certain crimes within the family. In addition to the disapproval of ancestors, recourse also may be had to the notion of taboo or pollution. Every society has a system of classification that imposes order on a chaotic universe. However, anomalies occur and menace the scheme of things: the pig that divides the hoof but does not chew the cud; the man that sleeps with his sister. These things bring pollution. As Mary Douglas explained in a remarkable book, one of the sources of ritual pollution can be "the interplay of form and surrounding formlessness." The danger of pollution lies in its attack on form. Because pollution rules, unlike ethical norms, are clear-cut, they can "settle uncertain moral issues" by bringing on the certain manifestations of pollution: disease, bad luck, and death.[30] In cases of incest or fratricide, there is often no mechanism for punishment. Among peoples like the Nuer, the ordinary procedure is to demand compensation in cattle for an injury done. That is impossible within the family. Instead, the man who kills his brother or mates with his cousin becomes polluted—no matter what his intentions or knowledge. Motivation may be taken into account by the law, but not by the powers that be. In ancient Athens, an animal that caused the death of a man would be tried before being killed, because Athenian homicide law remained until fairly late as much concerned with pollution as with ethical notions of justice. It is the absolute quality of pollution rules, then, that makes them so effective a form of social regulation.

Ritual and taboo serve chiefly to prevent disorder by strengthening social solidarity and holding out supernatural sanctions against misbehavior that might otherise go unchastized. Under some conditions, it can be a means of reconciling antagonisms that have actually developed—chiefly by affirming the unity of the community. The Orthodox and Uniate Greek Christians tried to hold joint services in Hagia Sophia during the last days before the Turks broke in to Constantinople. In Australia, aborigine "doctors" may exploit the threat (or occasion) of illness to heal social breaches. John Cawte describes a quarrel that broke out between two families in a Walbiri settlement. When one of the men developed a strange illness, Cawte (an M.D.) convinced the village councillors that sorcery, arising from bad feelings, was to blame. The councillors took the hint and arranged a reconciliation.[31]

In some cultures, ritual may be the only unifying force able to resolve disputes. The African Ndembu are a nation of individualists with an unstable social structure, always threatened with fission. Rituals carried out by lineages and villages can only produce a temporary and insufficient sense of harmony, because the quarrels are usually between lineages and villages. However, rituals performed by cult associations that cut across boundaries of kindred and village keep "the common values of Ndembu society constantly before the roving individualists of which it is composed." What unity there is derives from the moral and religious instruction given to children. One of the functions of Ndembu ritual is to handle disturbances in the social structure caused by the change in status of individuals who are made the principal actors in the ritual. Since ritual participants may belong to rival villages or lineages, their participation in the common rites serves to bond together the jarring groups and individuals.[32] Unfortunately, many nations, like the Byzantine Empire and the United States, often are as divided as united by religion, and it is necessary to look elsewhere either for more secular expressions of community identity or for more direct avenues of redress.

Self-help

"The lance is back of every demand of importance." Barton's brief statement of the first principle of Ifugao law holds true for a great many peoples as diverse as the Nuer, the Pygmies, and the Comanche Indians. Self-reliance was the ultimate resource of American duellists like Aaron Burr, the celebrated Col. McClung, and Jim Bowie (who liked to arrange imaginative contests involving a locked, darkened room and a single knife stuck into the floor). It was among the oldest and most enduring elements of Roman law that a man had the right to use violence to defend himself from violence: "Roman legal procedure was originally modelled on ritualized self-help, and for its successful functioning it relied on self-help."[33]

Not every act of individual violence can be described as self-help. At the very least, it must be undertaken in the name of right; second, it is the intransigent side of conciliation.[34] The fear of what a man might do can have the same effect on a would-be malefactor as Dr. Johnson attributed to execution — "It concentrates his mind wonderfully." Roger D. McGrath gives the same reason for the low burglary rate in the mining town of Bodie, California: "The low number of burglaries is at least partly explained by the willingness of Bodieites to fight to protect their property."[35]

If primitive society — including, perhaps, life on the American frontier — resembled Hobbes' state of nature, we would expect "a war as if of every man against every man" to be the rule, but such is not the case. However, self-help is almost universally the one sanction that can always by relied upon when all else fails. The Ifugao ordinarily demand compensation for damages when an injury has been done, but the same pride that drives the injured man to demand payment also instructs his adversary not to accept any punishment too eagerly or too tamely. It is not safe, anywhere, to acquire a reputation for meekness.

No orderly society can afford to give free rein to an individualized pursuit of justice. Self-help procedures are often formalized and ritualized in a number of ways. Among the most familiar is the duel. In the varieties of Code Duello, which governed European and American duels, it was not necessary for one of the parties to be killed: a drop of blood or the discharge of pistols often was enough to satisfy the requirements of honor. As Redfield observes of Australian aborigines, most groups provide for "regulated combat in which the blood of the offender is shed."[36] The accused meets his adversary, armed and painted according to tradition, and attempts to ward off a certain number of weapons hurled at him. The Ifugao provide a variety of duels and ordeals as the customary means of settling otherwise irreconcilable disputes: retrieving a pebble from hot water, duelling with eggs, wrestling. Perhaps the most bizarre are the Eskimo song duels, in which the adversaries engage in an extended battle of words—what American adolescents call a "rank-out."

Among the commonest methods of formalized self-help is a system of compensation. The Nuer, for example, are quick to seek revenge in a duel, but tradition—and the interests of the community—often deflect the act of vengeance to the more harmless alternative: payment of cattle. Among various peoples, a sort of nonbinding arbitration is used. Village elders or influential relatives try to arrange an amicable settlement. Such agreements are not always possible. The Comanche used a similar bargaining process but never forgot the first principle: "The ultimate power was the resort to force." It was difficult for a coward to seek redress from a brave warrior, unless he could find someone like a warchief to take up his cause. There was more to the problem than might making right; justice required that the parties' general merits be considered as much as the merits of the case.[37]

There is a more positive side to bargaining. Giving a gift or performing a favor has a way of obligating the recipient. Marcel Mauss in his *Essai sur le don* viewed reciprocity as an essential element in society that continues to operate in the modern world. Failure to repay a gift degrades the recipient. The expectation of reciprocation and the punishment of cheating formed the basis of the most successful strategies in prisoner's dilemma tournaments. Reciprocity plays an obvious role in all communities. Michael Taylor described it as a "combination of . . . short-term altruism and long-term self-interest."[38] It is only when reciprocity fails to operate that men must seek redress by the most direct means at their disposal. The very fact that self-help flourishes in stateless communities, where families are strong, may lead to wider problems.

When a man's family and kindred share responsibility for paying damages or getting revenge, a breakdown in the arbitration process can have more serious consequences than a duel between individuals. It may lead to a feud between families or between clans. The serious social consequences of feuds probably explains their relative scarcity. Indeed, their occurrence is probably symptomatic of more serious underlying problems of social organization. But when all other approaches fail—including the police power of the state—a society may be forced to flex its muscles. To enforce the general will and ensure domestic tranquility, communities may have to take collective action against those who infringe their customs and sense of propriety.

Collective Action

A society organized along the lines of kinship has one serious problem built in: a quarrel can pit one descent-group against another. In a series of BBC talks, Max Gluckman developed an idea advanced by T. S. Eliot in *Notes Toward a Definition of Culture*. His subject was "the social cohesion, rooted in the conflicts between men's different allegiances." The cross-cutting loyalties of ritual associations among the Ndembu is one good example. The exogamous marriages of the Nuer are another. In the Nuer social organization, what counts is the agnatic descent group (people related in the male line). The agnates are the group that takes vengeance for an injury done to one of its members and likewise must bear responsibility for offenses committed by its members.[39]

At first glance, it might be supposed that Nuer history would be nothing but a series of feuds and wars between kindreds. One deterrent to feuding, however, lies in their system of exogamy — obligatory marriage between, as opposed to within, descent groups. In addition to the natural friendly relations that might spring up between a man and his wife's family (from whom he has, after all, purchased a daughter), there is the belief that a maternal uncle has the power to bless or curse his nephew. Therefore, when quarrels erupt, some members of each group usually have an interest in making a settlement — if only to get peace from their wives.

These palliating circumstances are not left up to accidents of affection. As Gluckman observes, "Differences of loyalty, leading to divisions in one set of relationships, are institutionalized in customary modes of behavior." Sometimes, the larger community is continually disrupted by political factions dominated by family alliances or clans. In the familiar case of Athens, Cleisthenes tried to forge a greater social unity by creating a new social system independent of kinship. While his experiment reduced political tensions, Cleisthenes' artificial tribes and demes inevitably reverted to kin-dominated structures. An even clearer example of the effects of cross-cutting allegiances is provided by the Tonga, who lack even the advantages of a social system based on lineage. Here, what social cohesion they have derives from the endless round of bickerings, and from the shifting alignments of "intricate and overlapping networks of relationships between individuals."[40] The Tonga groups described by Elizabeth Colson also use community rituals to express their recognition of common interests. All members of the community are required to participate. Failure to take part could bring on mystical sanctions against the entire group and thus invite a collective action against the individual.[41]

A familiar ceremony of collective action is the rough music of the *charivari* or shivaree. Although in the United States shivarees are now restricted to the riotous jokes and pranks carried out at the expense of newlyweds, it was formerly used to exert community control whenever social unity was threatened with disruption: the privacy of mourning, the intimacy of marriage, the scandal of men who show they are not men either by conniving at their wives' adultery or by beating them without justification.[42] The Roman version, the *flagitium* — a repetitious and abusive chant with alternating parts — had political as well as social uses: on one uproarious occasion described by Cicero, the aristocratic gangster Clodius succeeded in publicly humiliating Pompey the Great with a particularly offensive set of questions, all answered by a mob chorus of POMPEY.

Ordinarily, however, the targets of a *charivari* are not victorious generals but unwed mothers or old men who marry young wives. A famous American *charivari* occurred in New Orleans in 1798, when a rich man's young widow remarried too soon. For three days, the home of the newlyweds was assaulted by crowds of rioters, many in disguise, beating time on kettles and shovels. Eventually, the widow atoned by giving $3,000 in hard money for the celebration of an outdoor mass.[43]

Participants of a *charivari* do not typically lay hands upon the victims or force them to take part. Stronger means are available: forcing unwed mothers to walk before the cart's tail, putting a scold in a ducking-stool, or the Gascon *azouade* — the custom of leading the victim through the streets backwards on a jackass whose tail he held in lieu of a bridle.[44] Rough music can give way to violent hands, the donkey replaced by a pole, songs by tar and feathers. The ultimate sanctions of a community are not ridicule but exile and death. Turnbull describes the Pygmies' response to a case of incest, that is, intercourse between cousins: The young man was pursued through the camp by other young men armed with knives and spears. The girls, also armed with knives but weeping loudly, joined the fray. Their victim eventually was driven into the jungle — to die, the Pygmies claimed, although he actually returned three days later. Many peoples, including the Pygmies, have recourse to exile or schism as the only means of maintaining harmony, and among certain East African tribes, men notorious for bad conduct may be killed, informally, by their own clansmen. Community consensus on such a measure amounts to a sentence of outlawry. If this consensus is arrived at informally or on impulse, the malefactor may find himself with a rope around his neck, surrounded by a shouting mob. Lynch law has its merits, but an orderly society will prefer more orderly methods.

If we turn, perhaps with relief, from Africa and New Guinea to our own United States, we shall discover that, despite the existence of government and a commitment to the forms of law, vigilante justice has flourished here as much as anywhere on earth. The South Carolina Regulators set the pattern for law and order movements across the South and Midwest in the late eighteenth and early nineteenth century. On the frontier, committees of vigilance that sprang up in California (the most famous in San Francisco) and Montana served as models for the West. It is difficult to generalize about such different places and circumstances: some movements, like the South Carolina Regulators and the San Francisco Vigilantes, turned political; others were used as a cover for settling private grudges and family feuds, but in the best case—as in Montana or in the mining towns studied recently by McGrath, these movements had a number of things in common: first, there was a real problem, an outbreak of violence or crime; second, there was a common—and valid—perception that the criminal justice system was not adequate to deal with the crisis; and third—what distinguishes a true vigilante group from a mob or terrorist organization—there was a community consensus arrived at in a solemn and deliberative manner. Richard Maxwell Brown, in his classic study, estimated that most movements were "socially constructive".[45] In Montana, the local authorities seemed unable to do anything to curb the outbreak of rustling and lawlessness. As it turned out, Sheriff Henry Plummer was the ringleader of a gang that was terrorizing Bannock and Virginia City. He was caught, made to confess, and hanged—along with accomplices—on his own gallows.[46]

A number of things help to explain the American affection for vigilantism. We cannot discount the very old European tradition—German as well as Roman—of self-help and community action. In addition, Americans, especially on the frontier, prided themselves on their self-reliance and their independence from empty formality. Law and government were all very well, but the first principle was defense of the individual, his family and community, and not adherence to due process. This conviction has very little to do with "democracy" or egalitarianism. It was more like a practical recognition of necessity. Roger McGrath makes an excellent point in his discussion of violence on the frontier. The citizens of the trans-Sierra mining towns were accustomed to rough young men shooting each other over a game of cards or an ill-timed jest. The killers, who might be better described as survivors, were invariably acquitted by a jury—to the approval of the town's best citizens. It was, after all, murder between consenting adults. But, on the rare occasions when an innocent man actually was murdered in cold blood and without justification, the citizens were not content with a due process that might turn loose the killers on a technicality. Of equal importance was their determination to turn the executions into a collective statement of opinion, a statement that the "Badmen of Bodie" would take to heart. A proper vigilante movement has all the elements of law and order: community support, a concern for the solemnities of due process, even adherence to traditional forms. However, vigilantes ordinarily carry out their work in the presence of (and sometimes with the connivance of) representatives of state authority. Their emergence usually signals a rift between community sentiments and the mechanisms of law and order.[47]

"When in the course of human events it becomes necessary for one people to dissolve the political bonds that have connected it with another . . ." Jefferson's language was a good indication that, for some people at least, the American

Revolution was already a *fait accompli* in July of 1776. To speak of Americans and Englishmen as different peoples suggests more than a political quarrel. It is a sign of an irreconcilable divorce.

When a system of cross-cutting cleavages and allegiances is not strong enough to prevent collective feuding, fission or secession may be the only answer. It appears to be the most common regulatory technique among peoples like the Mbuti, the Hazda, and the Brazilian Indians studied by Levi-Strauss. On the smallest scale, it may be hard to distinguish fission from exile (voluntary or not). At Athens, one of the most powerful clans was exiled for violating sanctuary during a civil war, and in the period before and after the Persian wars, the Athenians repeatedly resorted to ostracism — a public vote to exile a prominent individual — as a means of reducing tensions and finding sufficient consensus to carry out policies. The Mixtecans use an informal ostracism — shunning — "one of the most realistic threats for compelling conformity."

On a larger scale, fission constitutes a kind of secession. It is assumed that most societies, before developing higher levels of organization, routinely fissioned themselves whenever their population reached an unwieldy size. However, once political leadership and control enters the picture, fissioning may not be so easy — as the thirteen American colonies (and later the states of the Confederacy) learned.

The course of human events that compel such a split result in a failure to see the advantage of union. In most developed societies, even those who are politically poles apart find it useful to collaborate on such matters as the common defense. When ideological concerns, however, become paramount — capitalism vs. socialism or slavery vs. abolition — secession or rebellion may be inevitable. Even the Federalists, Hamilton and Madison, insisted on the legitimacy of secession if the central government should ever invade the privileges of a state.

Apart from the legal and constitutional questions, rebellion and secession are justifiable whenever a significant part of society ceases to view itself as belonging. Excise taxes hardly constituted a legitimate reason for rebellion in 1775. The offenses of king and parliament were trivial, but a great many people (by no means all) had come to view their country as Virginia or Massachusetts. Eighty years later, the Virginians felt the same way, but most Americans outside the South considered their country to be the United States. Under the circumstances, rebellion seems inevitable.

In such cases, it does no good to speak of legitimacy as something abstract or universal. It is a concrete manifestation of historic experience. If enough people forming a corporate group perceive themselves as victims of oppression, they will rise up. After the Civil War, there was a great clamor that Jefferson Davis should be tried for treason, but such a proceeding proved to be impractical. The government was advised that a man did not commit treason by following the wishes of his state. The amnesty given to draft evaders in the Vietnam

War and the light sentences handed out to civil rights workers made no sense in law, but they were a dim recognition that America had gone through a low-grade civil war in the 1960s.

Any of these informal methods of social control can serve as a countervailing force against an oppressive state. Powerful families that are free to conduct their own affairs will not put up with tyranny. In many African states, the ruler's mother or agnatic relatives had the right to rebuke him.[48] Public opinion — under some degree of manipulation — has been thought to be the destroyer of the regimes of the Shah of Iran and Richard Nixon. The power of religion to influence politics or resist the state (for reasons good and ill) is a fact of life not only in Zimbabwe, where Robert Mugabe was rumored to be a powerful witch doctor, but also in the modern West — as shown in the careers of religious leaders from Thomas à Beckett to Martin Luther King Jr. There is probably no point in offering a detailed account of the familiar activities of protestors and rebels who remind us, from time to time, that rulers may lose touch with their subjects.

Most of the natural social mechanisms function in every conceivable type of society. Evidence of exceptional societies only proves the rule. The Ik studied by Turnbull in *The Mountain People* seem oblivious to all family or social obligations — they laugh if a baby sticks its hand in the fire. But the Ik have suffered under three generations of externally imposed social disruption and routine starvation. They illustrate all too well Aristotle's statement that asocial men must be either lower animals or gods. The Ik are not divine.

Something similar is going on in American society, but the cause may be too much, rather than too little law. At the turn of the century, Kropotkin, in his *Mutual Aid*, argued that the modern state, by absorbing every social function, promoted the development of selfish individualism. In fact, the decay of family functions was to become a major theme in the writings of American sociologists like W. F. Ogburn and Carle Zimmerman. This degeneration was neither accidental nor inevitable but was related to the rapid growth of the centralized state since the Renaissance. Apologists for the state, from Hobbes to Rousseau, always based their arguments on individual rights: Only a powerful, centralized authority can preserve us in our liberties. The danger, as they saw it, lay in all those social forms that lay between the individual and the state — family, church, and corporate associations.

Much of this social transformation is related to the development of an administrative bureaucracy that has come to play an increasingly activist role in political affairs. While ordinary individuals may complain about invasion of privacy or infringements upon their freedom, defenders of the modern managerial state frequently argue for its greater efficiency. Centralized planning results, it is said, in a more equitable and more efficient redistribution of resources. One underlying assumption of welfare state politics must be that the state is better able to provide for widows and orphans than families, communities, or voluntary associations like churches.

Altruism is a healthy force in society so long as there is the possibility of reciprocation. Paternalism is more one-sided and assumes the inability of its dependents to provide for themselves or to return the favor. In a cross-cultural analysis of paternalism, Grace E. Goodell argues that state paternalism destroys the autonomy and cohesion of traditional social institutions:

> Paternalism inspires no loyalty in its "beneficiary," who not only has no stake in the transaction but, worse, has been used — often willingly — to collaborate in his own social negation.[49]

The state is not, in fact, necessary for effective social regulation and the growth of state power seems inevitably to undermine all other forms of social control. Perhaps it is significant how many legends of state formation or dynastic change feature some act of family violence like incest or parricide. The ancient tales of Oedipus and Gyges, not to mention the whole bloody saga of Tontalus, Pelops, Atreus and Thyestes, Agamemnon, and Orestes — effectively hint at the dangers inherent in state power.[50] Community life depends on reciprocity between individuals and, more importantly, between corporate groups like families and lineage. The groups are helpless to resist the overpowering generosity of state bureaucracies.

Part of the problem may have to do with the politicization of government administration to which M. G. Smith has drawn attention. While politics should involve a competition for power, administrative government is inherently hierarchic. The political process encourages individuals to work through groups — hence the familiar and misguided complaint about "interest groups" — and may actually serve to confirm traditional social institutions, while the administrative side of government is more static and monolithic.[51] When administrative structures begin to decide on questions of policy (which happens in the Soviet Union and increasingly in the managerial states of Europe and the United States), government begins to regard the various corporate groups as divisive and will seek to liquidate them. The American legal system exemplifies this evolution from community to bureaucracy. Increasingly, the official legal system has come to be invested with all authority for maintaining order and resolving conflicts. There is, it seems, an "inverse relationship" between law and less formal methods of social control. The more police there are, the more we rely on them, and the more we rely on the police, the less able we are to resolve our problems. Recently, a number of students of American violence have come to the conclusion that neighborhood organizations may do a better job than the police of maintaining security in the inner city. In the words of Paul J. Lavrakas, "a caring and vigilant citizenry" should be the first line of defense and the police held in reserve "as *fall-back* mechanisms when things go wrong."[52]

Laws, of course, have a function. As societies develop greater complexity, it becomes increasingly necessary to discover more formal mechanisms for resolving problems. Writing down the customary law or drawing up a new code often constitutes a major breakthrough that can only be performed by culture heroes like the Sumerian Urukagina, the Babylonian Hammurabi, the Athenians Draco and Solon, to say nothing of emperors like Justinian and Napoleon. It usually takes a man of blood and iron to reform the law. This is due not to the wickedness of rulers so much as to the conservatism of lawyers. Law may arise in response to social needs, but it soon comes to have a life of its own. Because it is "the culture of lawyers,"[53] legal professionals tend to look upon the law as "the true embodiment of everything that's excellent," rather than as a series of decisions and compromises arrived at by fallible judges arbitrating petty quarrels. Legal philosophers like John Austin wrote of their subject as if it could be reduced to abstract rules, while Ronald Dworkin continues to assert that judges must arrive at their decisions on the basis of principle, a view that elevates the courts above all political debate and makes them the only proper forum for settling the most serious questions of social ethics.[54]

By converting law into a set of abstract and universal principles, divorced from its historic context, legal philosophers contribute to the process by which a legal system is transformed from a tool for resolving conflict into a weapon of government power. The less we rely on prescriptive right and the traditions of our communities, the more prone we are to accept the state as "a mortal god" whose authority does not lie in the circumstances of life lived together, generation after generation, but from abstract principles of right, which the god discovers and enforces.

Even among civilized peoples, a great deal is left up to informal methods. In his *Anabasis*, Xenophon describes how an army of 10,000 Greek mercenaries in the heart of the hostile Persian empire managed to fight their way out. After the death of their Persian commander, they turn to a Spartan general, Clearchus, whom they obeyed:

> Not because they had chosen him, but because they saw that he alone had the necessary wisdom.

When Clearchus and the other generals are treacherously murdered by the Persians, the soldiers find new leaders — one an experienced Spartan, the other an Athenian amateur and student of Socrates, Xenophon himself. The remarkable thing about the retreat of the 10,000 was not so much their military victories but their ability to elect leaders and obey them. By necessity, they submerged their inter-Greek hostilities (Sparta and Athens had recently been at war) in a common front against "barbarians." In their speeches, the generals dwell on two themes over and over: the superiority of the Greeks and the favor of the gods. Not only have armies repeatedly defeated barbarian hosts many times their number, but now they will have divine support since the Persians have violated their oaths. Their sense of unity must have been powerful, since Xenophon was to spend most of his life as a naturalized Spartan.

One more example: I spent eight years in a Southern fishing village with a population of about 500. The great questions that agitated the natives included domestic disputes, a fight over zoning, plans to pave dirt roads, and a struggle for control over churches and the school. In nearly every case, disputes were resolved by appeals to family loyalty, gossip (women over coffee, their husbands down at the dock), threats, and even something approaching a shivaree, in which teenagers bombarded the school principal's house with garbage and firecrackers. The law was rarely called in. If a boy vandalized a store or the school, a few older men met with the offender and his parents to work something out.

Much of the trouble came from outsiders, men of authority whose views differed sharply from the community's: the doctor, several ministers, and the school principal. The response of both sides varied, but the community usually won in the end. The doctor was, of the outsiders, the most stiff-necked but also the most necessary. For his own sanity, he and his family stayed in their house in the woods and had virtually no influence on community decisions. Preachers with strange ideas, on the other hand, were not indispensable. In the Methodist Church, it was possible to wait a man out, since their ministers usually were transferred in two years. The democratic Baptists were more direct and fired, at the drop of a hat, any preacher they took a disliking to. The Presbyterians, confronted with a likeable but moderately liberal minister, fissioned, while the tiny group of Episcopalians simply went to the Bishop when a man got too arbitrary and continued to hold services at the inconvenient (especially during summer) hour of 11:00.

Shame remained the most powerful force. Talking to a group of teenagers about MacBeth's passion for his wife, I heard one of the girls pipe up with, "You mean like Norma's mama and my uncle." Norma blushed, but what could she say? Everybody knew the story. At least three different people claimed to be the only one to know the reason why a distinguished old man never entered the church so long as the old warden was alive—the warden knew the dark secret of his birth. Men and women who did something foolish would be punished by hearing the "funny story" the rest of their lives. Some moved away for years (like Norma's mother) to escape, but they generally returned. Newcomers, on the other hand, often could endure the community for no more than two years. Charmed by the quaint old houses and close family ties, they moved in desperately to recover a lost sense of *Gemeinschaft*, but the harder they tried to fit in, the unhappier they became. Real communities are all too much like the religion of Zoroaster. You can never join, you must be born into them.

Informal methods continue to play an important role in American society. They may prove to be preferable, in many instances, to the coercive powers of the state. Their continued existence illustrates the futility of any political philosophy that takes, as its first principle, the anarchic individualism of the natural man.

"Man, born in a family, is compelled to maintain society" is Hume's answer to the social contract — echoing Aristotle, St. Thomas, and Sir Robert Filmer. No society can function without some means of enforcing norms or finding redress for injuries. The notion of individual rights, as useful as it may be in some settings, obscures the true bases of civil order by investing these rights in the individual, instead of in family, kin, and community. Nor is it any use to appeal, like Epicurus, Hume, and certain social psychologists, to natural necessities as the roots of society. It is not primarily the need for food and protection that makes the Mbuti sociable. Man born of woman cannot live without other men, and, since he must live with them, he has been designed as a social animal.

Our social nature is not something we are free to choose: it is a given. Revolutionary projects that begin by declaring the absolute freedom of the human species degenerate rapidly into the anomic bestiality of caged rats and street hoodlums. The anthropologist Elizabeth Colson, reflecting on her experiences at Berkeley during "the Revolution," concluded that "we may be free to negotiate with our fellows about a great many things, but one thing we are not free to negotiate and that is the freedom to do as we will."[55] Whatever our moral freedom consists of, it is closer to the stoic conception of living in accordance with nature than to Rabelais', "Do what you will."

To this extent, Edmund Burke's probably tongue-in-cheek *Vindication of Natural Society* is correct:

> The mutual Desires of the Sexes uniting their Bodies and Affections, and the Children, which were the Results of those Intercourses, introduced first the Notion of Society, and taught its Conveniences. . . .

Society is natural. How far we may go in considering the specific mechanisms of political society as natural is another question. However, at least two elements of political organization appear to have a basis in nature: leadership and group identity. There is substantial evidence that human males, like other primates, have a natural tendency to assert themselves at the expense of others, to pursue positions of higher status and influence. The pursuit of power can be hindered or even checked by cultural forces — as among the Hopi and the

!Kung — but the existence of celibate priests does not discredit the naturalness of sex.

A leader without followers does not amount to much. Since the 1950s, sociologists and social psychologists have been studying the tendency of individuals — even those brought together randomly or in laboratory situations — to form social groups.

If, even apart from families, we have a natural tendency to form groups, promote leaders, and develop rules and status systems — as studies of group formation and hierarchy seem to indicate — then we have to wonder still more about man in the natural state. Were Adam and Eve, along with their children, ruthless individualists like the Ik, or were they inclined, as we are, to share and cooperate, to lead and to follow? What we know of man leads us to believe that the roots of government were buried deep in the earth of Eden or the savannahs of Southern Africa, where anthropologists now locate the Garden.

Notes

1. Robert Nozick, *Anarchy, State, and Utopia* (New York: Basic Books, 1974), 26 ff.
2. See "Tangled Tale" in *The Wall Street Journal*, 15 September 1986.
3. M.J. Meggitt, *Desert People: A Study of Walbiri Aborigines of Central Australia* (Sydney: Argus and Robertson, 1962), 251.
4. Lucy Mair, *Primitive Government* (Bloomington: Indiana University Press, 1962), 55.
5. M.G. Smith, "On Segmentary Lineage Systems," *Journal of the Royal Anthropological Institute* 86 (1956), 13–70.
6. E.E. Evans-Pritchard, *The Nuer* (Oxford: Clarendon Press, 1940), 5.
7. Robert A. and Barbara B. Levine, "Nyasongo: A Gusii Community in Kenya," in Beatrice Whiting, ed., *Six Cultures: Studies of Child Rearing* (London: John Wiley, 1963), 36 ff.
8. Robert MacIver, *The Web of Government* (New York: Macmillan, 1965), 20.
9. Meyer Fortes and E.E. Evans-Pritchard eds., *African Political Systems*, (London: Oxford University Press, 1940), 83 ff.
10. K. Oberg, "The Kingdom of Ankole in Uganda" in Fortes and Evans-Pritchard *op. cit.*, 130 ff; and John Roscoe, *The Banyankole* (Cambridge: Cambridge University Press, 1923), 20.
11. Lloyd A. Fallers, *Bantu Bureaucracy: A Century of Evolution Among the Basoga of Uganda*, 2nd ed. (Chicago: University of Chicago Press, 1965), 227 ff.
12. Max Gluckman, "The Kingdom of the Zulu in South Africa," in Fortes and Evans-Pritchard, 36 ff.
13. R.F. Barton, *Ifugao Law*, repr. from 1919 ed. (Berkeley: University of California Press, 1969), 92.
14. Laura Thompson, *Culture in Crisis: A Study of the Hopi Indians* (New York: Russell and Russell, 1973); Dorothy Eggan, "Instructions and Affect in Hopi Cultural Continuity" in Y.A. Cohen ed., *Man in Adaptation: The Institutional Framework*, (Chicago: Aldine, 1971).
15. R.D. Black, "Hopi Grievance Chants: A Mechanism of Social Control," in D. Hymes and W.E. Brittle, eds., *Studies in Southwestern Ethnolinguistics* (The Hague: Mouton, 1967).

16. Colin M. Turnbull, *The Forest People: A Study of the Pygmies of the Congo* (New York: Touchstone/Simon & Schuster, 1962), 114.

17. Robert Redfield, "Primitive Law" in Paul Bohannon, ed., *Law and Warfare: Studies in the Anthropology of Conflict* (Austin: University of Texas Press), 15.

18. William J. Goode, *The Celebration of Heroes: Prestige as a Control System* (Berkeley: University of California Press, 1978), 141.

19. Jean L. Briggs, *Never in Anger: Portrait of an Eskimo Family* (Cambridge: Harvard University Press, 1970).

20. Elizabeth Marshall Thomas, *The Harmless People* (New York: Alfred Knopf, 1958).

21. Fred Eggan, ed., *Social Anthropology of North American Tribes* (Chicago: University of Chicago Press, 1937), Vol. I, 49 ff.

22. E. Adamson Hoebel, *The Cheyenne Way*, 84 ff.

23. William Wyatt Brown, *Southern Honor: Ethics & Behavior in the Old South* (New York: Oxford University Press, 1982).

24. Anthony Wallace, *The Death and Rebirth of the Seneca* (New York: Knopf, 1970), 25.

25. Beatrice Whiting, ed., *Six Cultures: Studies of Child Rearing* (New York: John Wiley, 1963), 611.

26. Roy A. Rappaport, "Ritual Regulation of Environmental Relations Among a New Guinea People," *Ethnology* 6 (1967), 17–30.

27. Meyer Fortes, "Pietas in Ancestor Worship" in Y.A. Cohen, ed., *Man in Adaptation*, 207–25.

28. C.K. Meek, *Law and Authority in a Nigerian Tribe* (London: Oxford University Press, 1937).

29. K.O.L. Burridge, "Disputing in Tangu" in Bohannon, *Law & Warfare*, 206 ff.

30. Mary Douglas, *Purity and Danger: An Analysis of the Concepts of Pollution and Taboo* (London: Routledge & Kegan Paul, 1984).

31. John Cawte, *Medicine is the Law: Studies in Psychiatric Anthropology of Australian Tribal Societies* (Honolulu: University Press of Hawaii, 1974), 37 ff.

32. V.W. Turner, *Schism and Continuity in an African Society* (Manchester: Manchester University Press, 1957).

33. A.W. Lintott, *Violence in Republican Rome* (Oxford: Clarendon Press, 1968).

34. Sally F. Moore, "Legal Liability and Evolutionary Interpretation: Some Aspects of Strict Liability, Self-Help, and Collective Responsibility" in Max Gluckman, ed., *The Allocation of Responsibility* (Manchester: Manchester University Press, 1972).

35. Roger D. McGrath, *Gunfighters, Highwaymen & Vigilantes: Violence on the Frontier* (Berkeley: University of California, 1984).

36. Redfield, *op. cit.*, 11.

37. E.A. Hoebel, "Law-Ways of the Comanche Indians" in Bohannon, *Law and Warfare*, 193.

38. Michael Taylor, *Community, Anarchy, and Liberty*, 36.

39. Max Gluckman, *Custom and Conflict in Africa* (Oxford: Basil Blackwell, 1956). Similar points have also been made by Georg Simmel and S.M. Lipsett; cf. E.E. Evans-Pritchard, *Kinship and Marriage Among the Nuer* (Oxford: Clarendon Press, 1959).

40. J. Van Velsen, *The Politics of Kinship: A Study in Social Manipulation Among the Lakeside Tonga of Nyasaland* (Manchester: Manchester University Press, 1964), 288.

41. Elizabeth Colson, *The Plateau Tonga, Social and Religious Studies* (Manchester: Manchester University Press, 1962).

42. Edward Shorter, *The Making of the Modern Family*, 218 ff.
43. William Wyatt-Brown, *op. cit.*
44. Christian Desplat, *Charivaris en Gascogne: La "morale des peuples" du XVI au xxe siecle* (Paris: Collection Territoires, Bibliotheque Berger-Levrault, 1982).
45. Richard Maxwell Brown, *Strain of Violence: Historical Studies of American Violence and Vigiliantism* (New York: Oxford University Press, 1975).
46. Thomas J. Dimsdale, *The Vigilantes of Montana* (Helena: State Publishing Company, 1915).
47. D. Black and M.P. Baumgartner, "On Self-Help in Modern Society" in *The Manners and Customs of the Police* (New York: Academic Press, 1980).
48. John Beattie, "Checks on the Abuse of Political Power in Some African States: A Preliminary Framework for Analysis," *Sociologus* 9, No. 2 (1959), 97–115.
49. Grace E. Goodell, "Paternalism, Patronage, and Potlatch: The Dynamics of Giving and Being Given To," *Current Anthropology* 26 (1985), 247–66.
50. Georges Balandier, *Political Anthropology*, trans. by A.M. Sheridan Smith (New York: Rand House/Pantheon Books, 1970), 57.
51. M.G. Smith, *op. cit.*
52. Paul J. Lavrakas, "Citizen Self-Help" in Lynn A. Curtis, *American Violence and Public Policy* (New Haven: Yale University Press, 1985), 88.
53. Alan Watson, *The Evolution of Law* (Baltimore: Johns Hopkins University Press, 1985), 118.
54. Ronald Dworkin, *A Matter of Principle* (Cambridge, MA: Harvard University Press, 1985), 33 ff.
55. Elizabeth Colson, *Tradition and Contract: The Problem of Order* (Chicago: Aldine Press, 1970), 4 ff.

8

The Federal Principle

There is a great distance between troops of baboons or stateless societies and the modern nations of Europe and America. And yet, if there is any force to the argument from human nature, it is circumstances and conditions that change, not man. It should be possible to address some questions of social and political ethics as universal codicils to the human constitution. A theory of natural politics, if it did not clarify the problems faced by citizens in the industrial democracies, would be little more than a curiosity, as interesting to practical men and women as stamp collecting or particle physics.

What can we say about any of the following pressing problems that come in and out of fashion? The North-South dialogue between industrial and underdeveloped nations, state regulation of private and religious schools, draft registration, forced busing, a national ban on abortion, censorship, anti-nuclear protest, illegal immigration? In one way or another, each of these issues is concerned with the responsibility of governments and the duty of citizens. An equally pressing problem — a favorite question for writers on social ethics — is posed by Third World poverty: To what extent do private citizens have a social obligation to help citizens of other countries?

Well-intentioned men and women make up their minds on these issues without troubling themselves overmuch with ethical theory. Those who call themselves "conservative" are likely to favor the draft and a ban on abortion while denouncing the "sanctuary movement" and forced busing. They will be typically more willing to help American allies like Israel but oppose aid to less friendly nations. Those who call themselves liberal will argue that the state has a legitimate role in guaranteeing social equality through forced busing, while individuals should be free to follow the dictates of conscience in opposing the state or buying a magazine. They are more likely to favor aid to Nicaragua or North Vietnam.

The important thing to note about these positions is not the differences but the points in common. Both presuppose a society of individualists acting under or against a nation state with broadly defined powers. The two views share a broad common ground: both sides wish to use the power of the state to advance an agenda. It is only on matters of detail that they part company.

This broad agreement is a tribute to the persuasive power of liberal ethics. For the purposes of this discussion, "liberal" refers to the ethical and political views of most philosophers since Hobbes, including Locke, Rousseau, the utilitarians as well as contemporary writers like Bernard Williams, John Rawls, Robert Nozick, Bruce Ackerman, and James Fishkin.

A figure typical in many ways is Adam Smith. Best known for his economic theory of free-market capitalism, Smith also was a moral philosopher of high repute. In *The Theory of Moral Sentiments*, Smith provided a deistic and liberal theory of morals that anticipated libertarianism but also appealed to conservatives like Hume and Burke. Although Smith's admirers like to point to his ethical theory as proof of a higher moral conscience than what appears in *The Wealth of Nations*, his thought is really all of a piece: the free and rational individual is everything. Throughout, the talk is of self-love, individual conscience, and the justice that prevails among equals. Men are fitted for society because they "stand in need of each other's assistance" — the standard Epicurean view; family relationships arise out of the habitual sympathy that results from living together, rather than from biological instincts: "I consider what is called natural affection is more the effect of the moral than of the supposed physical connection between the parent and the child." For Smith, the highest type of morality is universal benevolence, which he elevates above the discharge of rooted responsibilities. Individual self-interest is at the heart of our decision making, while the ultimate arbiter of our conduct is the hypothetical "impartial spectator," to whom he appeals repeatedly.

Individualism, rational self-interest, habit (as opposed to nature), universality, and impartial judgment — are all prime requisites for liberal theory. Individualism has received special emphasis from Bentham and Mill, while universal benevolence has been stressed by Marx, Rawls, and Bruce Ackerman; but these are variations on a theme. Outside of a few distinguished dissidents, liberalism has been established as the language of ethics.

Much of this writing is highly abstract, filled with symbolic formulas and hypothetical cases: Suppose an individual (I) in a leaking lifeboat with his pregnant wife, Mahatma Gandhi, and a German Shepherd. He must get rid of at least 40 pounds of passenger (P) to save the boat from sinking. Whom (or what) is he to sacrifice? Various answers might be given, depending on the order of priorities. In the view of some (say, Tom Regan) the dog has a higher claim, at least, than the unborn child, and perhaps more than all the rest: as a dependent and exploited creature, he must deserve our loyalty. In another view, it is the saintly Gandhi (or Dr. Schweitzer or Mother Teresa) who must be saved because of his service to mankind.

Now, the response of an ordinary decent man might be something like this: Feed the dog to your wife and unborn baby and, if necessary, tell the foreigner to swim for it. Put simply, natural obligations are felt to take precedence over any general principle. From the previous discussion, it should be clear that his argument is not only natural but comes closer to moral reality than the tortured arguments of some academic philosophers.

The obligation of men to take care of wives and children is at the root of the social order. Marriage and the family are a special relationship, both natural and social, which impose peculiar obligations on husbands and wives, parents and children. Without these primary, natural obligations, no other form of rights or duties makes any sense. The course of human life is something like the progress of social evolution: we begin life utterly dependent upon the family and ignorant of any other mode of existence. Little by little, we become aware of cousins and neighbors, of our town and region, and eventually form some concept of a nation to which we owe our allegiance. If we live long enough, we begin to see that even the nation is bound up in social and moral relationships with other nations, and that these international relations may impose a burden upon us as citizens—to subsidize an ally with tax money or to fight in a war, which, at first sight, seems to concern us very little. A major shift seems to occur on the threshold of adolescence, between the ages of eleven and thirteen. Younger adolescents are egocentric authoritarians who cannot grasp the concept of institutions or social obligation: "As adolescence advances, the youngster is increasingly sensitive to the fact of community and its claims upon the citizen."[1]

In a broad way, our ethical ontogeny recapitulates the social phylogeny of the human race, and the ethical concerns of ordinary people reflect the social evolution that most of us have undergone. A proper theory of social responsibility—the heart of all serious political discussion—should take account of this natural development, and a proper political system would incorporate and utilize the facts of life rather than try to conceal or destroy them. These concerns put us back on the familiar ground of natural law.

Since a healthy family background is a primary requirement for the development of children into ethically responsible adults, one primary political postulate emerges: Governments should make no law, pursue no policy, whose anticipated effect will be to diminsh the integrity or responsibility of the family in its legitimate sphere of activities. A corollary to this principle would read: Wherever any law or policy proves to be destructive of the family, it ought to be reversed as quickly as possible.

Among the government policies that deserve scrutiny are: no-fault divorce, compulsory school attendance, social security, aid to families with dependent children, sex education and values classes in public schools, and any "equal rights" legislation that calls into question the distinct functions and duties of mothers and fathers. All of these matters were taken up in the course of discussing the family, but it is important now to see them in a broader context, in which the family is not so much a valuable institution in its own right as it is the indispensable foundation for human life seen in its moral, social, and political aspects:

> The value of the family depends on its value as the foundation of the moral order. . . . The family is not only the most common moral net but inherently the strongest, by reason of its foundation in human social instincts. [Whatever a society's values] . . . it will practice those values better if it expects the family to impart them to the children.[2]

The usual arguments must, in this light, be reversed: it has been common to say that, while family unity is basically a good thing, a sentimental concern for traditional institutions must not interfere with higher social obligations: children must be educated, after all, and old people taken care of. Now, however, we should learn to say that education and welfare are good things, but we must not allow sentiment or piety to undermine the very foundations of all social life; that it would be better for large numbers of children to grow up ignorant (although that by no means follows) than to destroy the possibility of children ever growing up at all. Our decisions ought to be governed, if the species is to survive and prosper, not by pieties — Marxist, liberal, and capitalist — but by the facts of life.

In our rough scheme of social evolution, it became evident that the political forces that go to make up the state collect around the two poles of community and society. Viewed historically, this distinction has serious implications for political life in advanced societies. The terms themselves are worth exploring.

Community is not an easy concept to define. One writer found 94 distinct definitions, the only common term being "people" — although a biologist would have something to say about that. The distinction between *Communitas* and *Societas* (or *Gemeinschaft* und *Gesellschaft*) is older than Toennies', who did so much to give the terms a useful philosophical precision. (My own usage will be rougher and depend more on common speech, but it does not differ materially from Toennies and his successors.) The underlying notion of community might be described as shared experience, while society usually implies purposeful association and affiliation.

Many writers have emphasized the organic, all-encompassing unity of community. Redfield speaks of "an ecological system," Marcel Mauss refers to social totality, and René König describes "a global society . . . a term of a order superior to family, neighborhood, profession."[3] Is there such a "thing" as community? In the social sciences, it is all too easy to confuse discovery with invention, to assume that, because a name has been found, there is a reality to match it. In this sense, community is sometimes written about abstractly and generically, as if it were an easily identifiable class of social relations. It is not so easy. The task is, instead, to walk in the footsteps of Toennies and Robert Nisbet, who tracked this chimera through the forests and marshes of historical experience.

One of the most useful investigations of community is Robert Redfield's *The Little Community*.[5] Rather than offering definitions or analysis, Redfield explored the interrelations between various levels of community identity in a small set of quite different examples. Following Redfield's lead, it is useful to look not for such a thing as community but for social relations that exhibit, to some degree, the hallmarks of community life. We are looking, not so much for an institution, (e.g. kinship structures or political forms) as a quality — like purpleness — which can turn up in a variety of circumstances. The difference is that, with a color, we know intuitively what we are looking for, since color perception is based on the spectrum and on human neurophysiology. For community, we need at least a few signposts.

Talcott Parsons, in his usual methodical fashion, once spelled out four characteristics of *Gemeinschaft* versus *Gesellschaft*: affectivity (vs. affective neutrality), particularism (vs. universalism), ascription (vs. achievement), and diffuseness (vs. specificity).[6] Put less schematically, community relations might be characterized by feeling and irrational attachments; they spring from and are connected to real people and places, rather than abstract and universal principles (people in a community probably could not tell you what a community is), and they encourage members to judge each other not so much on the basis of what they've done but of who they are as members of the community. In this connection, Maine's old distinction between status and contract can be used as a tool for distinguishing between community and society: Status is inherited from the community, while contracts are achieved by allies, partners, colleagues — *socii*, i.e. members of a society.

The purest forms of community are those relationships into which we are born and which we grow up accepting as the natural conditions of our existence. (Thomas Bender speaks of "the we-ness" in a community.) In this sense, the immediate family is the communal institution par excellence, but the extended family is typically taken for granted in much the same way. In a static, traditional culture, the most intimate social experiences appear to be the family written in ever larger (albeit fainter) letters: the clan, the hamlet, the village, the tribe.

Even in the more mobile circumstances of modern life, children take the neighborhood for granted as a familiar place and may learn to feel a sentimental identification with their town or region. Others may not. Many rural Southerners and Texans not only express a warm attachment to their state, but also profess loyalty to their region, while city-dwellers in other regions tend to be more cosmopolitan in their outlook. Under the circumstances, it would be futile to distinguish precisely communal social identities and institutions from societal ones. Consider the case of religion. Many, if not most, Catholic and Orthodox Christians grow up regarding their church as an inevitability, a community of faith that is a family tradition more than a body of doctrine. Most (but not all) serious Protestants, on the other hand, make a formal pledge to a certain set of principles like the Augsburg Confession or the 29 articles. The most extreme cases are the separatist communities of the Amish, but other ethnic churches have retained a sense of inherited community with remarkable tenacity. Dutch Calvinists, for example, while continuing their history of secessions and reunions, have still maintained their religious identity to a considerable degree, particularly in the Western states.

> For Dutch Americans religion has been *the* medium of culture, and thus also of acculturation; the many issues, divisions, and change of both have consistently registered in religious terms. . . . As congregations became the heart of each locality, so denominations have been the networks binding together the Dutch communities across the country, and church-related colleges and periodicals have provided the main forms of intellectual activity.[7]

Dutch Americans are united by religion, but they are also divided by the fissioning of churches that is a long-standing tradition in the Netherlands. English Protestantism has gone through a similar process as the Anglican church threw off Puritan Presbyterians, Baptists, and Wesleyans. Protestantism is particularly susceptible to schism because of its insistence upon individual understanding and personal commitment. Still, even the most traditional Catholic has usually made a decision to remain a part of the Church, while the most doctrinaire Southern Baptist or Reform Presbyterian comes to feel himself a part of the church community.

Professions are more strictly societal than churches, but even they sometimes exhibit communitarian symptoms.[8] Choice of a career is typically a voluntary and conscious decision, but family tradition can play a part. The sons of physicians often follow the father's profession, and the ministry of certain churches were dominated — like English politics — by the same names for generations. Country music provides the most obvious illustrations in the contemporary United States: Since it is, in the words of Hank Williams Jr., a "family tradition" for the children to follow in the footsteps of illustrious relatives, Nashville offers an almost feudal spectacle of family dynasties.

There are sons (Hank Williams Jr.; and Rex Allen Jr.), daughters (Roseann Cash), brothers (David Frizell), sisters (Crystal Gayle, Louise Mandrell), and whole families like the Stonemans, the Whites, and the Carter family. There are even dynastic marriages, e.g., June Carter and Johnny Cash. In some cases, sons may simply find it easy (and profitable) to make use of their fathers' influence and position, but it is impossible to rule out a sense of family loyalty.

Communal relations then, convey a sense of natural inevitability. Ideally, they are also intimate and depend on the face-to-face contact typical of families and villages. Plato and Aristotle obviously thought of the *Polis* as a community (rather than a state) when they put limits on its size. If community conflicts are mediated by emotional bonds (as in families),[9] then the community must be small enough to allow such bonds to develop. Perhaps the defining characteristic of community is this: While a societal institution is composed of individuals who have banded together for some purpose, a community consists of families. To the extent that an organization or institution is family-based, it is also communal. Membership will be inherited (or virtually); the range of activities will include both sexes and all ages; and individuals will not expect to find themselves opposing other family members on important issues. Professional organizations, then, lie near one extreme as an almost strictly societal association, while church congregations, neighborhood groups, and certain social clubs, e.g. the Elks, are more nearly communal.

Communal institutions are, in essence, the instruments by which families cooperate and resolve differences. At the intimate, face-to-face level, communities require very little in the way of government and coercive mechanisms, since there is a broad array of informal social controls open to them — up to and including the ridicule and harassment that is aimed at exiling the offending members. These measures are not only natural but also inherently egalitarian, since they do not exalt individuals or endow them with more decision-making powers than others are willing to grant them on a day-to-day basis. If informal community pressures are adequate to the task of local social control, then the burden of proof must always be on those who would deprive communities of their powers and invest them in a government body. In fact, most forms of moral regulation over adultery, bastardy, pornography, use of alcohol and drugs, are traditionally exercised communally and locally.

Small towns and villages provide the best opportunities for communal regulation through town meetings, school boards, and churches as well as the usual mechanisms of shame and public pressure, although small towns are increasingly subject to the same pressures as the rest of society. As Nisbet makes clear in *The Sociological Tradition*, the decline of community was a central theme for the reactionary and conservative intellectuals who founded sociology in the nineteenth century. The conditions of urban life depersonalize human relationships. The first American "sociologist" (actually, more a political pamphleteer), George Fitzhugh, defended slavery on the grounds that it was a personal bond between master and men. In *A Sociology for the South*, Fitzhugh argued that the doctrine of liberty and equality set up a struggle of individualists:

> The war of the wits, of the mind, which free competition or liberty and equality beget and encourage is quite as oppressive, cruel, and exterminating as the war of the sword, of theft, robbery and, murder. . . . Where men of strong minds, of strong wills, and of great self-control come into free competition with the weak and improvident, the latter become the inmates of jails and penitentiaries.

The conservative theme of community decay was converted into a formal thesis as part of modernization theory. While it is true that traditional social practices have been strained in modern times (as indicated by the rates of family dissolution, the high numbers of aged parents who do not live with or near their children), the theory is itself built on sand — specifically, historicist sand. In the case of the family, modernization is supposed to have destroyed the extended family and replaced it with the isolated nuclear household. But the nuclear family is, in fact, universal, and urbanization did not uniformly or inevitably disintegrate the extended family. The same is true of community.

Even under the most unlikely circumstances, the community principle tries to reassert itself — in housing projects, Indian reservations, and planned suburban neighborhoods. Robert V. Hine studied the resurgence of community on the American frontier in a variety of settings: on wagon trains, in mining camps, in farm settlements. In each case, the countervailing pressures proved to be either too powerful, or at least subversive. Settlers of the frontier came from diverse backgrounds, spoke different languages, and held — in some cases — sharply divergent worldviews. In many cases, the men who went West, miners especially, were competitive spirits, eager to get rich and get out, hardly the sort of men to form communal bonds. Predictably, the dominant relationship was partnership (a clearly societal bond). The presence of women, and families, inevitably changed things. Women couldn't abide all the moving and insisted on settling down, and with families some form of community life becomes inevitable.[10]

We ought to regard *communitas* as neither an abstract concept nor a specific and historical invention, but as an institution like the family (from which it is developed): the natural outgrowth of families interacting on a limited scale. If all forms of community association — including the family — were destroyed by the total state, they would be naturally reconstituted automatically, like origami flowers plunged into water, as soon as the human survivors were revived in more natural circumstances.

Society has less appeal for the utopian imagination, but it is no less natural than community. If communal relations have their source in the family, societal organizations seem closer to the multimale groups that have been discovered in Chimpanzee groups and in most human societies. Men with a common purpose — the hunt, war, religious rites — are banded together in a secret society, which, typically, excludes all women and children as well as immature and superannuated males. Much of the formal and informal politicking of the male world is conducted by such societies: youth gangs, the U.S. Senate, the Rotary Club, and the Marine Corps.

The masculine nature of societal relations comes out clearly in certain stereotypical attitudes. Women, it is frequently said (no longer in mixed company), are incapable of friendship; they are not good sports and don't play by the rules. Schopenhauer thought the "fundamental fault" of the female character was the lack of a sense of justice. He also observed that, on the street, women look at each other like Guelphs and Ghibellines. An American German, H.L. Mencken, compared women kissing to prizefighters shaking hands. The germ of truth in these invidious masculine epigrams lies in the lower level of competitiveness and greater strength of affection that is more typical of women.

Young women at work seem almost routinely to defy the stereotypes. In my impression, they are often "good sports," willing to take on extra work or stay late. They are just as loyal (if not more so) to the firm or their boss as male employees. What is more, they are ambitious and compete strenuously for success. Many of them turn into magnificent career women. More, however, marry and bear children. While some mothers continue to compete aggressively, many do not. Their loyalty is transferred to their home, and, even if they continue to work, it is often for the salary more than for success.

As more women enter management, it is not uncommon to hear complaints about the masculine style of doing business. Several women executives interviewed in 1986 for the CBS series "After the Sexual Revolution" expressed a preference for a less hard-nosed approach. Men, they suggested, would do anything to get ahead, but women were more indirect, played fewer games, and worked harder at simply doing their jobs right. The presence of large numbers of women probably would mute the societal competition of the marketplace and in some measure transmute it into a more familiar (probably more bureaucratic) style of doing business.

This would be a major change, since market relations are preeminently societal: the capitalist vision of the free market emphasizes the unfettered competition of individuals who seek to maximize their own self-interest. Considerations of family, charity, and social welfare apply only to what is done with profits. If they have a moral view, most capitalists would argue, along the lines of Mandeville's *Fable of the Bees*, that private vice is public virtue. Pure capitalism has never functioned, but in nineteenth century Britain and the United States, considerable pressure was exerted to give industrial capitalists the freedom they needed for success. The results were astonishing in two senses: in one sense, it was a period of unprecedented economic growth and of almost unparalleled improvement in the amenities of life; in another sense, it was a period of social disintegration, family dissolution, in which large fortunes were amassed by Jay Gould and J.P. Morgan, men who displayed little talent for business but an enormous appetite for wealth and power. Much of twentieth century history is an attempt to come to terms with the legacy of capitalism — of liberty without equality or fraternity.

In at least one aspect, political organization is an outgrowth of male groups: the conduct of war and the regulation of religious mysteries are traditional male preserves. Such relations are relatively more hierarchical, because they are rooted in competition and aggression. War and the political arena provide occasions for men to seek higher status and advance their fortunes. In small groups, these ambitions are curtailed and thwarted at every turn by communal restraints: scolding wives, contemptuous old men, and mocking children — all employing the age-old weapons of shame. But the further removed is the seat of power, the weaker are such restraining influences. A senator at home in rural Idaho or suburban Ohio has to watch his step and avoid the appearance of arrogance or the suspicion of vice, but once he is back in Washington he can vote his conscience (more often his interest), make dates with pages of either sex, and freeze his nostrils in the bathrooms of the Hart building with little fear of exposure. He is free to start immoral wars or run from necessary and just conflicts. Men, without women and children, leaders without community, constitute a real danger to themselves and to others.

The competition for power is the most frequently remarked upon feature of political life. Individuals strive to enhance their own access to wealth, dominance, and women; social classes struggle to maintain or improve their positions; and entire nations compete with other nations for a greater share of the world's goods. Whether the systems are described as democratic, republican, socialist, or monarchical matters very little: the essence of the political process is the rise of selected male groups, which set the tone for a civilization.

It is possible to moralize against the *libido dominandi*, and in certain contexts it may be important to give vent to outrage. But the contest for power fulfills certain vital functions for which the state was called into existence. Most obviously, a vigorous leadership backed by energetic younger men is a positive requirement for the defense of civil society (i.e. the national community viewed in its relation to the state). If a people succeeded in eliminating all competition and conflict, it would fall prey to the first rival that proved to be less successful at ridding itself of aggression.

Men will compete. Since that is so, it is better that there should be means of institutionalizing and ritualizing aggression in the form of political and military contests. Some will inevitably resist the process, especially in the conditions of civilized life: high population density, combined with an elaborate set of rules and restraints on the natural passions. Since the state, in this aspect, holds a near-monopoly on the use of force (and results, in part, from competition for power), one of its prime functions must be the regulation and punishment of violence. In its societal aspect, then, the state is an instrument for regulating the use of force: it defends itself against foreign aggression and controls (and mobilizes) aggression within the society. In Treitschke's definition, it is the public force for offense and defense.

If the state possessed only strictly societal powers, the libertarian night watchman government might seem attractive; however, the state has everywhere broader powers than maintaining defense and keeping the peace. Even the American Constitution declares as one of its aims, that the federal government will "provide for the general welfare." Setting aside the complexities of a federal structure, it is clear that governments do, on occasion, help to feed the hungry, house the homeless, and regulate the morals of the citizens. Since these are essentially communal and familial functions, there is at least a conceptual problem in turning them over to cohorts of competitive males. In smaller scale societies, no larger than a Greek polis, the "confusion" of roles presents few problems: the rulers and the ruled, the state and the community are close to being one. (But even the Greeks had problems, especially in cities like Athens and Sparta, which grew to depend on the economic and military contributions of subject peoples.)

The problems become more serious in the age of empire and the modern bureaucratic states that behave like empires. In Britain, France, the United States, and the Soviet Union, the centralization of power removes the communal functions from their natural local settings and transfers them to the control of ambitious men in distant capitals, rulers who are often aloof from the concerns of the scattered towns and cities they are charged with governing.

The most powerful analysis of America's political transformation remains James Burnham's *The Managerial Revolution*. In breaking with the Trotskyist wing of the Communist Party, Burnham applied the analysis of Italian political theory — Macchiavelli, Mosca, and Pareto — to modern political developments. In the twentieth century, Burnham argued, political, social, and economic power was shifting from capitalists to managers. As a result, a new type of social organization was emerging, exemplified (like all societies) by the characteristics shared by the dominant elite. As examples of managerial revolutions, Burnham instanced National Socialism in Germany, the Soviet Union, Fascist Italy, and the New Deal in the United States.[11]

One way of looking at some of the social and political changes in the United States is as an attempt to recommunalize the social structure. If the state rests upon two conflicting principles of family/community and societal competition, then one of the central political concerns must always be with maintaining a balance. Capitalism, by overemphasizing individualism and competition, inevitably invites a communalistic response. In the great age of capitalism, conservatives like Walter Scott as well as utopian socialists like Fourier (and his disciple Auguste Comte) repeatedly expressed their yearning for a more communal, perhaps medieval social order. "The quest for community" as Robert

Nisbet has shown, is one of the hallmarks of modern social experimentation. Unfortunately, as Nisbet recognizes, these experiments are always misconceived. Put simply, it is more than a serious mistake to confuse community with society: it is the origin of the worst political evil—the idea of the total state.

The totalitarian urge is more than a desire for power: it is a passion for virtue, for doing right with people's lives. Dostoevsky's Grand Inquisitor, as Mihajlo Mihajlov has shown more than once, foreshadows much of the twentieth century's rejection of freedom.[12] Mihajlov and Dostoevsky both view the problem in essentially mystical and moral terms: Despair of divine grace drives good men to create a society that compels men to be good. But there is, equally, a secular and more strictly political side to the matter. The state, when it presumes to act in our interest, has fundamentally changed its nature.

Formerly, the familial image of the state (at least in most Western societies) was paternal. Government was supposed to behave like a laissez-faire father, who gives his children enough freedom of action to do well or ill, above all, to make their own mistakes. Rewards were administered for success, punishments for failure. The managerial state continue to perceive its role as familial, but it is to motherhood that it turns for a model. Mothers are far more absorbed in the lives of their children. No matter how old or grey a man gets, his mother continues to regard him as hopelessly incapable of managing his own affairs. A father will promise his children a dollar a piece for raking the yard and roll over to continue with his nap. When he gets up, he either pays them for their work or spanks them for their idleness. A mother, however, is more likely to hover about, giving instructions and clucking disapproval: she rejects the idea that the children can fail. She insists—affectionately or rigorously—upon their performance, step by step, hour by hour.

European languages themselves hint at an Aristotelian conception of government. When a popular song of 1980 asked Americans to join the Navy and protect "the motherland," it struck a peculiar note. It is true that words for earth and country are typically feminine in Indo-European tongues; and a homeland has as clear a title, as any college, to be called alma mater; indeed, it is the most obvious metaphor in the world to call the language of our birth—mother. Still, the history of language is against it.

While fatherland is attested at least as early as the reign of James I, for motherland—in the sense of native country—we have to wait until the declining years of Queen Victoria. There is a basic rightness about fatherland, even though it has fallen into some disfavor by the disgrace of its German cousin, *der Vaterland*.

In fact, the notion of a fatherland is ancient. The Greeks with *patris*, the Romans with *patria*, the French, the Germans, the Spanish, the Italians, even the Serbs and Croats speak, as one concordant Babel, of the fatherland—although the Serbs and Croats may not have quite the same father in mind.

The ancient Greeks on Crete are the exception that proves the rule. They were peculiar, not merely for their word *metris*, motherland, but also for the kind of state nurture made more famous by the Spartans. Our country is the land of our fathers who have given shape and identity to our traditions. If government was created in the image of fatherhood, then we can have no reason to fear a properly constituted paternalism. Of course we could fall into the error of supposing that political power is identical with the power a father has over his children. This line of thought, as Locke suggested, leads inevitably to the excesses of hereditary monarchy and was refuted long ago by Aristotle. A father's authority over his family was adjusted to meet the needs and abilities of his subjects. Aristotle made the elegant distinction between paternal power over children, which is monarchical, and over wives, which is republican; and the Dutch jurist, Hugo Grotius distinguished still further between a child whose judgment is immature and one whose "judgment is mature but he is still a part of his parents' family." The main point of a father's care is to rear the children to be independent adults, men and women capable of governing their own families and of doing without parental guidance. A government formed in such an image would have a parallel object: the guarantee of the citizens' rights to direct their own lives insofar as they were able.

In the past, the form of government has often made little difference in the life of the people. Such diverse governments as the Athenian democracy, the Roman or American Republic, the British monarchy, all assumed their citizens were capable of conducting their own affairs. They all restricted themselves in the exercise of governmental benevolence, the "Grace that comes by force," which Aeschylus attributed to the gods. As much as we might deplore "statism" in all forms, whether under the Caesars or the Bourbons, it is important to remember that a Nero's or a Sun King's interference into private life was both capricious and confined very largely to the upper classes. Until recently, only philosophers and priests imagined a society in which the ordinary citizen would be so carefully trained and so strictly controlled as to be rendered incapable of sinning against God, against himself, or against the people.

Government's benign neglect of its people has been attributed to the want of means — the technical resources of coercion — but it is just as likely to have something to do with the paternalistic cast of traditional societies. C.S. Lewis once described fathers as foreign ministers for their families. A father insists that justice be done to outsiders as well as family members, whereas "a woman is primarily fighting for her own children against the rest of the world." Fathers are fond of setting rules and of making sure that they are obeyed or that punishment is administered to those who break them. They like to reward children for doing their duty and to chastize them for failure or disobedience. Fathers allow children to make their own mistakes — even at the risk of life and limb —

believing that it is better to break an arm falling out of a tree than to grow up too timid to climb.

A genuine paternal government would pursue a similar policy of making laws, punishing criminals, rewarding the virtuous and patriotic, executing or expelling traitors, but it would never take steps to guarantee virtuous behavior or to prevent crime. It would only rarely stoop to spying on its children, tapping their phones, opening their mail, nor would it assume that because firearms, tobacco, alcohol, and automobiles can be misused by the careless and the foolish, that such things must be regulated or forbidden. It could never conceive of manipulating the minds, even of its worst criminals, through sleep-teaching, hypnosis, or drugs. Such a society would not regard the law as an insurance policy against every human ill. A paternal government would rely on the good sense of its citizens, and if that fails, they must take the consequences.

If fathers are the judges and foreign ministers of their families, then mothers are supreme advocates for their children, "the special trustees of their interests," as Lewis called them. Our mothers love us with eyes open and in spite of our unworthiness. Their bodies have given us life and nourishment. For years they watched over almost every moment of our lives and understood us far too well ever to trust us to our own devices. For our own good, they have held us all night in the dark, forced us to take nasty medicine, and not only told us what to do and how to do it, but stood over us until we had done it the right way, their way. Even when we have sprouted gray hairs, they recall our childhood with some foolish nickname or episode we had long forgotten and worry constantly whether our wives or husbands are taking proper care of us. A mother's love will not even shrink from snooping through drawers or opening our mail or making us unhappy, all for our own good.

But what works in the family, with the counterbalance of paternal judgment, will not necessarily be a successful ordering principle of a society. In a maternal society, in a country whose image of government is essentially female, considerations of freedom and justice will necessarily give way to a concern for the welfare of the citizens. Such a government will hover over its people like a mother hen, making sure that they keep out of trouble, preventing them from making mistakes.

I have been told stories of my widowed great-grandmother, a woman who ruled her grown sons with an iron hand, beat them when they erred, confiscated their pay, and at their weddings gave them houses that she paid for out of their accumulated earnings, which they otherwise would have squandered. I am quite sure that her sons benefited from this benevolent despotism, one which had been made necessary by their father's death. But at the core of all such kindness is the unwillingness to regard grown men as anything but irresponsible children, sprung up miraculously to a height of six feet.

What is sometimes called the welfare state mentality is not at all paternalistic, as is sometimes claimed, but maternalistic. Orwell's "Big Brother" — better, "Big Mama" — looks out for our welfare and does everything it can to prevent failure. One means of ensuring success is to impose a familial and communal form upon essentially societal functions. Equality and fraternity replace liberty as primary concerns. Competition becomes stigmatized as unhealthy, social concerns infect market relations as quotas are imposed upon hiring practices and school admissions.

Conservatives and capitalists complain of these developments without taking into consideration either the social conditions that led to the managerial revolution or the basic conceptual changes that have allowed such a wholesale transformation of society.

It is not welfare policies or bureaucracy per se that constitutes the problem. Any great state is bureaucratic by nature and subject to the control of one or another ruling class. No decent healthy society can or should neglect any reasonable opportunity to clothe and house the poor and feed the hungry. If the Pygmies can take care of their own, there is no excuse for Americans. But welfare is, as I have argued, an essentially communal function — whether it is provided formally (by government) or informally (by friends, relatives, and churches). The problem with welfare lies not with whether it is a sound idea, but with how properly to arrange it. No means could be more bizarre and less appropriate than a great nation state whose governors — even in the act of communalizing society — are imperious males who have escaped from the moral restraints of their home communities.

Here, then, is a serious issue to grapple with: how to distribute and exercise the communal functions of the state? The growth of empires is almost always at the expense of rival forms and levels of social regulation. Down to the third century A.D., the Romans made a valiant effort to preserve the powers of municipalities. Civic responsibility, unfortunately, was burdensome. Participation in municipal government came to mean personal liability for local revenues. In any event, while local conditions varied, the decline of the empire is matched by the decay of local government.

In modern times, the most obvious example is the consolidation of the French central government, first under the Bourbons and then under the governments of the revolution. Alexis de Tocqueville, who comments forcefully on this development, was also among the first to admire the American federal experiment in self-government. Tocqueville traced the peculiar virtues (and vices) of the American system to "the principle of popular sovereignty!" The belief that each man was the best judge of his own interest radiated upward through the municipalities and states:

The townships are only subordinate to the state in those interests which I shall term *social*, as they are common to all the citizens. They are independent in all that concerns themselves.[13]

In Tocqueville's opinion, the many levels of responsibility acted as buffers against the tyranny of the majority that ordinarily characterized democracy. The United States possessed a centralized government but not a centralized administration.

To what extent American self-government was an outgrowth of the federal constitution, or merely a byproduct of their habits and experiences, remains to be seen. This much, however, is clear: no subject so agitated the founding fathers as the possible loss of local responsibility under a federal government. The new constitution had to be designed in a way that maximized state autonomy. As Hamilton put it in *Federalist* 62, "The equal vote allowed to each state [i.e. in the Senate] is at once a constitutional recognition of the portion of sovereignty remaining in the individual states, and an instrument for preserving that residual sovereignty."

Although Hamilton favored a centralized economic authority, he argued that the federal government could not legitimately use the taxing power as an excuse to interfere in the internal government of the states. In *Federalist* 28, he argued that state militias would be called out to resist invasions of sovereignty. Madison concurred, and in *Federalist* 46 suggested that the states would band together to prevent such encroachments. Even the archfederalist John Marshall declared (in McCulloch v. Maryland) that "no political dreamer was ever wild enough to think of breaking down the lines which separate the states, and of compounding the American people into one common mass."

This was more than a question of states' rights. Hamilton regarded the federal principle — at all levels — as the result of the human character. In *Federalist* 17, he argued for the "known fact in human nature, that its affections are commonly weak in proportion to the distance or diffusiveness of the object." These would be strongest in families and grew progressively weaker through local communities, to the states, and up to the union. In 1801, the poet and propagandist Joel Barlow declared "to his fellow citizens" that the federal principle (along with representation) was an indispensable foundation of the American system.

Despite the Federalists' spirited defense of their principles, many Americans were fearful that the limited government of the Constitution would be invested with too much power. Patrick Henry struck at the first words:

The question turns, sir, on that poor little thing — the expression, *We*, the *people*, instead of the states of America.

Even state officials, Henry argued, were capable of oppressive acts. "If sheriffs, thus immediately under the eye of our State Legislature and Judiciary, have dared to commit . . . outrages, what would they not have done if their masters had been at Philadelphia or New York?"[14] Interference in the life of local communities had been one of the complaints against the royal government. The anti-Federalists were afraid that, by adopting the Federal Constitution, they were saddling themselves with another absolutist regime.

Mass democracy, as Tocqueville realized, was dangerous. It was also impossible, but voting by constituencies was not. One anonymous pamphleteer in Charleston argued for a system of "assembling the parishes separately. In which way, matters of constitutional concern . . . should be duly deliberated on and fairly submitted to vote, and a final issue may be taken in general assembly on a certain majority of vouched and recorded parochial decisions."[15] By consolidating the federal government in New York or Pennsylvania, the anti-Federalist argument ran, the middle states would possess unfair advantages. The greater the distance, the likelier the possibility of abusing power.

One fear seemed to haunt the anti-Federalists, although it was never clearly articulated: consolidation of power would diminsh the autonomy of natural communities. Timothy Ford, writing as Americanus in Charleston (1754) came close. Society, he suggested, was not made up of individuals in a state of nature, but of communities of interest — farmers, planters, manufacturers. None of them has a right to infringe upon the rights of the others, even in the name of majority rule.[16] Such a concern for diversity showed up in many ways. The Continental Congress, for example, in urging Quebec to join the revolution, insisted upon the restoration of French law in civil cases, liberty for Catholics, and a local parliament. The anti-Federalist Federal Farmer envisioned a Federal system in which each state was sovereign over its own affairs, while at the same time respecting the counties, towns, citizens, and property within its borders.[17]

Perhaps the most thoroughgoing exponent of federalism was the Federalists' great opponent, Thomas Jefferson. While the aristocratic Federalists were skeptical of the people's ability to govern themselves responsibly, Jefferson was equally suspicious of all concentration of power. His remedy was a ward system of government. In his proposal to the Virginia legislature for a system of education, he drew up a plan for dividing the counties into wards like the New England Townships. As he explained to John Adams in a letter of 1813:

> My proposition had, for a further object, to impart to these wards those portions of self-government for which they are best qualified, by confiding to them the care of their poor, their roads, police, elections, the nomination of jurors, administration of justice in small cases, elementary exercises of militia; in short, to have made them little republics with a warden at the head of each for all those concerns which, being

under their eye, they would better manage than the larger republics of the county or State. A general call of ward meetings by their wardens on the same day through the State would at any time produce the genuine sense of the people on any required point and would enable the State to act in mass, as your people have so often done and with so much effect by their town meetings.

A few years later, Jefferson sketched out an entire system of government originating in the ward:[18]

The way to have good and safe government is not to trust it all to one but to divide it among the many, distributing to everyone exactly the functions he is competent to. Let the national government be entrusted with the defense of the nation and its foreign and federal relations; the State governments with the civil rights, laws, police, and administration of what concerns the State generally; the counties with the local concerns of the counties, and each ward direct the interests within itself. It is by dividing and subdividing these republics from the great national one down through all its subordinations until it ends in the administration of every man's farm by himself, by placing under everyone what his own eye may superintend, that all will be done for the best. What has destroyed liberty and the rights of man in every government which has ever existed under the sun? The generalizing and concentrating all cares and powers into one body, no matter whether of the autocrats of Russia or France, or of the aristocrats of a Venetian senate. And I do believe that if the Almighty has not decreed that man shall never be free (and it is a blasphemy to believe it), that the secret will be found to be in the making himself the depository of the powers respecting himself, so far as he is competent to them, and delegating only what is beyond his competence by a synthetical process to higher and higher orders of functionaries, so as to trust fewer and fewer powers in proportion as the trustees become more and more oligarchical. The elementary republics of the wards, the county republics, the State republics, and the republic of the Union would form a gradation of authorities, standing each on the basis of law, holding every one its delegated share of powers, and constituting truly a system of fundamental balances and checks for the government.

The Bill of Rights, which was designed to placate the opposition, included a states' rights provision, but most of the amendments were written in such a way as to prevent Congress from interfering in the rights of individuals. As the sectional controversies heated up — over tariffs and slavery especially — the question of communities of interest was bound to revive. John C. Calhoun, in an attempt to defend the interests of his native state (South Carolina) and section, elaborated the only important American contribution to political theory in the nineteenth century: his idea of constituent majorities. Put broadly and simply, Calhoun rejected the individualist tradition of natural rights embedded in the Declaration in favor of a vision of natural communities whose rights and privileges could not be violated or overriden by a numerical majority. While Calhoun was primarily concerned with defending the rights of Southern slave-owners, his theory was much broader. It can even be extended to include the rights of ethnic and religious minorities to be the judge of their own interests against a potentially tyrannical majority. What is equally important is that Calhoun was not speculating *in vacuo*. He was simply giving shape and philosophical substance to the traditions of American social and political life. Calhoun's theory is simply the federal principle extended across the artificial boundaries of government to include natural communities of interest.

Much of the American experiment is unique to the United States, but a great deal of it is an outgrowth of European — specifically British — experience. Various elements of the federal principle were expressed in antiquity, not only in the arrangements of the various confederacies that arose in the Hellenistic period (e.g., the Achaean League), but also in Aristotle's teleological theory of state formation. In the *Politics*, Aristotle described the *Polis* not as an agglomeration of individual citizens but as the result of a natural evolutionary process of households, banding together in villages, and villages uniting in a city-state.

The most elaborate discussion of federalism was made by Johannes Althusius, a German Calvinist lawyer, in his *Politica Methodice Digesta* first published in 1603. Althusius' *Politics* is a curious work — partly scriptural, partly Aristotelian, and imbued throughout with Roman law. The root concept is the *consociatio symbiotica*, the natural association of people living together. A few sentences from the opening of his work are worth quoting:

> Politics is the art of allying people together for creating, cultivating, and preserving a social life among themselves. For this reason we may call it symbiotic. . . . All government is held together by sovereignty (imperium) subjection; the human race right from the beginning proceeded from sovereignty and subjection. For Adam constituted lord and monarch by God over his wife and all of those who were born from her and the rest. . . .[19]

Althusius repeats Aristotle's arguments that man is a social animal and begins his discussion of social organization — quite properly — with the family, "private and natural symbiotic association," and its extension into broader kin relations. From here he turns to civil associations — e.g., corporations — then to public associations: city, province, empire. The key to Althusius' federalism, as Carl J. Friedrich points out in his introduction, is that, on all levels, the union is composed of the units of the preceding lower level. In this sense, the constituent members of a state are not individuals but the political units of cities and provinces. If there is a failure at some point in the chain — suppose a ruler dies without heirs — it is not up to the individuals of the realm to choose a successor; rather, it is the responsibility of the constituent members, i.e. barons or mayors.

Althusius' federalism is not entirely something new under the sun. The Aristotelian inspiration connects it, at several points, with the social philosophy of the Catholic Church.[20] In the Middle Ages, some defenders of the

Church's political authority developed arguments of popular sovereignty and limited government. The organic metaphor of the body politic was taken quite literally to mean that each member had an important function and that it was on the coherence of the members that a proper constitution was based.[21] In this respect Pope Pius XI was not entirely misstating the case when he referred to "a fundamental principle of social philosophy . . . that one should not withdraw from individuals and commit to the community what they can accomplish by their own enterprise and industry . . . [nor] transfer to the larger and higher collectivity functions which can be performed and provided for by lesser and subordinate bodies."[22]

This principle of "subsidiarity," already implicit in Pius XI's predecessors (especially Leo XIII) was used by Catholics in the twentieth century as an argument against the growth of government and state socialism. Brilliantly simple in conception, subsidiarity shares a fatal flaw with Catholic natural law theory: a rationalistic and antiempirical bias. By stating the principle in abstract— rather than concrete and historical terms—Pius XI left it exposed to misuse. Almost inevitably, the modernizing John XXIII turned subsidiarity on its head and used it to justify state ownership[23] and even intervention into national and local affairs by "the public authority of the world community."[24] For all its virtues, subsidiarity is a less-useful concept than federalism.

The system of Althusius also can be compared at several points with American federalism. Friedrich suggests that Althusius' federalism stands in contrast with the American constitution, which unites individuals as well as states, but that is only on one interpretation of the constitution. Hamilton—to say nothing of Madison, Jefferson, and Calhoun—would not have gone so far in asserting the importance of individuals. In the minority tradition, from Patrick Henry to states' rights Democrats, the constitution approximates an Althusian theory in action. Althusius' thorough-going and radical federalism has two advantages over less rigorous versions:

1) Its theoretical lucidity makes it applicable to a variety of situations. While originally conceived in relation to the Holy Roman Empire, its basic principle can be applied to the United States or to an emerging African nation, especially since they consist of more than one tribe.
2) Because it is historical and organic, such a federalism is rooted in the actual experience of social evolution. A true federal system is designed to recapitulate the phylogeny of the state; at the same time it provides a series of concentric spheres of political behavior into which individual citizens are able to grow.
3) It makes possible a theoretical answer to all those questions of authority and responsibility discussed at the beginning of the chapter, since questions of tyranny and treason can easily be restated as violations of natural (as well as constitutional) federalism.

Power naturally seeks its own level. Conflicts within families can best be settled inside the household, while conflicts between families can be resolved within the neighborhood, the congregation, or in the context of local government. Local governments would be given the management of their own affairs — as they were in the New England townships (described by Tocqueville) and Southern parishes. The governments of states (or provinces or districts) would have powers to regulate all public business that involved more than one community: e.g. transportation, commerce, communication, and — especially in a mobile society — a system of courts. The federal or national or imperial government would have something like the jurisdiction granted to it by the American Constitution before the Fourteenth Amendment turned the Bill of Rights on its head and converted Constitutional assurances of liberty into a program for equality.

Notes

1. Joseph Adelson, *Inventing Adolescence: The Political Psychology of Everyday Schooling* (New Brunswick, NJ: Transaction Books, 1986), 194–95.
2. Raoul Naroll, *The Moral Order: An Introduction to the Human Situation* (Beverly Hills, CA: Sage, 1982).
3. George A. Hiller Jr., "Definitions of Community: Areas of Agreement," *Rural Sociology* 20 (1955).
4. René König, *The Community*, trans. by Edward Fitzgerald (New York: Basic Books, 1768), 27.
5. Robert Redfield, *The Little Community: Viewpoints for the Study of a Human Whole* (Chicago: University of Chicago Press, 1955).
6. Talcott Parsons, in Parsons, Bales, and Shils, *Working Papers in the Theory of Action* (New York: Free Press, 1953).
7. James Bratt, *Dutch Calvinism: A History of a Conservative Subculture* (Grand Rapids: Eerdmans, 1984), 37–38.
8. William J. Goode, "Community Within a Community: The Professions," *American Sociological Review* 22 (1957), 194–200, attempts to define professions as a "community without physical laws" but only succeeds in muddying the waters.
9. Thomas Bender, *Community and Social Change in America* (New Brunswick, NJ: Rutgers University Press, 1978).
10. Robert V. Hine, *Community on the American Frontier: Separate but Not Alone* (Norman, OK: University of Oklahoma Press, 1980).
11. For a thorough discussion of Burnham's Thought, especially in relation to his Italian sources, see Samuel T. Francis, *Power and History: The Political Thought of James Burnham* (Lanham, MD: University Press of America, 1984).
12. Mihajlo Mihajlov, "Dostoyevsky on the Catholic Left" in *Underground Notes*, 2nd ed. (New Rochelle, NY: *Caratzas Brothers*, 1982), 51–59.
13. Alexis de Tocqueville, *Democracy in America*, I.V.
14. Patrick Henry in Herbert J. Storing, ed., *The Complete Anti-federalist* (Chicago: University of Chicago Press, 1985), 5.16.2.
15. "Rudiments of Law and Government Deduced from the Law of Nature," reprinted in Charles S. Hyneman and Donald S. Lutz, *American Political Writing During the Founding Era, 1760–1805* (Indianapolis: Liberty Press, 1983), Vol. I, 565–605.

16. Americanus, "The Constitutionalist: or An Inquiry How Far It Is Expedient and Proper to Alter the Constitution of South Carolina," reprinted in Hyneman and Lutz, Vol. II, 900–35.
17. In Storing *op. cit.*, 2.8.1–14.
18. Letter to Joseph C. Cabell, 2 February 1816.
19. *Politica Methodice Digesta of Johannes Althusius* (Althaus), with an introduction by Carl Joachim Friedrich (Cambridge, MA: Harvard University, 1932).
20. See, for example, St. Thomas, *Summa Theologiae* II, 1, a. 105.
21. See the discussion in Giercke, *op. cit.*, 22 ff.
22. *Quadragesimo anno*, 78–77.
23. *Mater et magistra*, 53.
24. See *Pacem in terris*.

9

Natural Remedies

Americans have always congratulated themselves on the uniqueness of their institutions. Historians even have a name for it: exceptionalism, a term that is used (in lieu of an explanation) to signify the absence of either an aristocratic right or a revolutionary left in U.S. politics. An American defender of federalism might plausibly be accused of converting the singular experiences of a young nation into a general theory of human political life. Global federalism, in this sense, would be as fatuous as global democracy, especially since federal structures seem to be the exception, rather than the rule for modern states. Even most "democratic" countries are, like Great Britain, structured more simply with a central governing body (such as the House of Commons) that speaks for the entire nation.

In such unitary states, some powers are, nonetheless, reserved to provincial and local authorities. An observer of British politics who left Scottish nationalism out of the picture (to say nothing of the pressures of militant Irish Protestantism) would conceive a highly distorted image. In addition to regional forces, other nongovernment groups frequently are drawn into the decision-making process. The influence of British trade unions upon the Labor Party (and its administrations) is only the best-known example. (Even in the United States, labor legislation has turned unions into "governmental agencies garbed with the cloak of local authority."[1]) One might point to the role of religious groups in Belgium and of economic interests (e.g. business and agriculture) in Scandinavia. In each case, important decisions may be arrived at by what Robert Dahl calls "a system of centralized national bargaining."[2]

The development of such semiautonomous constituencies is inevitable, even in the most totalitarian states. They are a clear indication of the impracticality of purely unitary democracy and a refutation of any liberal/utilitarian theory that restricts politics to an interaction between individuals and the state. As Dahl (a zealous proponent of democracy) concedes, "It seems doubtful that a country could long exist under a democratic government if its citizen body consisted of merely rational actors acting from conscious and rational "collective interests."[3]

The trouble with democratic theory — Dahl's is only the most intelligent current variety — is one that besets all liberal political theory: it confuses aspirations with reality and universalizes the peculiar circumstances of developed Western nations in a 100-year period. Equality of civil rights may well be, in the absence of countervailing ethical principles, a reasonable goal for a modern country like the United States or Sweden, but it cannot serve as the foundation for either political theory or a national constitution. It raises too many questions. Is democracy, for example, a genuine *summum bonum*, such that it overrides all other considerations, like religious freedom or basic physical needs? Would a 90 percent Protestant majority, for example, be justified in outlawing Catholicism or refusing to share food supplies with non-Christians during a famine? Given the choice between defending American interests or those of a demonstrably more democratic state, which has prior claim on our loyalties — the ties of blood and experience or allegiance to a political theory? To most people, the answers seem obvious: Democracy is not an end in itself.

If democracy is only a qualified or secondary good, then it can hardly be used as the sole basis either for deriving other political principles or for concrete political action. Considerations of fairness and self-interest will always weigh heavily in our calculations — as they ought to. Most frequently, democracy is held up seriously as an absolute only by political actors and propagandists with suspiciously undemocratic objectives, e.g. the exclusion of extremist dissent from both the right and the left. In the Reagan years, Lt. Oliver North was the biggest democratic globalist in the administration.

Modern democracy is of recent origin: it is about 100 years or less since the United States could safely be described as essentially democratic and less than three generations since women were enfranchised. This modern version of democracy, so far from being a *fons et origo* of all our social and political institutions, took shape under the only possible conditions — those of the liberal state and free enterprise capitalism. (MacPherson calls democracy the "topdressing" of liberal society.)[4] However, the success of democratic states (like modern West Germany or ancient Athens) suggests that citizen participation and representation appeal to something in our nature, a quality previously discussed as "cooperation." Since cooperation is a familial, communitarian virtue that, in origin at least, has little to do with the mechanisms by which competitors divide up political power, it is possible that democracy, viewed as a political system, rests upon a fundamental confusion. By applying the mechanisms of family life to the pursuit of power, democratic theory and democratic practice may be guilty of the besetting sin of the totalitarian mind: the attempt to impose community by creating a maternal state.

To some extent, this objection to democracy has some validity. Of what else does the tyranny of a majority consist than the creation of artificial unity out of real diversity? The Athenian democracy became a proverb for popular misrule, so passionately did the assembly react to anyone who threatened its values or authority. On the other hand, it is still not clear what most Americans mean when they celebrate the glories of democracy. Experience suggests that they are thinking not so much of elections (only a minority actually votes) as the right to govern their own affairs without undue interference from uniformed officers of the state. No one asks to see their papers—at least not yet—and, apart from high taxes, few people really feel the pinch of the welfare state.

It seems nothing short of miraculous that American citizens are willing to pay their taxes without coercion. This low level of resentment against the state stands in sharp contrast with many other nations. It was, after all, certain questions of taxation (and interference in local affairs) that caused the signers of the Declaration of Independence to label poor George III a tyrant. Tories, even those who criticized North's administration, considered the charge ridiculous. The British opinion was summed up by Samuel Johnson's "Taxation No Tyranny," and "The Patriot": "He that accepts protection stipulates obedience." The American colonists, by demanding and receiving protection from Britain had obligated themselves to pay for at least some of the expense. Charles Townshend, as well as other supporters of stamps and taxes on tea, sugar, etc., based the government's claim principally on the high cost of defense, and argued that it was high time for the Americans to help shoulder the burden. In the eyes of Johnson and other Tories, the colonists were "a race of convicts that deserved hanging" and not only for their enormous treason against the British crown. A more sympathetic writer like George Chalmers (a Scottish emigré to the New World) thought the root of the problem lay in the indulgence, rather than the harshness of British policy.[5]

For many Americans who became revolutionaries, the actual money involved was not the principal issue. Their main complaint, as James Otis summed it up in his memorable phrase, was that taxation without representation was tyranny.[6] They used two lines of argument to defend this position. The first, which was without any legal merit, was based on natural rights: By coming to the New World, the Americans had reassumed the rights to which they were entitled in a state of nature. Therefore, their relations with Great Britain had to be governed by original documents of incorporation, e.g. their charters. The second argument, which was really their only sensible line of defense, was based on Common Law and English tradition. By tradition, argued John Dickinson of Pennsylvania in the second of his *Farmer's Letters*, the regulation of trade (including taxes and tariffs) aimed at promoting prosperity and fairness; the Stamp Act, on the other hand, was only designed to raise revenue. *The Decla-*

ration of Colonial Rights and Grievances (1 October 1774) complained that the extension of the Admiralty Courts not only worked a hardship upon Americans: they were deprived of the Common Law right to a trial in front of one's peers.

Official answers always fell back on the observation that the colonists were no worse represented in Parliament than the majority of Englishmen. The obvious colonial rebuttal was that the Americans were simply not like other Englishmen. Their unique position was even recognized by the Lords of the Privy Council, who (as Richard Bland of Virginia pointed out) declared that "acts of Parliament made in England without naming the foreign Plantations will not bind them."[7] Even in Parliament, the friends of the Americans, while affirming the right of taxation, were well aware of the different circumstances. In Britain, a member of Parliament had to live with neighbors (voting and nonvoting alike) who had to endure — along with the member himself — the consequences of legislation and taxation.[8] A similar sentiment was expressed by William Pitt in the Stamp Act crisis. Pitt made a distinction between legislation and taxation by pointing out that it is only lawful to give of one's own. In a speech given 14 January 1766, Pitt sarcastically outlined the process by which, "We, Your Majesty's Commons of Great Britain, give and grant to Your Majesty, what? our own property? No . . . the property of Your Majesty's Commons of America." It was, Pitt declared, "an absurdity in terms."

Not everyone saw the conflict as a clear-cut case of treason or tyranny. American moderates and British Whigs condemned the misguided policies of Britain and proposed two sensible remedies. The Whigs saw no reason for Americans not to sit in Parliament, while colonial moderates like Joseph Galloway argued for a self-governing union of colonies under the British crown. Although firebrand preachers in Massachusetts tried to portray the conflict in the colors of natural rights and resistance to tyranny, it is doubtful how many soldiers and their families were enthralled by such abstractions. One argument, however, is stated repeatedly both in the sessions of Congress and in the diaries and letters of simpler people: Americans were used to running their own communities and they perceived any intrusion, by a far-off imperial Parliament, as an act of tyranny.

After two centuries, the question of colonial rights vs. British tyranny may seem entirely academic, but it is worth considering for two reasons: first, because it is the foundational myth upon which the American order rests — and most important political disputes turn on such stories; second, such a well-known and hotly disputed case — with effective arguments on both sides — provides an apt example for any general discussion of the rights of subjects and the duties of governments (and vice versa).

Tyranny

Some anarchists regard any (or almost any) exercise of government power as illegitimate, especially if it requires the surrender of personal wealth or income. Even in the American Revolution, Tom Paine found an audience, in Britain as well as America, for his radical individualism. In his pamphlet "Common Sense," Paine declared government to be "even in its best state . . . but a necessary evil; in its worst state, an intolerable one." He felt so little allegiance to any of the governments he lived under that he proclaimed, in *The Rights of Man*, "My country is the world, and my religion is to do good."

This sort of individualist anarchism — and there are those who carry it much further than Paine — is one logical end product of an emphasis on natural rights. Most individualists concede the necessity for some "minimum state," a set of core functions required of any modern government, but we run into problems with this concept almost immediately. Attempts to define the central core are capricious in the extreme, more the product of current fashion than theoretical rigor. For example, while most individualists are concerned with economic rights, Robert Nozick in listing the duties of the minimal state includes the redistribution of wealth to the extent that some people are required to pay for the protection of others.[9] If, however, civil society is nothing more than a contractual association of individuals, it is hard to see why such an association may not freely expel any member who falls behind in his dues. Exile may no longer be a practical remedy for economic inequity or social strife, but no one in his right mind demands practicality of a political theory. At best it can serve as a set of idealized guidelines, a platonic form by which we can judge the everyday. It seems pointless to build in absurdity and contradiction at the very heart of a republic.

Less philosophical individualists are more concerned with limiting the day-to-day functions of existing governments. Brian Crozier in *The Minimal State* confines himself to drawing up a list of largely economic rights that any government might be expected to guarantee: In addition to protection at home and abroad, the minimum state should undertake to secure the right to stable currency, to make property transactions, to keep what we earn apart from what the minimum state needs to keep going, and so on. Oddly enough, Crozier's minimum state also includes the regulation of marriage (the right "to marry the person of our choice, subject only to mutual free will"), provision of elementary schools, and freedom from union intimidation.[10]

Under some circumstances, Crozier's list may be entirely reasonable and praiseworthy, but it points to the problem of all individualist analysis: From the very beginning, it equips the state with the power to intervene in family life (by preventing arranged marriages) and limit the activity of corporate associations. Trade unions may be entirely vicious in the United Kingdom, but their evil influence surely has much to do with their virtual control over one major party and with their privileged legal position. It is not at all clear why the state should have the power to curb or regulate an association of working-men, so long as such associations confine their activities to the purposes for which they exist. Closed shops may be inefficient or even unjust, but surely — from a libertarian or individualist perspective — that is a matter for the parties to work out among themselves rather than an invitation for the minimum state to increase its power. This reliance on the state is an almost universal feature of political individualism. Freedom of the press, for example, is interpreted by libertarians to mean the obligations of ordinary people to pay taxes to support the police who protect pornographers from outraged citizens. Individualists are in favor of "privatizing" schools, utilities, and sometimes, even national defense; however, the one thing they stick at is the most obvious: the privatization of justice, in the form of duels and vigilance committees.

Nearly everyone, even individualists, concedes the state's monopoly on legitimate use of force. The state, as Treitschke noted, exists primarily for offense and defense. It is not, he went on to say, "an academy of the arts." Trietschke particularly feared the rise of universal theories of morality that threatened the existence of the national state: "If it neglects its strength in order to promote the idealistic aspiration of man, it repudiates its own nature and perishes." Such an enfebling idealism he described as the political "sin against the holy ghost." Without accepting any of Treitschke's absolutism (much less his fear that moralism would undermine the state's authority, since in the short run it seems to have the opposite effect), we may concede his main point. The state has legitimate functions, which ought not to be compromised by a relentless search for hypothetical justice.

For some political philosophers, any systematic denial of justice constitutes tyranny. The violence used by national liberation movements in the Third World is justified, it is argued, by the injustice of the regimes they oppose. South Africa, for example, by refusing to allow blacks to participate in the political process, abrogates any claim to legitimacy. Similarly, Woodrow Wilson refused to meet with Wilhelm II on the grounds that the Kaiser had not been elected by the German people. What would have been Wilson's response to a suffragist who pointed out to him that women were systematically deprived of voting rights in America or to a Marcus Garvey, who might have brought up the delicate question of Negro suffrage? By the standards of the 1980s, it is not only the South African regime that is illegitimate; indeed, there is hardly a government in the history of the world that would not qualify as a despotism.

By pinning legitimacy to procedural details, we run a serious risk of sacrificing a greater to a decidedly lesser good. Anarchy and ruin may always be justified on the grounds of majority rule or social justice. The question came up a number of times during the American Revolution. When the authority of Britain collapsed, it was not always replaced immediately by duly elected colonial government. In Western Massachusetts, people took advantage of the situation by declaring the dissolution of all courts and in Pittsfield, a Committee of Safety assumed jurisdiction over civil actions (such as debt collection). In a period of civil war, it is not hard to imagine the inconvenience occasioned by the disappearance of legal authority. As William Whiting told the men of Pittsfield,

> "You loudly proclaim yourselves to be Sons of Liberty. Pray, what kind of liberty is it you contend for, against Great Britain? Does not your conduct testify . . . that you contend for the same thing, for which all tyrants contend with each other; viz: that each one may monopolize the whole empire of tyranny to himself."[11]

The men of Western Massachusetts had this in common with the Irish Republican Army and the African National Congress: all three are sticklers for procedural legitimacy and are willing to risk (or sacrifice) the lives and property of a great many people to fulfill the letter of some imagined law. The relentless opposition to tyranny on procedural grounds leads inevitably to a justification for tyranny. A more cautious approach to the subject might be to look at a few familiar examples and classical observations on tyranny.

Many of Herodotus' most interesting political reflections are concerned with tyranny. When Darius the Great succeeds in overthrowing a tyrannical pretender to the Persian throne, Herodotus takes the opportunity to devise a symposium on the ideal form of government. One Persian nobleman speaks for popular government against monarchy that makes it possible for one man to do whatever he likes, answerable to no one. While under popular government, people have equality before the law, the monarch will overturn ancestral laws and customs, violate women, condemn people to death without trials. Throughout his *Histories*, Herodotus provides memorable portraits of such tyrants as Polycrates and Periander.

Periander was once sent a request for guidance from another strongman facing political difficulties. Periander said nothing but took the messenger out to a field of grain and lopped off the tallest stalks. Aristotle commented on this action as an instance of tyrants' hatred of excellence. While legitimate kings, who base their rule on honor and merit, must reward the excellent, tyrants look out for their own interests. Tyrannies are propped up by a number of means, Aristotle adds: elimination of all prominent men; prohibiting of social, political, and cultural organizations (because they might promote high-mindedness and trust); distraction of the populace with war (and high taxes to pay for military expenditures); and civil strife between the classes. Other typical signs of a tyrannical regime are the rising power of women and impudence of slaves.[12] Both Aristotle and Plato regarded tyranny as the natural end product not of monarchy but of democracy.

While Herodotus and Aristotle provide interesting testimony to the character of the Greek *Tyrannis*, obviously, not all their observations are relevant for a more general definition. But there are a number of threads worth holding on to: the hatred of merit, the attacks on social organizations, the reliance on war and civil strife, and the liberation of dependent classes. All of these characteristics can be found in Marxist dictatorships, and many of them also apply to the military despotisms of the right. Mussolini and Hitler, for example, relied on foreign wars as an instrument for unifying and mobilizing the populace, while nearly all absolutists regard the independence of churches, universities, and trade associations as a threat to their own authority.

Althusius tried to express this fundamental aspect of tyranny as the dissolution of society's "foundations and bonds." Mere abuse of power is not enough to earn the label "tyrant," he argued, just as every wrong committed by husband and wife is not grounds for divorce — only adultery. Like Herodotus, Althusius pointed to the overthrow of fundamental laws and traditions, but — within the framework of his own system — he was more concerned with the destruction of the Commonwealth's corporate bodies: family, church, chartered municipalities, and so on.[13]

Most later writers on tyranny have concentrated on the violation of individual rights. This tradition is summed by Robert Dahl: "Tyranny is every severe deprivation of a natural right," a statement designed to express the view of James Madison.[14] James Fishkin, in criticizing and developing this position, introduces the notion of personal autonomy. Each of us has a "life plan" on which our happiness depends. To carry that plan we need to be able to live but, what is more interesting, we build our lives around a "structure of commitments." A significant interference with those commitments, especially where there are less damaging alternatives, constitutes tyranny.[15] It is not necessarily tyrannical to draft a would-be physician out of college; however, if all medical students were systematically prevented from completing their studies, or if blacks and Southerners were kept out of medical school, that would be an instance of tyranny.

It is not necessary to limit this line of reasoning to the individual. Families, communities, and associations have their own structures of commitment, their own autonomy that cannot be seriously infringed without inflicting damage, not only to the institution but to the entire commonwealth. These actions are preeminently tyrannical. When families cannot pass on their traditions and beliefs, when local governments are required to conform all their decisions to national regulations, a more systematic tyranny is involved than in the case of medical school discrimination.

The history of most modern states is a record of predatory intrusion into the lives of families, communities, and the intermediate jurisdictions of local and provincial governments. Rather than rehearse the changes in family law or, in America, the impact of the Fourteenth Amendment on state and local government, one issue — public education — can illustrate the gradual transformation of a federal republic into a bureaucratic empire.

In 1987, the United States celebrated the 150th anniversary of public education. It was in 1837 that Horace Mann became (the first) secretary of the Massachusetts Board of Education. Early historians obscured some of Mann's significance by pointing to the common school legislation in Colonial Massachusetts, but those early experiments were the product of a theocratic Commonwealth in which the distinctions between public and private, secular and religious were hardly made.[16] In 1837, children in the American states were educated in a variety of settings; in classical academies or log cabin school houses, in religious schools, in schools established and supported by private philanthropy (notably the New York Public School Society), and at home.[17] Tax-supported common schools, where they existed, typically were controlled and supported entirely at the local level. Since the eighteenth century, Massachusetts had had school attendence laws, but enforcement varied from lax to nonexistent. Besides, social control in a small, homogeneous Puritan township is closer to the model of a Mbuti band than it is to twentieth century Boston.

In all the varieties of schooling, parents were assumed to have the primary and major responsibility for educating their children, and hardly anyone comtemplated the enforcement of government schooling against parental objections. The exception was Horace Mann himself. As a legislator in Massachusetts, Mann had evinced "concern for state action"[18] and shortly before taking up his position as secretary, he wrote in his journal, "When will society like a mother take care of *all* her children?" (27 May 1837). Mann was deeply impressed by what he had read — and seen — of the Prussian system of state education and was determined to extend its blessings to his own country. This meant a shift — subtle, at first — in the balance of responsibility for education. In Mann's view, some parents were incapable of making wise and disinterested choices when it came to their children's minds. In earlier generations, parental folly had to be endured as a necessary evil, but Mann viewed education as an inalienable right, which was being denied to some children. The remedy lay, inevitably for the Puritan-turned-deist, in the mortal god, the state. In his Tenth Annual Report (1846), Mann wrote:

> I believe in the existence of a great, immutable principle of natural law . . . which proves the *absolute right* of every human being that comes into the world to an education; and which, of course, proves the correlative duty of every government to see that the means of that education are provided for all.

How easily the reformer slips from individual right to government obligation! But if the state is obliged to provide "free," i.e., tax-supported, schooling, this entails an obligation upon parents to take advantage of the benefit being conferred. For much of the nineteenth century, the constant complaint of school officials was truancy. School attendance laws assume parents do not know what is best for their children or, if they do know, they do not care. However, there is little evidence to suggest that parents of unschooled children did not have their children's interests at heart. There is, on the contrary, ample evidence to show that public schooling was a tool of middle class upward mobility. Opposition to high schools, for example, came not only from poor rural families but also from skilled artisans who were deaf to the appeal that education was necessary for training industrial workers. In that light, public schools could be seen as a vehicle for an industrial revolution that was reducing craftsmen to the level of proletarian employees. Farmers also were afraid that schools would alienate their children from the values and occupations of rural life.[19]

Anxieties over school indoctrination were legitimate, since one of the main efforts of the first 100 years of government schooling was directed toward assimilating minorities and civilizing the lower classes. The poor needed to be disciplined and taught useful skills, while the immigrants had to be indoctrinated into the American way of life. Foreigners, it was believed, posed a serious threat to liberal democracy. The prevailing attitude in school circles was that "the immigrant had to be educated for his own good and that good was defined by the mores of the new liberal."[20] Nativist fervor reached a peak in the 1920s, when Oregon passed a law requiring attendance in public schools. The law was overturned by the Supreme Court in 1925, but the push for social uniformity and liberal ideology was a central theme of twentieth century progressives, especially John Dewey.[21]

A special target of assimilation was offered by the Catholics, although religion was a controversial topic even in Horace Mann's career. As a Unitarian deist, Mann opposed the introduction of Trinitarian (i.e., authentic Christian) doctrine in the schools. Individual districts couldn't decide on a curriculum of religious doctrines, because these doctrines would be at the whim of temporary religious majorities. Critics pointed out that Mann's program of nonsectarian Christianity really amounted to the establishment of Unitarianism as a state religion. Actual practice varied, in Massachusetts as well as elsewhere, but the Christological controversy soon took second place to the anti-Catholicism generated by the arrival of Irish immigrants in big numbers. By insisting on Protestantism, the schools eventually forced out the Catholics who, nonetheless, had to pay taxes to support the government schools.

If the first century of government schooling constituted a kind of majoritarian tyranny over the poor, Catholics, Jews, and ethnic minorities, after World War II it became increasingly a tyranny of an elite class over the majority. The official ideology became increasingly radicalized until, by the 1970s, it provoked the "values" controversy. Old-fashioned Christians (as well as Orthodox Jews and

Mormons) were outraged by what they saw as an antireligious, anti-American bias and by classes in values, which seemed to undermine both parental authority and traditional morality. Some Christians began to call for value-neutrality in schools, others for the reintroduction of religious "values" into schools; still others call for a disestablishment of the government monopoly on schooling and the construction of a pluralist system through education vouchers or tuition tax credits.[22] The details are not so important as a general feeling that parents are kept out of the whole process of education.

The most bitterly contested issue of the 1980s was school-based health clinics that provided pregnancy testing, distribution of contraceptives, treatment for venereal diseases, and counseling on sex and abortion. Critics charge that parents are virtually excluded from the process (in some cases they are allowed in at the child's request). Setting aside the controversy over whether sexual counseling retards or increases sexual activity, even a neutral observer would conclude that government schools no longer operate merely *in loco parentis*, but to a large extent have assumed primary responsibility for the socialization of children.

When parents complained about such practices, they were routinely sent from counselor to principal, from school to superintendent and board who refer to state laws and federal guidelines. This centralization of power is neither recent nor accidental. It is not a causal byproduct of the centralizing tendency of modern government. It is the result of generation after generation of deliberate policies that can be traced back to Horace Mann's obsession with state authority and Prussian models. In the midnineteenth century, local control was still the rule rather than the exception, but centralization was the constant theme of school reform. Education had to be isolated from the contagion of politics by reducing the size of school boards and consolidating the districts. Since even school boards, however, could reflect the reactionary inclinations of ordinary people, education increasingly was turned over to professionals who could inculcate democratic values while being — at the same time — removed from the democratic process.[23]

Long before the United States had diminished the authority of sovereign states and the autonomy of local governments it had erected a system of schools that would push, with ever-increasing force, for centralization. By 1937, the Lynds were observing that Middletown's schools were witnessing an increase of state and federal spending, and "spending entails control."[24] Social services and welfare have followed similar evolution: a decay of parental rights, the collapse of neighborhood government and the rise of centralized urban administrations, and the gradual transfer of social responsibility from local jurisdiction first, to state, then national.[25]

Local governments, of course, vary widely in the United States. However, centralization and consolidation have been progressive themes for many years.

In the early 20th century, the ward system of municipal government came in for sharp attack. A city councilman's district often coincided with the boundaries of an ethnic neighborhood, encouraging the rise to power of ethnic leaders and corrupt politics. When councilmen lived in their own districts, neighbors could confront them regularly on such pressing problems as garbage pickup and sewer lines. Such locally responsive politicians, it was alleged, never developed a citywide loyalty and stood in the way of reform.[26]

The solution lay in the consolidation of districts or the creation of an at-large system of representation. Both effectively liberated the councilman from constituent pressures. In the ward system, minority groups were able to win early recognition, but under the reformed systems the politicians became less responsive and the entry into office of ethnic groups was retarded.[27] Eventually, the Civil Rights Movement caught on to municipal reform. Moderates launched an attack on at-large representation, while more radical black leaders began demanding community control over neighborhood government and over the housing projects into which progressive municipal governments had crowded them.[28] Even "conservative" Republican black leaders, like Robert Woodson, made responsible self-government the basis of their political program.

Neighborhood control and government of the people have a fine democratic ring, but there is small evidence of progress in decentralizaiton. "Home Rule," i.e. the empowerment of urban and county governments, became a popular slogan for a time, and in 1970, Illinois included a Home Rule provision in the new state constitution, giving cities of over 25,000 automatic power to regulate the "public health, safety, morals, and welfare; to license, to tax; and to incur debt." Interestingly, the state's second largest city voted in a referendum to give back their newly won autonomy — a clear vote of no confidence in the city government. William Colman concludes that "though its rhetoric continues to be heard in bargaining between mayors and governors . . . city home rule has lost most of its functional significance.[29]

Since more and more people live in cities and under consolidated metropolitan governments, the decline of local autonomy becomes a natural characteristic. There are, of course, mitigating factors, such as the autonomy of many suburban villages and the competition between rival municipal jurisdictions. Still, American social and political life continues a pattern of centralization for which schools (followed by social services) would seem to have paved the way. There is an interesting sidelight on these developments: the position of women. Throughout the nineteenth century, women had assumed an important role in all the communitarian offices covered by the Departments of Education and Health & Human Services. Not only were female teachers rapidly becoming the majority in the lower grades, but charitable organizations were dominated by female volunteers. Of course, the idealization of the feminine had something to do with the increasing numbers of women who entered teaching and social work, but the "feminization" of these functions is also related to the gradual decline of domestic responsibilities among the affluent and the devaluation of women's work. But there is also an even more basic explanation. Women are by nature more nurturant. Since teaching and social work are only extensions of ordinary maternal responsibilities within the home, it was entirely predictable that (in the absence of restraint) they should assume control of these functions once they were extended to the public sphere.

But there were restraints. Wherever money is spent and authority exercised, males will be sure to sniff it out. In the case of social services, the males were not typically of the highest available quality—effeminate socialists and "spoiled priests" for the most part, but they were all the more eager to assert their male right to rule. As a consequence, women were relegated to lower levels of prestige and authority. We had female elementary teachers and social workers, but male principals, administrators, and officials. The inevitable result was a two-way contamination: the state became feminized as it sought to provide communitarian services, but at the same time, social services became a battleground for politicking males. The net effect of this attempt to impose community is, as always, a benign-appearing tyranny.

It does not matter that there may have been, from time to time, majoritarian support for the establishment of a social services bureaucracy or that the support was occasionally expressed by means of democratic elections. Even a national plebiscite would not justify the extermination of a disagreeable minority, much less the forced erosion of the subsidiary institutions on which any state (not just a federal republic) ultimately rests. George III's limited campaign to diminish the autonomy of his American colonies pales in comparison with the tyranny the descendants of his former subjects have imposed upon themselves. For antecedents we must look back to the great tyrants of legend: to Gilgamesh, who separated sons from families (presumably to fight his wars) and who claimed the first-night privilege of every bride; to Louis XIV's centralizing policies that corrupted all the estates of France; to Cromwell and his Roundheads, who overturned religion, law, and tradition in their attempt to establish a rule of the Saints; and finally to Stalin, whose genius it was to compel women to work in factories while they managed their households. However, even Stalin would have been disturbed by American sex education—not because he was puritanical (although to some extent he was), but because he had seen the effect of state-liberated sexuality in his own country.

Treason

If a government is engaged in tyrannical behavior, what is the appropriate response? A conventional modern answer would be couched in the language of civil disobedience or conscientious refusal: no government should coerce an individual to perform acts that violate his conscience; individuals have the right — indeed, the obligation — to disobey unjust laws and regulations. The simple answer to law-breaking for conscience's sake is a matter of prudence: if everyone can decide which laws he will obey and which he will violate, then each man becomes "the judge of his own case" — a position reserved for absolute monarchs. There is no civil order without obedience, and no morally grounded obedience without a recognition of the state's legitimacy.

The issue, however, is considerably more complex. Let us return to the tax-protesters of 1776. Many (although by no means all) colonists regarded the taxes on tea and other commodities (to say nothing of the extension of Admiralty Courts) as tyrannical. Granting the justice of their cause — purely for the sake of argument — what should they have done? A conscientious objector simply would have refused to pay the taxes or drink the tea. (He also would have paid his fines or gone to jail.) A civil disobedient might have gone further and engaged in provocative acts. He might have gathered together a group of protesters who (disguised as Indians) might dump tea into Boston Harbour. He and his friends might have engaged in still more serious acts of hooliganism — throwing ice balls and rocks at British soldiers. In this latter case, the so-called Boston Massacre of 1770, the soldiers who fired (in self-defense) upon the mob were defended successfully by John Adams and Josiah Quincy, neither of whom were lukewarm in their attachment to the incipient rebellion.

What the Americans actually did, of course, was to establish thirteen colonial governments claiming to represent legitimate order. These, acting in concert, withdrew from the empire and waged a successful war to maintain their claims to independence. Eighty-five years later, a group of Southern states tried to do precisely the same thing. Their social institutions were threatened, they claimed, by an imperious central government that imposed unfair taxes (in the form of protective tariffs) upon the agrarian South. In one important sense, the Confederates were on stronger ground than their grandparents, because in most cases they did not have to establish new state governments. The old governors, legislators, and senators simply transferred their states' allegiance from one national union to another. Northern politicians and journalists, who had been vocal in urging Southerners to secede, now cried treason. However, after the war it proved impractical to try even the Confederate President for treason, since — constitutional theories aside — the Southern states had withdrawn as states.

The federal principle, therefore, provides a partial answer to the problem of tyranny and treason. If the question is one of community or states' rights, then the community or the state is the only proper level of action. If the federal courts, for example, interfere in the administration of local schools, it is clearly up to state and local governments to take a stand. No individual conscience or theory of obligation can justify the resistance of individual citizens acting as individuals or as members of conspiratorial groups. The tyrannical centralization of government in the United States has met with little organized resistance since 1865. While this apathy may provide cause for exclamations of *O tempora, o mores*, it does not justify any private enterprise rebellions.

The same argument can be applied to most illegal tax-revolt. Under a federal system of government, a national tax on income (prohibited by the Constitution of 1789!) would appear to be illegitimate and yet there is no denying the fact that the states themselves ratified the Sixteenth Amendment.

So long as state and local governments connive at the collection — sometimes in brutal disregard of due process — of federal taxes, an individual's only recourse is to hire the best accountant he can afford.

Individuals have a limited range of responses to a government that commits acts of tyranny. One area of moral freedom, however, lies in the realm of family autonomy. While we may object to Social Security taxes or school taxes, they do not directly threaten a family's existence, so long as grandparents are not forbidden by law to reside with their families and so long as children are not required to attend public schools. However, direct state intrusion by "aggressive outreach," whether it is the seizure of students in a religious school or removal of children from homes on trumped-up child-abuse charges, may and ought to be resisted by any means available. While the use of violence is never to be recommended, it is always preferable to submission.

The simple answer Federalism may not resolve all the questions that continue to be raised concerning the conflicting duties of conscience and obedience. It is the special quality of legitimacy that it commands not just obedience (an armed robber can do that) but the willing obedience of a volunteer-soldier. On the one side is the liberal view of man as an individual with rights; on the other is the apparently necessary civil order represented by the legitimate state. It has proved very difficult (in fact, impossible) to link the two with chains of moral obligation.

None of the liberal theories of the state — contract theory, rules theories, etc. — can supply a convincing reason for obeying a difficult law, if we think we can get away with it. The only satisfying substitutes for legitimacy lie at the extremes of individualism and universalism. It is possible, after all, to reject the whole idea of obligation. If, as the utilitarians urge, the state exists only to further certain interests of individuals who make up the citizenry, then respect for laws is obviously a good idea on practical grounds — but no more. As Kurt Baier points out, this amounts to a theory of obedience, not obligation.[30] While doing away with the problem of obedience, however, a utilitarian theory of the state rests upon a series of interlocking counterintuitive assumptions.

The other possible repudiation of obligation also lies in the context of "rights," namely the universal right of everyone to live like an upper-middle class Swede, with guaranteed health care, education, and minimum income as well as a nice apartment and the right to choose among two or three parties who quibble over details of administration. Until everyone in Ethiopia lives on such a level, it is our obligation, as moral individuals, to work and sacrifice for the welfare of the Third World. Whether we are Rawlsians or Christian Marxists, we shall not let the petty dictates of antiquated nation states stand in our way.

Liberal universalism also rests on the counterintuitive principal of individualism (i.e., that the circumstances of birth and life-experience mean nothing), but, more irrationally, it replaces the limited obligation of national loyalty with the unlimited obligation of universal ethics. For the unreligious, there is not even the consolation that these moral principles are transcendent. Christian socialists, however, quickly run aground on the theological bedrock of a faith that commends them to "render unto Caesar the things that are Caesar's" and to revere all authority because it derives from God. Believers who reject orthodoxy on these points forfeit all the advantages of their claim to follow transcendent principles.

While these universalist arguments are rooted in the repudiation of ordinary experience, they play an important role in the major uprisings against state authority. In the 1980s, there have been at least three types of civil disobedience that attracted serious attention from journalists: protests at military installations, the so-called sanctuary movement, and the bombings of abortion clinics. Since the sanctuary movement combines the religious rhetoric of the right-to-life protesters with the political philosophy (and affiliation) of the antiwar protesters, it can serve as the focal point of discussion.

Since there is no "right of sanctuary" in U.S. law (it was abolished in Britain before there was a United States), there is no point in examining that aspect of the case. However, religious arguments play an important role (as they do also for right-to-lifers). In what sense do churches have the right or obligation to resist the state? Jim Corbett, one of the founders of the sanctuary movement, insists that he and his friends are "following the traditional Judeo-Christian injunction to minister to those in need." This injunction seems to involve more than the obligations of an individual conscience; Corbett regards his actions as "the work of the faith community." As he told the *Christian Science Monitor* (February 7, 1985), "You can't do it as an individual." The bishops of three Lutheran synods (neither Missouri nor Wisconsin) have declared that the sanctuary churches are fulfilling obligations derived from Scripture. These are, therefore, the corporate acts of congregations rather than merely individual decisions. When an individual breaks the law, he is either a criminal or a civil disobedient or both. When a church body is involved — a congregation or a national organization — it is presumably a more serious business. But in American constitutional law, churches have rather few rights. The First Amendment expressly forbids the state establishment of religion, by which is meant either a strictly national church, like the Church of England, or an international church with legally recognized rights and privileges, like the Catholic Church in France under the *ancien regime*. No church in the United States enjoys special constitutional privileges, apart from the right of individuals to establish an organization or worship as they please — so long as their activities do not conflict with laws. (Druids are, for example, not permitted to practice human sacrifice.) Where it has seemed appropriate, we have seen fit to confer special privileges on religious groups. By the mid-nineteenth century, many states had passed laws exempting certain communities of faith from military service on the stipulation of making an equivalent contribution in money. More recently, clerics are exempt from military service, although that was not always the case: During the Civil War, the Episcopal Church petitioned Congress to exempt their priests from the draft. Their petition was denied.[31]

The Supreme Court has repeatedly affirmed that draft exemption for conscientious objectors is a privilege rather than a right. In fact, Madison's proposed addition to the Second Amendment exempting any "person religiously scrupulous of bearing arms" from military obligation was rejected.

Still, the most familiar justifications for conscientious objection are a refusal on religious grounds to serve in the army, swear an oath, or comply in any way with the demands of the states. Even in the time of revolution, states granted exemptions to Quakers who did not wish to fight for conscience's sake. With national conscription during the Civil War, the problem became acute. Congress was reluctant to exempt any class of the population from the draft — especially since requirements could be satisfied by paying for a substitute. Members of certain religious groups — Quakers and Mennonites, for example — were regularly pardoned. But exemption based on church affiliation seemed to many people patently unfair. What of the tender consciences of Baptists and Methodists who might have scruples about bearing arms? In modern times, the problem is even more acute. Refusal to obey the law cannot be based simply on religious or moral conviction. Civil disobedience is, as John Rawls points out, a political act, and even acts of conscience must be political in a country where there is no unanimity on religious questions.[32]

As a practical matter, we did, until recently, have a rough-and-ready idea of religious norms in America and of which groups "had a right" to refuse to serve. By the 1960s, that consensus was gone, and the Selective Service was flooded with appeals from conscientious objectors whose church affiliation was either bizarre or nonexistent. It became fairly obvious that religion could not be the test. Perhaps it never should have been, except in a very restricted sense. Rheinhold Niebuhr, once a leading pacifist, was right to censure the inconsistency of religious pacifists who enjoyed all the fruits of civil order but insisted on their right to let others bear the burden. Groups that left the world — Shakers or Trappist monks — were one thing, but worldly and prosperous Quakers were quite another.[33] Writers on ethics are likewise reluctant to grant special status to religious groups. Most of them are, at best, indifferent to religion, but — more to the point — they are hostile to any attempt to treat individuals as members of a traditional status group, such as a family, a church, or a privileged class.

In democratic, pluralist, and — we might even add — secular America, the mere fact of religious affiliation can never be used as a legal shelter from the due process of the American legal system. Members of churches may, of course, choose to carry out their support of church doctrines to the point of breaking the law by refusing to inoculate their children against certain diseases, by performing animal or human sacrifices, or by assisting illegal immigrants. As with all acts of civil disobedience, those who break the law must be prepared to take the consequences.

Some Christian activists are prepared to accept punishment, because they claim their religion explicitly requires them to resist the state whenever the state acts against the teachings of the Scripture. The case of conscientious refusal is fairly clear-cut. If Caesar orders Christians to worship him on pain of death, then, by respectfully declining, the faithful will incur martyrdom. Beyond such refusals, it becomes more difficult to justify Christian resistance. The central biblical text is Paul's Epistle to the Romans, I. 13:

> Let every person render obedience to the governing authorities, for there is no authority except from God, and those in authority are divinely constituted, so that the rebel against the authority is resisting God's appointment . . . For magistrates are no dread to the person who does right but to the wrong doer. You do not want to fear the authority, do you? Do right, and you will earn its approval . . . but if you do wrong, then be alarmed, for it does not carry the sword without reason . . . It behooves us, therefore, to be submissive, not only because of punishment but also for conscience sake.

It is well to remember that Paul told his Roman friends to "be submissive for conscience's sake" in a period when Rome was ruled by Nero, the emperor who initiated the persecution of Christians. For the next three centuries, Roman Christians continued to be law-abiding citizens of the empire that persecuted them. Because it is difficult to base a religious doctrine of resistance on the Bible alone, many advocates of "holy disobedience" fall back on the teachings of Thoreau, Gandhi, and Martin Luther King, none of whom is an exemplary role model for Christians. Neither Thoreau or Gandhi were Christian, and Dr. King, while professing the faith, was afflicted with certain moral weaknesses that cannot command the respect — much less the reverence — of serious believers. If Christians wish to engage in acts of resistance, then, it is on other than purely religious grounds.

For most of the participants in the sanctuary movement, the defiance of U.S. law is an act of civil disobedience. In the eyes of Eric Jorstad, an American

Lutheran Church pastor, it is "an act of resistance against what its supporters believe to be the unjust foreign policy of the United States towards Central America."[34] Civil disobedience is a murky term, which can be made to include everything from a conscientious refusal to salute the flag or take an oath up to the decision to perpetrate acts of organized terrorism. In most strict definitions, however, civil disobedience is distinguished both from conscientious refusal and from an outright resistance to the regime as such.

Traditionally, conscientious objectors have insisted only on their right not to perform acts that violated their religious convictions. Those who assist illegal immigration are engaged in more than a conscientious refusal to comply with INS regulations. They are actively involved in what they see as a campaign of civil disobedience against our treatment of Central American refugees. The civil rights and antiwar protests of the 1960s are an obvious historical parallel. Civil disobedients, in the strict sense, do not simply disagree with government policies, nor do they, on the other hand, seek to subvert the system. While agreeing with the essential fairness of the system of justice under which they live, they object to specific lapses in the application of justice. They appeal not just to their own conscience but to the conscience of the nation or, as John Rawls puts it in *A Theory of Justice*, it is "a political act addressed to the sense of justice of the community."[35]

Most civil rights workers acknowledged the rightness of the American principle of equal rights. What they protested was the fact that blacks did not seem to enjoy the same legal protection as the rest of society. Although there is a diversity of opinion among ethical philosophers, there is something like a liberal consensus on civil disobedience. Martin Luther King put the case eloquently in his "Letter from the Birmingham Jail." King argued that citizens were only obliged to obey just laws, which are "rooted in eternal and natural law." Unjust laws, which violate the laws of nature (and nature's God), we were free to violate in a "loving" spirit. By this criterion, he argued, any laws imposed by a majority upon a minority that did not bind both groups equally were unjust. In King's view, these were laws that degraded the personality. He and his followers believed that their nonviolent revolution would raise the conscience of the American people and result in changing the legal system.

King was an activist, rather than a philosopher, and there are many problems with his theory (derived from Thoreau by way of Gandhi). In the first place, the revolutionary threat was always implicit and sometimes explicit in his rhetoric. The liberal historian Herbert J. Storing, while expressing sympathy for King's aims and ideals, insisted that civil disobedience quickly gave up its civility as black-power advocates repeated only one side of King's call for nonviolent revolution.[36]

A more attractive feature is King's appeal to natural law. Conscience may oblige us to disregard a law in flagrant violation of natural law — say, Herod's edict to kill the children of Israel or a law compelling children to inform on their parents. Unfortunately, King's interpretation of "natural law" was so loose that it opened the door to every conceivable form of lawlessness.

There is nothing remotely similar either in Scripture or in the recognized natural law tradition to King's argument about the dignity of persons or the rights of minorities. The same reasoning, if applied to wives and children, would undermine fundamental provisions of revealed and natural law. On the basis of this argument, it is easy to ask by what right adult males legislate against adultery or forbid their children to have sexual relations? It has been suggested more than once that "patriarchal" moral codes are all an affront to the dignity of children. In King's version of civil disobedience, there is nothing to prevent such "victims" from violating the law or, worse, from rising up in rebellion.

Although civil disobedients like to lump their activities together with the more traditional forms of conscientious objectors, their cases are different. Acts of civil disobedience must meet stiffer requirements than conscientious refusal. Since they are challenging the application of justice in the name of fairness, civil disobedients must, as Ronald Dworkin insists, "exhaust the normal political process . . . until these normal political means hold no hope of success." They must also take into consideration the possible negative consequences of their actions: it is entirely possible that the result of all this protest will be a rising tide of hostility against all immigrants from Latin America.[37] Another effect of frivolous disobedience, one that is not perhaps entirely unintended, would be what Rawls describes as "a breakdown in the respect for law and the constitution."[38]

The more radical elements in the movement have already answered to such criticism: It is not only the injustice of INS policies that they seek to change, but our entire policy in Central America. Sister Darlene Nicgorski declared that she would continue to bear witness to the truth because the Pentagon was waging a "technological, clean, and distant" war in Central America.[39] Most of the leaders repeatedly excoriated the Reagan administration for its "genocidal" policies.

While insurrection and revolution fall outside almost anyone's definition of civil disobedience, they are often lurking in the wings. Willful violation of the law tends to undermine lawfulness, in the criminal class if not in the entire society. As early as 1838, Lincoln professed to being disturbed by the growing tendency to fanaticism and the "increasing disregard for law . . . the growing disposition to substitute the wild and furious passions, in lieu of the sober judgements of the courts."[40] Lincoln hoped to make reverence for the laws into "the political religion of the nation," but it is his fears, rather than his hopes, that have been fulfilled.

Systematic defiance of the law is a kind of revolution that puts the individual or his movement on the same footing as the state. Howard Zinn, whose *People's*

History of the United States is quoted as scripture by some sanctuary activists, rejects the notion that the state has privileges denied to ordinary citizens. He argues that just as the United States decides which international laws it will obey, we should all be free to pick and choose among the laws: to abide by the ones we like and to defy the ones we don't. Furthermore, Zinn holds that civil disobedients should not submit to punishment because submitting to unjust punishment is a form of collaboration with the enemy. He also rejects nonviolence in favor of revolution and argues that any rules or privileges that apply to states must also apply to individuals and vice versa.[41]

Confusion of roles — of individual and state — is really at the heart of the discussion. Robert Nozick, the libertarian philosopher, highlights this confusion in his brief discussion of civil disobedience as a form of lawbreaking. Crime, in Nozick's view, is the result of the criminal's disconnection from "correct values," and punishment is a process by which he is reconnected. The civil disobedient, however, tries to reverse the roles by attempting to punish society. In flouting the laws and values of his country, the conscientious lawbreaker claims to be affirming correct values: "He is sending us a moral message."[42]

Is there no difference, ethically speaking, between the citizen and the state? In the current political context, the answer seems to be no. Private citizens like Jesse Jackson go from country to country as free-lance diplomats in a flagrant abrogation of sovereignty. On the other hand, federal and state agencies increasingly take it upon themselves to decide questions of religion and child-rearing that were formerly reserved to families. Meanwhile, the impassioned rhetoric of politicized preachers and celebrity fund-raisers has convinced a significant number of Americans that they owe a personal responsibility to the people of poor countries like Ethiopia — a burden that was previously shouldered by the American people collectively working through the federal government.

The ethical case for sanctuary finally boils down to a similar argument: as individuals and small groups, American citizens took it upon themselves to decide questions of foreign and domestic policy, specifically the Reagan administration's Central American policy and the INS's enforcement of its regulations. Each sanctuary worker becomes, in effect, his own state and a law unto himself. All that separates such activity from treason is their apparent (sometimes) willingness to subject themselves to the judicial process.

Socrates gave the classic response to civil disobedience when he refused to escape from jail and execution on the grounds that he owed his birth and education to the laws of his city. Continued residence in Athens, as Plato represents his argument in the *Crito*, was a sufficient proof that he consented to be a part of his native commonwealth. He had, by his refusal to leave, abrogated any right he might have had to break or evade the laws. Socrates viewed the citizen as a family member in the larger community the Greeks called the *polis*. Citizenship, as Aristotle would later argue, is a national condition from which the only escape is exile, since even in death we remain part of the community. The responsibilities and obligations of citizen and city are, therefore, quite different. The city, that is, the community, far from being a mere collection of individuals, is the necessary condition of ordinary human life, while the state, as we understand it, is nothing more nor less than the expression of community will.

One of the most influential contemporary writers on political ethics, Michael Walzer, rejects Socrates' argument for civil obligation. Although an enthusiastic supporter of civil disobedience in every form, he is uncomfortable with the idea that private conscience by itself can serve as justification. For Walzer, a conscience raises the same problems as religious convictions—both are personal. In fact, the appeal to conscience is most often part of a larger religious perspective. Without divine sanction, conscience might be a euphemism for willfulness or perversity. For somewhat different reasons, Walzer concludes that if conscience can be appealed to on social questions, then it is "a form of moral knowledge that we share not with God, but with man." For Walzer, "disobedience . . . is almost always a collective act."[43]

Walzer's point of departure is the familiar doctrine of John Locke enshrined in the Declaration of Independence:

> We hold these truths to be self-evident, that all men are created equal, and endowed by their creator with certain unalienable rights, that among these are life, liberty, and the pursuit of happiness; that to secure these rights governments are instituted among men, deriving their just powers from the consent of the governed. That whenever any form of government becomes destructive of these ends, it is the right of the people to alter or abolish it . . .

The right of civil disobedience rests, in the first place, on the right of the people to repudiate laws to which they do not consent and, in the second, on the obligations they have incurred by joining a group. "Commitments to principles," he declares, "are usually also commitments to other men, from whom or with whom the principles have been learned and by whom they are enforced." What Walzer calls "the duty to disobey" arises when the aims of a small group are in conflict with the duties owed to the state. There may be a *prima facie* obligation to obey the law, but that only means we should not engage in unjustified acts of disobedience.

Subordinating the national interest to the ideals of a party is not always recognized as a high ethical principle. Jeb Stuart Magruder, a young man who put loyalty to President and party above respect for law, was asked at the Watergate hearings if he had any ethical principles. Yes, he insisted. He had been taught ethics at Williams College by William Sloane Coffin. Magruder felt loyalty to the President and his administration took precedence over loyalty to country—a perfect illustration of Walzer's theories (and Coffin's preaching).

Against the Socratic vision of the community nurturing its citizens with laws, liberals like Walzer portray a scene in which individuals struggle for their rights against an impersonal government under which they are accidentally born. Citizenship is not willful, he argues, because many of us simply can't leave our country. Prof. Walzer, who now has a chair at Princeton, might well find it inconvenient to leave — but impossible? Hardly. Like so many bourgeois radicals, philosophers of civil disobedience prefer to live in comfort in a society they claim to regard with revolutionary disdain. In his most recent book, Walzer tries to apply the story of Exodus to the current political situation. He concludes with a set of lessons:

—first, that wherever you live, it is probably Egypt;
—second, that there is a better place, a world more attractive, a promised land;
—and third, that "the way to the land is through the wilderness." There is no way to get from here to there except by joining together and marching.[44]

Ironically, by "marching" Walzer does not have in mind the fine democratic custom of voting with his feet but organized demonstrations that would violate the law. Walzer's more radical view of civil disobedience has obvious implications. Small group loyalties exactly describe the sanctuary movement and other high-minded groups like antinuclear protestors and abortion-clinic picketers. All the apologists for radical civil disobedience — Walzer, Zinn, and the sanctuary activists — are intentionally confusing disobedience with rebellion. Locke and Jefferson did not defend at any time any supposed right to disobey — lovingly or not — the laws and constitution of Great Britain or the United States. On the contrary, they were upholding the right of rebellion against despotic regimes. Even a high Tory like Dr. Johnson recognized that "there is a remedy in human nature against tyranny," one that did not depend either on form of government or political theory. What the sanctuary churches and their spokesmen seem to be telling the American people is this: "Your constitution and legal system are so badly flawed, your democratic process so tyrannical, that only rebellion offers a way out." If this is so, they should violate the laws. They should also evade punishment not only through the legal methods they have so far used, but also by whatever means possible. As soon as they find the courage of their convictions, they should take up arms against the government of America and liberate us from the tyranny of Republicans and Democrats. Anything short of rebellion would constitute cowardice and hypocrisy.

Dr. Johnson's "remedy in nature" is a highly interesting phrase. It does not suggest a natural right to engage in rebellion and tyrannicide. On the contrary, we know that Johnson was a Jacobite legitimist who repudiated the Glorious Revolution, whose principles Edmund Burke, Johnson's friend, worked up into a political myth that has proved to be the fountainhead of Anglo-American conservative thought. How the invasion of an ambitious Dutch homosexual and a king's disloyal daughter got incorporated into conservative politics is only one amusing incident in the history of ideology. Johnson, however, would not have been more amused by Burke's Old Whig ideology than he was by the "patriotism" espoused by Burke's political opponents. That doctrine of rights, progress, and universalism, he rightly termed "the last refuge of a scoundrel."

The great revolution in France for the rights of man, which so appalled Burke, would have struck Johnson as a natural redress for the centuries of misrule. The murder of Louis XIV and his wife were, after all, a remedy in nature, even if they were arranged by patriotic scoundrels. From a federal perspective, French history offers the interesting spectacle of progressive centralization interrupted by periodic fits of anarchy and despotism. Despite the variety of local traditions, the rulers of France since Louis XIV have gradually imposed a uniform structure of government in which even local officials serve the national government. So little respect is paid to local tradition that the language and customs of the Bretons have been all but exterminated (in World War I, Breton conscripts were sometimes shot for not giving the password in French). For several centuries, at least, French administrations have tried to annihilate the federal principle and, since the 1790s, to institutionalize a revolution against human nature. The result has been a pathological instability and a history marked by the imperialist follies of Napoleon and the abject cowardice of the French nation throughout the course of World War II. When it is realized that France is *the* great nation of the West to whom the English and the Germans owe their civilization, her political suicide becomes an even more distressing spectacle.

France is hardly an exceptional case. The violent experiences of the Germans and Russians in this century — to say nothing of the galloping decadence that has afflicted Britain — are, if anything, more appalling. None of this, however, should occasion surprise. A creature designed to live in small, face-to-face societies has constructed vast imperial nations, while investing central governments with almost familial powers. The more governments deprive their peoples of moral and social autonomy, the more they compel their subjects to behave as infantilized dependents. Carried to its conclusion, progress should result in a one-world bureaucratic utopia somewhere between *1984* and *Brave New World*.

These scenarios are highly unlikely, so long as man is man. Only genetic engineering holds out the prospect of human beings liberated from violence, greed, and lust. But a designer species will inhabit a world as inhumanly dull as *Walden II*; their morals and politics will be studied not by the poet or the philosopher but by the computer: only artificial intelligence suits an artificial species.

But the biological utopia is, I believe, even less likely than the political. Most of us do not wish to be perfect or even better — what would be the point? For all our powers of imagination, we are what we are and will resist any effort to change us. That, too, is part of the resiliency of our nature and a provision of the natural law.

Natural law is, as I have argued, something more than the invention of right reason: it is a law of nature. The natural differences between the sexes, that issue into institutions of family, community, and state, delineate the contours of a healthy organic political system. For some time now, Western man has been engaged in a systematic effort to undermine the natural foundations of the state, while increasing the power of the deracinated state to the point that ordinary people begin to challenge even the legitimate functions of legitimate government.

Under these circumstances, we have reason for alarm but not, perhaps, for the apocalyptic terrors held out by the great modern prophets. If famine, suicide, divorce, infanticide, and environmental pollution are nature's revenge against Prometheus and his creatures, chaos and social disintegration are ultimately nature's remedies. Every dark age is a period of slow and painful healing. If man born in a family is, as Hume observed, "compelled to maintain society," as the social animal he is even more compelled to maintain the family. Two young Americans plucked from a singles-only apartment house in San Diego and set down upon a deserted island would reinvent the family, and their offspring would inexorably recapitulate the social history of the human race. The laws and decrees enacted by human government are mutable and sometimes tyrannical, but the laws of human nature, curled tight within the spirals of the genetic code, are unchanging and just. More than just, they are justice itself in this sublunar sphere.

Notes

1. Clyde Summers, "Union Powers and Workers' Rights," Michigan Law Review 49 (1951), 805; cf. discussion in Howard Dickman, *Industrial Democracy in America: Ideological Origins of National Labor Relations Policy* (La Salle, IL: Open Court, 1987).
2. Robert Dahl, *Dilemmas of Pluralist Democracy: Autonomy vs. Control* (New Haven: Yale University Press, 1982), 71.
3. Robert Dahl, *op cit.*, 96.
4. C.B. MacPherson, *The Real World of Democracy* (Oxford: Oxford University at the Clarendon Press, 1966), 5.
5. George Chalmers, *An Introduction to the History of the Revolt of the Colonies*, Jared Sparks, ed. (Boston: J. Monroe, 1845).
6. James Otis, "The Rights of the British Colonies Asserted and Proved" (Boston 1764) in Bernard Bailyn, ed., *Pamphlets of the American Revolution, 1750–1776* (Cambridge, MA: Belknap Press of Harvard University Press, 1965), 409–505.

7. Richard Bland, "An Inquiry into the Rights of the British Colonies" in Merrill Jensen, ed., *Tracts of the American Revolution, 1763–1776* (Indianapolis: Bobbs-Merrill, 1967), 108–26.

8. See Jared Ingersoll's letter to Governor Fitch of Connecticut, 11 February 1765, reprinted in Richard B. Morris, *The American Revolution, 1763–1783: A Bicentennial Collection* (Columbia, SC: University of South Carolina Press, 1970), 64–70.

9. Robert Nozick, *Anarchy, State, and Utopia*, 26 ff.

10. Brian Crozier, *The Minimum State: Beyond Party Politics* (London: Hamish Hamilton, 1979), 45–46.

11. On Pittsfield disturbance, see Lee Nathanael Newcomer, *The Embattled Farmers: A Massachusetts Countryside in the American Revolution* (New York: Columbia University Press, 1953), 99 f. Whiting's speech is reprinted in Hyneman and Lutz, *op. cit.*, I, 461–79.

12. Aristotle, *Politics*, D. 9.2., 131ba-15b.

13. Althusius, *op. cit.*, Ch. 38.

14. Robert Dahl, *A Preface to Democratic Theory* (Chicago: University of Chicago Press, 1956), 6.

15. James Fishkin, *Tyranny and Legitimacy* (Baltimore: The Johns Hopkins University Press, 1979), 12 ff.

16. For early American education see Lawrence A. Cremin, *The American Common School, An Historical Conception* (New York: Teachers College Press, 1951).

17. Michael B. Katz, "From Voluntarism to Bureaucracy in American Education," *Sociology of Education* 44 (Summer, 1971), 297–332.

18. Jonathan C. Messerli, "Localism and State Control in Horace Mann's Reform of the Common Schools," *American Quarterly* 13 (Spring 1965), 104–18.

19. See Michael B. Katz, *The Irony of Early School Reform: Educational Innovation in Mid-Nineteenth Century Massachusetts* (Cambridge, MA: Harvard University Press, 1968).

20. Clarence J. Karier, "Liberal Ideology and the Quest for Orderly Change" in Clarence Karier, Paul C. Violas, and Joel Spring, *Roots of Crisis: American Education in the Twentieth Century* (Chicago: Rand McNally, 1973), 84–107.

21. Pierce v. Society of Sisters, 268 U.S. 510 (1925).

22. See, for example, Rockne McCarthy, et. al. *Society, State & Schools: A Case for Structural and Confessional Pluralism* (Grand Rapids, MI: Eerdmans, 1981) and Connaught Marshner, ed., *A Blueprint for Education Reform* (Chicago: Regnery/Gateway, 1984).

23. Joel Spring, "The Evolving Political Structure of American Schooling" in Robert B. Everhart, ed., *The Public School Monopoly: A Critical Analysis of Education and the State in American Society* (San Francisco: Pacific Institute, 1982), 77–108.

24. R.S. and H.M. Lynd, *Middletown in Transition: A Study in Cultural Conflicts* (New York: Harcourt Brace, 1937), 129 n.

25. Michael B. Katz, *In the Shadow of the Poorhouse: A Social History of Welfare in America* (New York: Basic Books, 1986).

26. See Kenneth Fox, *Better City Government: Innovation in American Urban Politics* (Philadelphia: Temple University Press, 1977).

27. Edward C. Banfield and James Q. Wilson, *City Politics* (Cambridge, MA: Harvard University Press, 1967), 91.

28. See Alan A. Altshuler, *Community Control: The Black Demand for Participation in Large American Cities* (Indianapolis, IN: Pegasus/Bobbs-Merrill, 1970).

29. William G. Colman, *Cities, Suburbs, and States, Governing and Financing Urban America* (New York: Free Press, 1975), 22–23.

30. Kurt Baier, "Obligation: Political and Moral" in J. Roland Pennock and John W. Chapman eds., *Political and Legal Obligation* (New York: Atherton Press, 1970).

31. See Edward Needles Wright, *Conscientious Objectors in the Civil War*, repr. from 1931 edition (New York: A.S. Barnes, 1961); cf. James F. Childress, *Moral Responsibility in Conflicts: Essays on Nonviolence, War, and Conscience* (Baton Rouge: Louisiana State University Press, 1982), 95–163.

32. *A Theory of Justice*, 365.

33. Reinhold Niebuhr, *Christianity and Power Politics* (New York: Scribner's 1940), Chapter 1.

34. "Sanctuary for Refugees: A Statement on Public Policy," *The Christian Century*, 14 March 1984, 274–76.

35. John Rawls, *op. cit.*, 64.

36. Herbert J. Storing, Jr., "The Case Against Civil Disobedience," in Robert A. Goldwin, *On Civil Disobedience: American Essays, Old and New* (Chicago: Rand McNally, 1968), 95–120.

37. See Ronald Dworkin, *A Matter of Principle* (Cambridge, MA: Harvard University Press, 1985), 104–16.

38. John Rawls, *op. cit.*

39. Quoted by Renny Golden and Michael McConnell in *Sanctuary: The New Underground Railroad* (Mary Knoll, NY: Orbis Books, 1986), 80.

40. Abraham Lincoln, "The Perpetuation of Our Political Institutions," a speech delivered 27 January 1838 before the Young Men's Lyceum, Springfield, IL, repr. in Goldwin, *On Civil Disobedience*, 1–9.

41. Howard Zinn, *Disobedience and Democracy: Nine Fallacies on Law and Order* (New York: Random House, 1968), 156.

42. Robert Nozick, *Philosophical Explanations* (Cambridge, MA: Harvard University Press, 1981), 390–91.

43. Michael Walzer, *Obligations: Essays on Disobedience, War, and Citizenship* (Cambridge, MA: Harvard University Press, 1970).

44. Michael Walzer, *Exodus and Revolution* (New York: Basic Books, 1984), 149–50.

Name Index

Subject Index